W9-BXS-193

Please remember that this is a library book,
and that it belongs only temporarily to each
person who uses it. Be considerate. Do
not write in this, or any, library book.

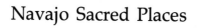

Navajo Sacred Places

NAVAJO

Klara Bonsack Kelley and Harris Francis

SACRED

INDIANA UNIVERSITY PRESS   BLOOMINGTON & INDIANAPOLIS

PLACES

The paper used in this publication meets the minimum requirements of American National Standard for Information Sciences—Permanence of Paper for Printed Library Material, ANSI Z39.48-1984.

Manufactured in the United States of America

Library of Congress Cataloging-in-Publication Data

Kelley, Klara B.

Navajo sacred places / Klara Bonsack Kelley and Harris Francis.

p.   cm.

Includes bibliographical references (p.   ) and index.

ISBN 0-253-33116-1 (alk. paper). — ISBN 0-253-20893-9 (pbk. : alk. paper)

1. Navajo Indians—Religion and mythology. 2. Sacred space—Southwest, New. 3. Navajo Indians—Land tenure. 4. Navajo Indians—Antiquities—Collection and preservation. 5. Economic development—Southwest, New—Religious aspects. 6. Southwest, New—Antiquities—Collection and preservation. I. Title.

E99.N3K3355   1994

979.1'3004972—dc20   93-49472

1 2 3 4 5 00 99 98 97 96 95 94

CONTENTS

Acknowledgments

Introduction   1

PART ONE

PLACES IMPORTANT TO NAVAJO

PEOPLE A SURVEY OF THIRTEEN

NAVAJO COMMUNITIES

1. Background   15
2. The Project to Consult Navajo Communities   26
3. Interpretation of Results   41

PART TWO

PLACES IMPORTANT TO NAVAJO

PEOPLE OTHER STUDIES

4. Other Studies: What They Did and How They
   Did It   53
5. Stories and Types of Places in the Other Studies   64
6. Preserving the Culture by Preserving the Land:
   The "Landscape" and "Piecemeal" Approaches   91
7. The Hidden Reservoir   105

PART THREE
NAVAJO CUSTOMARY LANDSCAPES
AND DEVELOPMENT LANDSCAPES

8. What Navajos Say about Cultural Preservation   135
9. Navajo Endangered Landscapes   149
10. Endangered Landscapes outside Navajo
    Jurisdiction   165

PART FOUR
HIDDEN AND MANIFEST LANDSCAPES
IN STORIES

11. Analytical Framework   187
12. Hidden and Manifest Landscapes in Two Stories   193
13. A Story about "Where Whiteshell Woman
    Stopped for Lunch"   205
14. The Land, the People, and Culture Change   221

Appendixes   229
Notes   235
References   239
Index   253

Illustrations follow page 112

LIST OF FIGURES

FIGURE 1.

Locations of the thirteen chapters in survey of
Navajo preservation concerns   14

FIGURE 2.

Locations of other projects   52

FIGURE 3.

Areas needing extraordinary preservation measures
wholly or partly within Navajo jurisdiction   134

FIGURE 4.

Lands in Navajo aboriginal use area outside Navajo
Nation jurisdiction   186

ACKNOWLEDGMENTS

In addition to the people named in this book, we say, "Aheehee" to the hundreds of Navajo people who have told us their stories over the years, and especially to family and neighbors Rose Francis, Albert Francis, Tom Claw, and David Kelley. We did most of the field work and drafted a good part of this book when we worked for the Navajo Nation Historic Preservation Department, and gratefully acknowledge the support of the Department Director, Dr. Alan S. Downer, and co-workers Dr. Alexa Roberts and Richard Begay. Hastiin Alfred Yazzie, Charlotte Frisbie, Dave Brugge, Jim Faris, and Beth King gave helpful criticism of our ideas, writings, or both. We mourn the loss of Leroy Jackson and his unflagging commitment to the life of the Navajo culture and environment.

Navajo Sacred Places

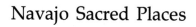

Introduction

I approve of your purpose in doing this
work, but I'm not sure I should trust
you. Maybe you will take my stories
and publicize them.

—Navajo woman from Sheep
Springs, 1988

American Indian places and the beliefs
that go with them have interested the non-Indian public for a long time.
American Indian communities have had a dense web of beliefs about
even the most minute parts of their homelands and surrounding territory. Navajos, like other Indians, say, "The whole land is sacred." This
statement evokes how soil, moisture, air, and light in human hands
become food that in turn becomes the people's flesh and blood. It also
evokes the social relations between mortals and the immortal "Holy
People" whose outer forms are landscape features, animals, plants, the
atmosphere, and celestial bodies. The statement is so succinct that many
miss its powerful meaning. On this land are certain places of special
power, where special processes and events—echoes, a miraculous escape from enemies—make the immortal people most evident or accessible to mortals, and the mortals who live on the land have a political
right to use these places for communicating with the immortals in ways
that sustain both.

Many Navajos believe that the whole earth is alive with socially interacting mortals and natural forces animated by human-looking immortal "inner forms." These places of special power are the most alive, and stories usually go with them. People visit the places to connect with their power. They use ceremonies to establish proper social relations with the Holy People who are, or have been, evident there. These places are sacred in the broadest sense of the word—they anchor the ways of Navajo life, the stories about the origins, and correct pursuit of those ways.

The stories that go with these places, and with the mortals and immortals who have come together there, are a large part of Navajo chronicles of the origin and evolution of the Navajo world, people, and customs. These chronicles are Navajo "history" as Navajos themselves have told it from older to younger, first by word of mouth, now also in writing.

Because the Holy People are so much a part of Navajo stories, and because they are associated with particular places, landscapes are strongly associated with these stories. Indeed, especially when Navajos passed down their chronicles mainly by word-of-mouth, the landscape provides a material anchor for those stories and thereby stores them. The landscape is a physical link between people of the present and their past. The landscapes and the stories that go with them depend on each other. In a sense, the landscape is part of the "text"—usually you can't grasp all the connotations of a story without knowing how the places in the story line up with each other, with other storied places, or with locations of other human events and natural processes like the movements of celestial bodies. One of the main points that we hope to get across in this book, in fact, is that places with stories, being part of the land-based life, are integrated into larger, living landscapes, just as the stories that go with each place are integrated into larger, living narratives.

We have been tempted to call this chronicle "Navajo history." Instead of extending the term "history" to cover what scholars commonly call "stories," however, we follow Gill's usage and extend the term "stories" to cover what scholars commonly call "history."

> . . . European-Americans and Native Americans do not differ as radically and clearly as is usually indicated by the distinction between history and story, a difference parallel to that between literate and nonliterate, civilized and savage. History is taken seriously, seen as connected with reality and with the true past. In contrast, story is usually seen as fictive, imaginative, nonhistorical, and, therefore, not to be taken seriously, especially if it is the story of the folk. . . . [T]he careful distinction between story and history is fundamental and essential, but . . . it does not

distinguish between Native Americans and European-Americans. . . . There is an important interdependence between story and history. Story is a manifestation of the power of the word to render history and, consequently, human life meaningful. As I have come to think of it, when the facts of history come together for someone in a way that reveals their meaning or in a way that enables their fuller meaning to be sought, a story is born. History lacks meaning without story. Story lacks substance and relevance without history. What distinguishes these traditions and those who bear the traditions is not that one presents history and the other tells stories, for they both tell stories; the distinction is the authority underlying the stories told. For the European-American story tradition the authority is history, even though the story is not strictly historical; for the Native American story tradition the authority is religious and outside of history, even though the story reflects history. (1987: 67–68)

The narratives in this work, then, are all stories, whether Navajo or non-Navajo, old or recent, ours or others', because all the narratives have taken what Gill calls "history"—information about the past, remote or recent—and have constructed stories—culturally meaningful narratives—around it.

Navajos, like other Indians, have responded to non-Indian curiosity about these places and the associated stories by trying to keep the locations and stories secret. In an oral tradition, the stories about the land contain (among many other things, all interrelated as multiple connotations of various story elements) almost a set of instructions on proper care and use of the land. You don't willingly pass such instructions to anyone whom you don't want to use the land. Non-Indians, or more accurately the businesses that profit from the unbridled consumerism in the twentieth-century United States, have a bad record of appropriating not just the land, but powerful cultural symbols to use in selling trivial consumer items.

But there is more to the secrecy. In the Navajo way, much lore about the land is esoteric, passed from a medicine man or woman to the few apprentices that he or she may have in a lifetime. Even old people who aren't specialists wouldn't pass on their most powerful stories, prayers, or songs until they felt ready to die. The reason in both cases is that indiscriminate spread of knowledge lessens its power. The person to whom you tell your secrets should already know enough about Navajo beliefs to use your secrets in the right way.

This system might have worked all right a century ago, when old people were the social and political leaders. But today's leaders in the Navajo Nation government and local communities are mainly middle-aged people, few of whom are studying with medicine people and many of whom the older people seem reluctant to entrust with their stories. Often the lack of interest is reciprocated. Many others, although they want to learn more about Navajo ways, have trouble combining modern family and community responsibilities with the situations in which such learning occurs—ceremonies, long periods out on the land with parents and grandparents. Even though middle-aged (and younger) Navajos have trouble building their knowledge of Navajo stories and customs, much of that knowledge is still widespread. So is the concern that more esoteric knowledge and practice stay alive and well through use.

Many other Indian communities seem to be the same. Since Congress passed the American Indian Religious Freedom Act in 1978, these communities haven't seen the hoped-for protection of their sacred places. Indian communities have turned to laws like the National Environmental Policy Act and the National Historic Preservation Act with mixed results. They therefore have started a new struggle to get new federal laws to protect these places. We believe that this will be one of the main Indian political issues of the 1990s. With the five hundredth anniversary of Columbus's voyage not long past, it is piercing to see how the land struggled over has shrunk from a whole continent to the isolated mountains, meadows, lakes, and springs that land developers say are not small enough to qualify for protection by law. It is painful to see, too, how the sovereign governments of these communities are reduced to seeking more benevolence in federal paternalism.

We have been part of the efforts of the Navajo Nation government, not just to preserve the places and the associated stories, but to encourage people to incorporate the old uses of these places and the stories into modern Navajo life. This book is a result of that work. Since the 1950s, as discussed in chapter 8, the Navajo Nation government has steadily expanded its cultural programs, laws, and policies to protect Navajo culture and cultural resources. One of the newer programs is the Historic Preservation Department, created in 1986 and staffed by only one person, its director. Partly at our suggestion, one of the first things this new program did was to organize a survey of people in a cross-section of Navajo communities to ask them what concerns they have about cultural resources and why. The stories that go with these places—sacred places—are part of the why and are themselves cultural resources.

We worked with the program's new director in designing the project. We also conducted most of the field work and wrote up our results. The results of this survey were supposed to help guide the program in setting its goals, policies, and methods of work. But perhaps more important than the information gained about specific places and how to protect them was the possibility of starting talk and work with these communities that would continue long after the project ended and that would eventually involve all Navajo communities. This effort and its results are the subject of part I of this book.

For various institutional reasons, the talk and work with the communities proved difficult to sustain and we were never able to extend this approach to other communities. Nor has it been easy to put across program goals, policies, and methods based on the lessons of this project. But as both professionals and people we learned a lot that we tried to apply to our more recent work that involved asking Navajos in certain localities about their concerns for cultural resources, especially sacred places, under certain problematic land-management regimes. These and similar studies by other people are described in part II of this book, which relates the findings in part I to those of other studies. The project described in part I, our subsequent work, and the work of others have made us more and more aware of what seem to be the dominating "grass-roots" Navajo opinions about, and efforts toward, cultural and landscape protection.

Part III brings out these dominant themes as Navajos express them in a variety of contexts beyond cultural resource management studies. In part III we also talk about the parts of Navajoland that all these sources (not to mention our own personal experiences of living and working in Navajoland, one of us for a lifetime and the other for more than twenty years) suggest are most in need of protection. These areas are where the old methods of secrecy within the family, local community, or network of medicine people need bolstering by new methods that involve newer institutions like Navajo Nation government, schools, and environmental organizations.

As we continue to help Navajo people put their concerns on record about protecting cultural resources and cultural rights, we grow more and more awed by the layers upon layers of meaning about the land and the culture that we discover in the stories. In part IV we try to impart some of this sense of unfolding discovery with a detailed discussion of two very short stories. We want to show how a story about a place specifies ("constructs") a culturally significant landscape and situates that place in it, often through implication rather than explicit statements. Even the short statements about locations that we discuss in this part are packed with information on the place's significance to the speaker and other Navajos. In part IV we also switch to an analytical viewpoint, outside the Navajo cultural frame as we have been interpreting it, to show that a story may contain information from which to make another story—one about the roots of Navajo culture.

Klara Kelley did most of the actual writing, based on discussions with Harris Francis that started before the writing and continued throughout it, not to mention the experiences that both authors shared through several years of working together. Harris Francis translated all the statements that we have reproduced from our own field work. He reviewed the entire work to make sure that it portrays accurately his own point of view as a Navajo and the viewpoints of the Navajos whom we interviewed. He also made the most likely interpretations of points of view of other Navajos in the printed sources we have consulted.

This book is not an inventory of Navajo sacred places, since most people who have taught us still regard secrecy as the first line of defense. These people wish neither to be objects of study themselves nor to have the places and stories dear to them made objects of study, at least not for purposes irrelevant to them. Instead, this book is about various ways in which these places have been, and still are, part of Navajo life. That these places truly are still part of modern Navajo life is evident from the concerns many Navajos express publicly in the face of the "economic development" juggernaut, which is the main thing that forces people to abandon secrecy and at least hint at their stories. Therefore, following Magubane and Faris (1985), we want this book to be not part of the problem, but part of the solution, not to exploit Navajos but to critique the exploitation of Navajos by showing how Navajo encounters with colonialism and "economic development" are affecting the landscapes and associated stories.

In keeping with our purpose, we have included some old stories that go with the landscape within the storytellers' larger statements of their concerns about modern life. But of course, the book is full of other, newer kinds of stories connected to the landscape through more recent events.

One reviewer of this manuscript (although generally sympathetic) noted our seemingly idiosyncratic choice of stories and use of sources of information, so we will explain these choices. First, regarding our sources. Sources lend authority, and what we have to say rests on the authority of our own experience as observers and participants as well as listeners and readers. This book is our attempt to make sense of all these things, to make what Gill calls "history" (or at least other people's stories) into our own stories. We believe in systematic examination of sources as an antidote to one's own wishes and prejudices, but we don't believe in the possibility of "pure," detached inductivism from all known sources. We hope that even a conservative reader can find our use of sources at least arguably valid in the light of our purpose, which is not to deliver the definitive work on Navajo sacred landscapes and economic development, but to stir up public discourse on the subject by speaking from our own experiences as witnesses to that encounter.

Part I is based on our own field work in thirteen Navajo communities. We tried to talk to a representative cross section of people concerned with culturally important places by picking a representative cross-section of communities and asking the community representatives to choose interviewees to represent this segment of their communities. We're not trying to give a cross-section of Navajo views on these places, only a cross-section of the views of people who care about them. That these caring people are a significant segment of Navajo society as a whole is evident from the support that they receive from Navajo institutions, as described in part III. We've also tried to suggest briefly how the places and stories that people mentioned fit with what has already been published (not including technical reports, the "gray literature," which we use in part II). We've reviewed what published sources we could find on places in each community that have religious or "historical" associations, including nearly all published works on the stories that go with specific ceremonies (which also make up most of the published works on the ceremonies themselves).

In part II we show how the places, stories, and policy concerns that people mentioned in our thirteen-community study fit with other studies most like ours in purpose and methods. We consulted reports (mainly technical) on all such studies that we could find. In part III we show how the policy concerns of our thirteen-community study and the other similar studies fit with other accounts of Navajo policy concerns about cultural and landscape preservation.

Our accounts of the developments that gave rise to the studies in part II and to the expressions of concern in part III are more or less coherent stories. In both their relative coherence and their relative succinctness, they hide the actual complexities of large numbers of people acting, reacting, and interacting in unfolding political ritual dramas in which people play roles that they may not entirely understand. So many ripples and loose ends emanate from the actual events under these "stories" that the intertwined sequences of events never actually end, only lead into various other sequences that one may describe through various other "stories." This is our view of the relationship between the processes of the real world and the stories that we all tell about those processes to gloss over the real world's unknowns, uncertainties, and irreconcilable contradictions.

The sources of information available about the problems we discuss are mainly (besides our own first-hand observations) newspaper stories,

technical reports, position papers of participants, and the like—sources
so ephemeral and prolific as to defy accepted scholarly methods of
reconstructing a story from all the available documentation. We use
these sources not only from lack of scholarly or "official" documentation about many of our topics, but also because scholars and officials
sometimes discount the people who express themselves through these
media, thus ignoring (or mischaracterizing) what they have to say.

Part IV first discusses connotations of two Navajo stories with heavy
reliance for esoteric meanings on Reichard's (1963 [1950]) rather ex-
haustive compilation of Navajo story and ceremonial elements. This
source reliably and thoroughly characterizes the literature on which it is
based, the literature on ceremonialism and stories cited in part I. Part IV
then compares elements in the Navajo stories with elements from stories
of neighboring Indian communities. We propose to account for the
elements that all these stories have in common with a brief story about
Navajo cultural change in relation to change in political economy. The
sources about the stories and ceremonial practices of other groups and
about changes in Navajo political economy are scholarly ones, which
one can theoretically review exhaustively but not within the scope of a
book like this one. (One of the authors is the co-author of a book
[Kelley and Whiteley 1989] about changes in Navajo political economy
and land use, although that book was written before the many recent
archaeological findings on early Navajos and consciously avoids relating
political economy to Navajo ceremonialism and the stories that go with
it.) Our purpose here is to propose a new way of looking at Navajo
cultural change and its relationship to neighboring groups, and show
that the story we propose deserves further investigation because it
accords with the work of some others.

Turning now to our choice of Navajo stories reproduced here: we
chose them to make a group that, read in sequence, would parallel our
own story, and to represent the range of Navajos who care about
keeping Navajo ways alive. These people vary in age, education, occupation; they vary in whether they express these ideas orally or in
writing, in Navajo or English, semiprivately to interviewers or publicly,
through retelling old stories or through their own syntheses of many
kinds of information about the past; they vary in rhetorical methods—
moral imperatives, apocalyptic predictions, and analysis. The order in
which we present these stories reflects partly the surrounding text,
which the stories illustrate, but also the chronology of Navajo history as
Navajos see it, from the episodes of the creation to the experiences of the
most recent generations. We've included stories we recorded and those
recorded by others, both recently and in the past to have a linguistic and

anthropological record of cultural forms that researchers and probably storytellers felt were dying out. Our format sets these nuggets apart from the surrounding text so that you can ignore what we have to say and read them in the sequence given or any other that you want. We want you to see for yourself what Navajos say, but of course we did the choosing for you.

Our rationale for choice and sequence of photographs is analogous—we've tried to show the different kinds of places important to Navajo people and the various types of development (including none) that are affecting them. The pictures and explanatory captions start with certain basic images you need to understand the significance of the images that follow, which are ordered roughly according to the parts of the Navajo chronicle associated with each. We've used only our own photographs, in keeping with our themes of speaking from our own experience and experiencing the past through the present.

The readers most interested in this book, we suspect, will be those concerned with environmental preservation, especially as it involves "indigenous peoples." In fact, we hope a good share of those readers will be "indigenous people" themselves. But we also speak to others, including "mainstream" folklorists, ethnohistorians, anthropologists, practitioners of disciplines "traditionally" concerned at least partly with "preserving indigenous culture" (if not among the people themselves, then at least in records).

Turning to terminology used (or avoided) throughout this book, first, we have tried to avoid "tradition." Navajos themselves (including one of the authors) often use this English word to translate Navajo terms that are more literally translated as "Navajo-way," "Navajos' own." Navajos themselves argue about what things in present Navajo life accord with the "Navajo way." The lives of most Navajos today involve much that is new and non-Navajo in origin. Navajos must struggle to integrate the useful (formal public education) into their lives without overwhelming the old ways and to keep out the harmful (teenage gangs), and even useful things have their harmful aspects. Navajos must grapple with how to view old ways that many consider harmful, such as witchcraft beliefs. In general, things widely recognized as being in the Navajo way figure in Navajo stories of the origin of the world, the Navajo people, their customs, and so forth. In addition, some things that came to Navajos from other groups a long time ago (silversmithing, for example) most Navajos probably also recognize as in the Navajo way because they are well integrated with other Navajo-way things. When we refer to Navajo ways or Navajo customs or Navajo culture, then, we refer to these kinds of things.

We have also been criticized in the past, by Navajos and non-Navajos, including our professional colleagues, for using terms like "religion," "sacred," "ceremony," "ritual," and so forth, because these terms connote a division of human life and activity into sacred and secular spheres. Perhaps the words even connote a sphere in which participants merely suspend disbelief, rather than believe. Such a division, they point out, is alien to the old Navajo way of life.

We don't want to get hung up on definitional hairsplitting, since we believe that all terms are ambiguous to some degree—they connote different things to different people, and the meaning of a term comes partly from the various contexts in which speakers of the language use it, contexts that the reader or listener may not know about. As we said above, according to old Navajo belief, the everyday world is filled with sources of power, the "inner forms" or Holy People in all places, species, and forces of nature. Many old Navajo practices, both everyday and for special occasions, tap these sources of power for human benefit by relating mortals socially to the appropriate Holy People. The theory behind how and why these practices work rests on such commonsense human ideas as that one can influence something at a distance because of such principles as "like begets like" and two things once physically connected can continue to influence each other when separated (ideas embedded in language as metaphor and metonymy). These practices, then, are as much applied science as they are religion or ceremony. To avoid vagueness, throughout this book we use "religion," "ceremony," and so forth, but also "beliefs," "knowledge," "ways," and "stories" instead of "religion" or "tradition," and "procedure," "practice," "activity," or "performance" instead of "ceremony" or "ritual." Through these usages we hope to remind the reader how pervasive these things have been in the old Navajo way of life.

Finally, and somewhat arbitrarily, we use the word *Navajo* rather than the people's own name for themselves, *Diné*. Writing in English, we have fallen into using the "English" name for the people.

We emphasize that we're not trying to replicate or otherwise render "Navajo truth"—how someone steeped in Navajo ways might see things (the importance of connotation in the meanings of words is one of many reasons why we believe that such a rendering is only possible in the Navajo language). Instead, in most of this work we're trying to interpret such a point of view for the great majority of readers not familiar with Navajo ways, and then, in part IV, to make our own story about Navajo stories by relating those stories to other sources of information about the past. We stand at a remove from the Navajo framework and use scholarly analytical methods, not because we think the scholarly framework is superior for any and all purposes, but because it lets us reach a particular group of our colleagues which we want to do because of concerns about protecting Navajo ways that arise from our work in a complex, multi-ethnic setting still riddled with colonialist power relations. And, to be more specific about where in relation to the Navajo framework we are situated: we speak from political positions critical of exploitation, not only of one human by another, but also of the natural world by humans, including humans whose exploitation of other humans forces the latter (even against their own best judgment) to exploit nature.

Even though we're writing "at a remove from" the Navajo framework, we're not, of course, entirely outside it. Not only is one of us a Navajo, but, as Bruner (1986:150) says, even when the anthropologist and the Indian community member differ culturally, "we share, at least partially, those narratives dealing with intercultural relations and cultural change," and that anthropologists and community members sort of find each other—each gravitates toward the other "whose narratives are most compatible with [his or her] own" (p. 151).

Finally, we aren't trying to exhaust our subject or write an authoritative work that claims to be the "last word." Our aim is the opposite, to start readers thinking. Therefore we've included many voices and much context in the form of statements by many people involved with Navajo sacred places. There is a lot of uninterpreted, unanalyzed meaning below the surface of each text (including our own) which interested readers will tap when they start seeing recurring themes, contradictions, or other patterns from one statement to another. There are thousands and thousands more hours of unpublished Navajo statements on record about the landscape and its stories, waiting for the day when others can't so easily exploit and misuse this information. The day when Navajos willingly give many such stories to others will come, however, only when the Navajo people themselves have gained both legal and practical control over land use in their homeland.

PART ONE

PLACES

A SURVEY

IMPORTANT

OF THIRTEEN

TO NAVAJO

NAVAJO COMMUNITIES

PEOPLE

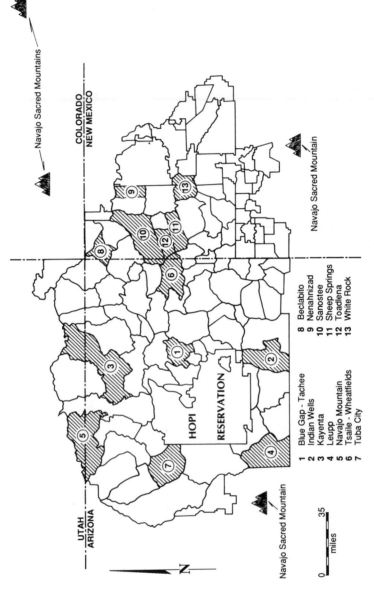

Figure 1. Locations of the 13 chapters in survey of Navajo preservation concerns (1987 boundaries).

1.

Background

In 1986, the Navajo Nation government created the Historic Preservation Department to help care for the cultural resources of the Navajo people—places and landscapes important to the Navajos and other American Indians, archaeological sites, historic buildings, objects, even "intangibles" like oral history and customs. The first task for the new department was to learn about "grass roots" Navajo preservation concerns. This section covers how we, as employees of the Navajo Nation government, tried to find out about those concerns and what we learned.

American Indian concerns about preserving Indian cultures led Congress to enact a joint resolution, the American Indian Religious Freedom Act of 1978 (AIRFA), which affirms the

> inherent right of freedom to believe, express, and exercise the traditional religions of the American Indian, Eskimo, Aleut, and Native Hawaiians, including but not limited to access to sites, use and possession of sacred

objects, and freedom to worship through ceremonials and traditional rites. (U.S. Congress 1978)

But this law hasn't been effective.

> The truly ironic aspect of modern land use is that during the past three decades, Congress has passed many laws which purport to protect certain kinds of lands and resources from the very developers who now seek to exclude Indian religious people from using public lands. The Wild and Scenic Rivers Act, the Wilderness Act, the National Environmental [Policy] Act [1969], the Clean Air Act, the National Historic Preservation Act [1966, and amended], and several other statutes all take definite steps to protect and preserve the environment in a manner more reminiscent of traditional Native American religion than that of uncontrolled capitalism or the domination of land expounded by the world religions. No real progress can be made in environmental law unless some of the insights into the sacredness of land derived from traditional tribal religions become basic attitudes of the larger society.
>
> At present, legal remedies for Indian religious practitioners are limited to those procedures provided by various environmental and historic preservation laws which, in some circumstances, may provide an indirect means for protection of sites. The only existing law directly addressing this issue, the American Indian Religious Freedom Act of 1978, is simply a policy statement with "no teeth." While it has led to some administrative regulations and policies providing for limited additional opportunities for input, it provides no legal cause of action to aggrieved practitioners. (Deloria 1991:6)

AIRFA has led federal agencies to consult American Indians formally about how proposed federal developments might harm sacred places, but the law doesn't provide any administrative mechanism for Indian communities to contest agency decisions on how to treat such places. Indian grievances are therefore thrown into the courts, an inhospitable forum given the law's failure to specify a legal cause of action to the aggrieved and a growing body of unfavorable case law.

Public concern about preserving the environment and Indian cultures, then, has produced laws that only partly or weakly protect natural and cultural resources. A cacophony of voices about places and whole landscapes important in Indian cultures, especially places considered "sacred," rises from Navajoland, as elsewhere in Indian country, about how Indians can use these laws to protect their customs about the land. To hear these voices more clearly, in 1987 and 1988, we talked with people in various parts of Navajoland about what kinds of cultural resources they think are worth preserving and why (Downer and others 1988, 1989).[1]

Before we started talking to people, we knew that Navajoland is full of places that figure in stories—by both Navajos and others—about the

Navajo past (not to mention stories by and about neighboring Indian communities). The results of our own field work, especially when combined with work of others (see part II) have given us more insights into stories about the Navajo past by both Navajos and others. We will refer to both types of stories repeatedly in this work.

The first written records on the region occupied by the Navajos— what is now northwest New Mexico, northeast Arizona, southeast Utah, and southwest Colorado—come from the Spaniards, who first visited the region with Coronado in 1540. References to Navajos, first ambiguous and then unequivocal, occur within the next century. Documentation, almost always by the colonizers or scholars working under their hegemony, becomes progressively more detailed through the end of the Mexican War in 1848, when the U.S. took the region from Mexico, through 1864, when the U.S. finally conquered the Navajos, and since 1864, as Navajoland has become economically, politically, and culturally tied more and more closely to the United States as a whole. Similarly, Navajo stories of their encounter with the colonizers, mostly unwritten until recently, becomes more detailed the closer one gets to the present. The following account is our synthesis of stories from these various sources.[2]

The Navajos Encounter Colonialism

Up to the conquest in 1864, most Navajos had lived by farming, herding mainly sheep, goats, and horses, hunting and gathering, and sometimes raiding. The Navajos got their first livestock from raiding the Spanish colonists. Much raiding was not for booty but in retaliation for the slave raids of the Spanish colonists (and the Pueblo Indians whom the Spanish forced to serve as auxiliaries). The Navajo tribe had no central political authority, but its members were all tied together in other ways. The tribe seems to have consisted of dozens of local groups, each with a dozen or more intermarried extended families with customary use rights to a shared, inalienable land base. Each group chose, by consensus, a headman who was often wealthy, and probably strategically placed in the kinship network. He settled disputes, mobilized the group for defense, and spoke for the group with outsiders. He also got together with other headmen over big questions like war and peace.

The Navajo tribe was bound together politically by a network of several dozen headmen of equal status, as well as by marriages between families of different local groups. Being a Navajo was (and still is) defined by one's ties to Navajo clans, named kinship groups whose members inherit membership from their mothers. In addition to the mothers' clans, Navajos also emphasize separate ties to the clans of their fathers and grandfathers on both mother's and father's side. Marriages among people of different local groups are common because Navajos are forbidden to marry a member of the clan of either parent and are also supposed to avoid marrying into the clans of their grandparents. A Navajo community might give in-married non-Navajos and captives new identities as Navajos by treating their previous ethnic, tribal, local, or non-Navajo clan affiliation as a Navajo clan.

In 1864, the U.S. Army ended Navajo political independence when Kit Carson and his troops and their Ute and Puebloan auxiliaries burned Navajo cornfields and starved the Navajos into submission. More than 8,000 Navajos, perhaps half the population, surrendered and went from their homeland to Fort Sumner, New Mexico, hundreds of miles eastward. They couldn't raise enough crops there to support themselves, however. Four years later, the headmen signed a treaty that created a reservation in a small part of their former homeland. Then they all returned home.

From 1868 until the 1930s, the Navajos lived under federal rule by raising livestock and crops, as before. Now, however, instead of each family consuming directly what it produced, families traded wool and other products to the trading posts that non-Indian colonists had established in Navajoland, especially after the transcontinental railroad appeared in 1881.

The Navajos had never confined themselves to the Treaty Reservation. They had tried to reoccupy their pre-conquest homeland only to find non-Indian settlers increasingly hemming them in. Piece by piece, the federal government added some of this area to the original Treaty Reservation. Today, the Navajo Reservation covers 27,000 square miles in Arizona, New Mexico, and Utah. Much of the pre-conquest Navajo homeland also remained federal land, however, and most of that is now under U.S. Forest Service and Bureau of Land Management jurisdiction. The resulting increase of Navajo population on the fixed land base, the lack of ways to make a living other than by stockraising (as the traders squeezed profits from the Navajos and invested them outside Navajoland), and lowering of the water table during the continuing cycle of downcutting and filling that has characterized the Southwest since prehistoric times, all contributed to denuding the range. Federal policy to curb the problem came, however, only after 1928. The resulting burden of silt in the Colorado River threatened the planned Boulder Dam and thereby the electrical power so dear to the hearts of Los Angeles real estate speculators.

The federal government reacted by passing the Taylor Grazing Act of 1934 to regulate grazing on public lands throughout the West, and by forcing Indians, including the Navajos, to get rid of much of their livestock. The Navajo livestock reduction, ultimately by half, probably owed more to the Depression, however. Wool and livestock prices that the traders paid fell faster than did the prices that they charged the Navajos for staple foods.

After stock reduction and World War II, stockraising was no longer the Navajo economic mainstay. The federal government administered the Navajo economy more actively along with the Navajo Tribal Council, which the federal government had set up in 1923 to sign oil leases and had reorganized and enlarged in 1937. Navajos came to depend mainly on (under)employment in federal and tribal governments and in oil and gas, coal, uranium, and electrical power industries that flourished during and after World War II to feed booming Los Angeles, Phoenix, and Albuquerque. These are the developments in and around Navajoland that bring attention to Navajo sacred places. They generate profits mainly for interests far outside Navajoland and don't give Navajos enough work or income to create a standard of living anywhere near the (however "mythical") U.S. "median" or "average." These "Third World" standards, the geography of exploitation, the history of conquest and expropriation, the fact that the federal government didn't recognize all Indians as citizens until 1924—all are reasons for our use of the term "colonialism" to cover Navajo relations with the U.S. political economy even to the present.

Nevertheless, through all these changes, Navajos have kept much of their pre-conquest homeland and also their pre-conquest land-use regime of extended families dispersed over the landscape, each with its own livestock, homesites, and seasonal herding camps and farms. Many Navajos today live and work in reservation government centers, border towns, or even distant cities. But they are still parts of extended families with other members (often parents and grandparents) herding and farming on the land that earlier generations of the same families have used.

Navajo Creation Stories
and Ceremonialism

The land-based family is the anchor for the Navajo stories about the Navajo past. These stories cover each family's use of the land and the places that the family has used in getting its living. They also cover the origin of the earth and sky, Navajoland, the Navajo people, their clans, ceremonies, and other customs. The Navajo way of life involves all the family's activities in these places to sustain and reproduce itself.

These land-based activities involve the family sometimes by itself and sometimes as part of the larger local "community," or network of interrelated and intermarried extended families (not to mention various immortal beings—Holy People—who live on the land). The activities include daily acts like herding, getting wood and drinking water, planting, cultivating, harvesting, and so forth, and the accompanying prayers and other small ceremonial acts through which one interacts with the Holy People while one is working. Less frequent activities are gathering plants, minerals, wildlife, and water for ceremonial use; and interacting with various immortal beings, the Holy People, through ceremonial performances to maintain or restore personal, family, and community health and prosperity or to protect the person, family, and community from various types of harm.

Daily life, land use, ceremonialism, and stories are therefore interwoven around the land-based extended family. Navajo stories recognize these interrelationships by illustrating how the land and everything on it are alive, permeated by a life essence of mingled air, light, and moisture. Each "thing" in this system, including landforms, individual plants, animals, natural forces, and so forth, has its own immortal humanlike "inner form" (Holy Person), which interacts with the other "things" in the system. There are also other Holy People, who move freely about the earth and sky. They are the main actors in Navajo stories about the origins of the world and Navajo life.

Directly or indirectly, the family is the main perpetuator of the Navajo way of life and stories. The older members of the family are supposed to tell younger ones about the family's past. Also, one's basic orientation to the land comes first through the family. This orientation is literal. Navajo geography recognizes the same four cardinal directions as do European-derived geographies, but east is the direction Navajos emphasize. Customary Navajo dwellings, called hogans, always have east-facing entryways (exits is a more literal translation of the Navajo in a terminological system that emphasizes motion outward or upward from the person). Navajo children in their cognitive development thereby become oriented to geographical space as soon as they become aware of the order in all dwellings. The Navajo creation stories describe the entire pre-conquest homeland as a hogan, with a sacred mountain in each of the four directions compared to a pole in the hogan's framework. So ingrained is this sense of geography that Navajos raised in the old ways will organize just about any domain of knowledge, even abstract or non-geographical or non-Navajo things, by associating the various components of the domain with the four directions.

Navajo beliefs also include a tremendous amount of esoteric knowledge that only certain medicine people possess. Much of this knowledge is organized into repertoires of ceremonial procedures, paraphernalia, prayers, songs, and the stories that explain how all these elements came together to form the repertoire. Each repertoire is directed at particular Holy People to engage their powers. These Holy People control natural phenomena and can alleviate the illness or other misfortune that they visit on a person, family, or community to express displeasure with certain deeds of one or more humans. Each repertoire has a name, which may refer to one of the main powers sought (Windway), or a distinctive feature of ceremonial acts in the repertoire (Nightway, for the all-night masked dancing), or a desired result (Blessingway). Each repertoire includes certain procedures that can be performed alone (prayers with medicinal substances and paraphernalia applied to the patient, for example) and require only hours. It also includes procedures that must be part of longer performances, and specifications for combining procedures into longer performances that may last as long as nine nights and days. All of these longer performances done according to a specific "way" (performances from the same repertoire) must include certain essential procedures in an exact order, but others are by choice. No two ceremonial performances from the same repertoire are exactly alike.

Navajo medicine people learn their specialties by serving apprenticeships to particular older specialists. There is no central authority, and until recently no organized groups of medicine people. No other hierarchy exists beyond the temporary difference in status between the apprentice and the teacher, which disappears when the apprentice completes the training. Some medicine people may know only one short procedure from one repertoire, while others may know in their entirety all the essential and optional procedures of several repertoires that can produce performances of up to nine nights. Most practitioners fall in between these two extremes. These people may gather their own raw materials from which they make medicines and paraphernalia. They may get these things from other medicine people who specialize in collecting certain materials, especially plants. There are also diviners who diagnose the source of a person's troubles and recommend a particular repertoire.

Most procedures and performances, whether short or long, require a patient. Even when the condition to be alleviated is something like wind or drought, a human act has caused it, and the Holy People must be persuaded to remedy the condition by making the offender (or representative) one of their own. The reason for asserting that the family is responsible at least indirectly for even the most esoteric parts of these repertoires is that it is the family that sponsors the performances of these repertoires. Most performances occur mainly in and around a hogan that belongs to the patient's family. The medicine person sits next to the patient and performs a series of procedures over the patient, including chanting, singing, prayer litanies, administering herbal medicines, having sandpaintings made, and applying other substances and paraphernalia to the patient. The medicine person also places various offerings in numerous places both near and far from the hogan. Other procedures don't involve a patient, like making offerings to specific Holy People at particular spots on the landscape that the Holy People frequent in exchange for taking plants and other materials, for rain, for the well-being of livestock that graze and for families that live within view of the offering place, and so forth.

Each repertoire has its own origin story, or at least a collection of stories about how various parts of the repertoire came about. These stories can be strung together in long chronicles, perhaps more in response to anthropologists' requests for "*the* myth of the such-and-such way ceremony" than for any other purpose [Faris 1990]. The stories are usually about a young Navajo man (sometimes a woman) who gets into a series of troubles and is helped or cured each time by one or more Holy People. In the course of the cure and in subsequent travels for self-education, the hero learns the various procedures and assembles the various materials and paraphernalia that are now part of the repertoire, and at the end teaches everything to relatives. The songs, prayers, sandpaintings, and other parts of the performance refer to these stories, although often only obliquely, or the stories explain or justify these elements. The order of stories in the complete chronicle is probably just as likely to be dictated by the order of songs, sandpaintings, and so forth in a performance as the other way around. Telling these stories isn't a required part of any performance, and some medicine people have learned the procedures without learning the stories that go with them. Others do tell the appropriate story from the repertoire before starting a particular procedure.

An important repertoire that differs somewhat from this general description is the Blessingway. Various choices from this repertoire are used at turning points in a person's life, for all sorts of major and minor occasions to insure continued well-being and prosperity, for making and renewing paraphernalia, and at the end of performances from almost every other repertoire to insure its effectiveness. The stories of the origin of Blessingway are the stories of the creation of the present earth and sky and of the Navajo people and the Navajo homeland, hereafter called the Navajo creation stories. Important episodes are the emergence of the people onto the present earth surface; placement of the four sacred mountains, which symbolize both the outer limits of Navajoland and the four cardinal directions (east, south, west, and north, to use the prescribed sunwise order) in which the movements of sun, moon, and stars orient one on the land; and the life of Changing Woman, perhaps the most trusted Navajo Holy Person. The origin stories of other ceremonies also include various parts of the creation stories. We will refer to these creation stories repeatedly throughout this work and therefore to the elements common to most versions here.[3]

In the beginning there was the Black World or the First World, in which essential substances combining air, moisture, light, and soil (or corn) formed into earth and sky, paired as female and male, and various other Holy People. The entire creation from this beginning involves the principle of complementary pairs, male and female. The beings were in human form but were immortals. Most inhabitants of the First World were tiny insects, but also included were (in some versions) First Man and First Woman. The people moved upward into the Second World, the Blue World. Bigger animals lived there. They went to the Third World, the Yellow World, and eventually to the present world, what we know as the White World or Fourth World. Various versions have different numbers and colors and creatures of lower worlds before the emergence onto the present earth surface.

Each time the beings left one world to move up to the next, their departure was caused by some kind of misconduct among the inhabitants, which brought on disasters like fire, drought, and wind. In the world below the present one, men and women quarreled and moved to opposite sides of a river. The women practiced "unnatural" sex acts that caused some of them to give birth to monsters. After the men and women reunited, Coyote stole the baby of "Water Monster" (a being that existed, according to some versions, since the First World, not one of the monsters born as a result of the separation of the sexes). The Water Monster took revenge by causing a great flood. The Holy People climbed into the present world inside the stalk of a giant reed.

First Man and First Woman created the first hogan and sweathouse, then placed on the present earth's surface various landforms, including the sacred mountains, which they reproduced from pinches of soil brought from the counterparts of these mountains in the lower worlds. The four mountains that symbolize the cardinal directions have associated colors and precious stones. Death originated at this time, and many of the Holy People became subject to it, therefore becoming human ("earth-surface people"). Then the monsters began killing them off. First Man and First Woman also performed certain ceremonial acts that preceded the appearance of the infant Changing Woman from clouds on top of Spruce Mountain. They thereby intentionally set in motion a series of events that would lead to the killing of the monsters so that the present earth surface would be safe for the Navajo people, who were yet to be created. Changing Woman took charge of the creation from First Man and First Woman. She gave birth to the Twins, Monster Slayer and Born For Water, whose father was the Sun (water was also involved in their conception).

The Twins later journeyed to the east to visit their father. After putting them through a series of trials, their father gave them weapons with which to kill the monsters that roamed the earth's surface. He was sad to do this because at least one of the monsters, Big God, was a child of his, too. The older twin, Monster Slayer, did the actual killing, while the younger twin, Born For Water, stayed at home on Huerfano Mountain near Spruce Mountain, monitoring his brother's success through divination in case his brother should need him. In some versions of this story, when the earth was free of monsters, Changing Woman (or Whiteshell Woman, whom some consider the same as Changing Woman) created progenitors of certain Navajo clans.

Later, the Sun persuaded Changing Woman to make her home in the west. She travelled from her home on Huerfano Mountain across Navajoland, a route marked by many places today. At her new home in the west, an offshore island or floating home, Changing Woman used the residues of her skin to create the progenitors of Navajo clans. These people then journeyed eastward back across Navajoland using essentially the same route as had their creator to join people that Whiteshell Woman had previously created there, or the few roving bands that had survived the monsters. These combined groups became the Navajo people. Still later, Changing Woman took two boys and taught them the Blessingway ceremonies. They returned to the Navajo people and taught these ceremonies to others.

Stories of the origins of various clans branch off this "main stalk" of creation stories, as small bands of Puebloans, Apaches, Utes, Paiutes, Havasupais, and many others joined up with the first clans (these bands were incorporated as clans). The origin stories of all ceremonial repertoires also branch off this main stalk. Besides telling these stories during breaks in ceremonial performances, people used to tell these stories on winter nights at home. Some still do.

Although most activities during a ceremonial performance are concentrated in and around the hogan itself, the repertoire involves, directly and indirectly, an extensive land base. The paraphernalia are made from an amazing array of rare plant, animal, and mineral materials that have been gathered over time from far distant places, even some (like seashells and buffalo scrota) outside of Navajoland. Other materials, especially medicinal plants, are gathered from a variety of places just before a performance. Still other materials, usually plants, are gathered during the performance, often with the medicine person directing members of the patient's family, who know the nearest places to find them. At the beginning of the performance, the medicine person places offerings outside, away from the hogan, to attract the appropriate Holy People. If the offering conforms faithfully to specifications detailed in the stories of the repertoire, the Holy Person *must* accept it. Acceptance in turn obligates the Holy Person to help restore the patient—this is part of the social contract between humans and Holy People. The medicine person and helpers place other offerings in various places near and far from the hogan at other times during the performance. They also dispose of substances used up during the performance in certain outdoor settings away from the hogan according to instructions in the stories of the repertoire. The stories of the repertoire also refer to many places through which the hero or heroine travels in assembling the repertoire, and which are the homes of various Holy People whom the repertoire engages. Between ceremonies, the medicine person may visit these places to make offerings and collect certain materials.

Each repertoire and each performance, then, requires various activities around large parts of Navajoland, which result in medicine people and others visiting a wide range of environmental zones and observing the condition of rare species and the land there. These activities allow medicine people to notice changes in the health of the ecosystems of Navajoland. These materials collected from all over Navajoland are then brought to the patient, thus symbolically bringing the resources of all Navajoland to benefit the patient and the family and community that the patient may represent. The daily activities of stockraising and farming (including individual and family prayers for plentiful herds and crops and personal well-being) root the Navajos in their family's land base by turning the land into food, which becomes their flesh. Ceremonial performances bond Navajos to the whole of Navajoland by engulfing them with the diversity of the land's natural products.

2.

The Project to Consult Navajo Communities

With the background given in the preceding chapter, we began our 1987–1988 project to learn about Navajo preservation concerns. The project involved thirteen local communities, called chapters, in New Mexico and Arizona. The chapter is the smallest unit of Navajo self-government. At the time there were 109 chapters (now 110), averaging 1,500–2,000 residents. Chapter meetings occur at least monthly. Each chapter has officers and a full-time chapter manager who administers daily chapter business. Each chapter makes up all or part of the district represented by a delegate to the Navajo Nation Council, the Navajo law-making body.

Figure 1 shows the locations of the seven chapters we chose in the Arizona part of the Navajo Nation: Navajo Mountain, Leupp, Tsaile-Wheatfields, Kayenta, Tuba City, Indian Wells, and Blue Gap-Tachee, and the six New Mexico chapters: Beclabito, Sanostee, Toadlena, Sheep Springs, Nenahnezad, and White Rock. We chose these chapters because they seemed to have a good geographical spread and range of economic development. The technical appendix shows more specifically how these chapters compare to the Navajo Nation as a whole and to each other.

Field Methods

We started field work in each chapter by contacting chapter officials—the officers, Navajo Nation Council delegate, or both. We followed up these first contacts by attending meetings of residents in some chapter areas. Some chapters assigned an official or volunteer to show us places of concern. But in most chapters, either the officials or the residents in the meeting gave us lists of people to interview. They apparently assumed that the concerns and places important to these people would adequately represent the chapter. We intentionally avoided imposing a uniform procedure for choosing people to interview in all chapters. Since our purpose was to find out the concerns of community members, we didn't want to prejudice the results by dictating how the chapter would give us the information.

Of the eighty-one people we interviewed, about one out of every four was a middle-aged chapter official, whose concerns were oriented toward community development. The rest were elderly people steeped in knowledge of the land and Navajo culture. (This latter group included a very few chapter officials.) Their concerns leaned toward preserving the land and culture. The interviews were "open ended," that is, after we explained why we were asking them for help, the interviewees would take control of the conversation. Most of the interviews were conducted in the Navajo language by a pair of researchers (usually the authors), at least one of whom is fluent in Navajo. Interviews were tape-recorded if the interviewee was willing, and most of the interviews occurred in the interviewees' homes. Whenever possible, we also visited the places with the person who told us about them. Otherwise, we visited the places on our own. We located all places on USGS topographic maps, photographed them, and made various field notes (including plan maps of archaeological sites).

The differences between the chapter with the most possible connections "outside," Tuba City, and the chapter with least such connections, Navajo Mountain, are worth noting. Because of the Tuba City chapter's centralized approach to identifying places (basically having one of the council delegates show us everything), we interviewed the fewest people and identified the most places per person there. Because of the Navajo Mountain chapter's extremely decentralized approach (giving us a list of a couple of dozen elders and having a chapter employee accompany us to introduce us), we interviewed the most people there and identified the fewest places per person.

It is tempting to think that the difference in the two chapters' approaches reflects differences in their connections to the outside world, but that is not our conclusion. Indian Wells and Leupp also took a rather centralized approach and yet are not as connected as Kayenta and Nenahnezad, which basically followed Navajo Mountain's approach. We don't know what caused some chapters take more centralized approaches than others, but we noticed that chapter officials tended to mention more "historic" (public) buildings and potential tourist attractions than did the old people to whom chapter officials referred us. The chapters where the largest proportions of "historic" buildings and tourist attractions were mentioned are the ones where chapter officials gave us the most information, but they are not necessarily the chapters most connected to the outside world.

Results: Concerns and Stories about the Land

The following statements typify the concerns that people expressed to us and the contexts within which people told stories. Most interviews unfortunately occurred in the spring, summer, and fall, when, as many people noted, one is not supposed to tell sacred stories.[1]

MAMIE SALT

[In December 1987, Harris Francis and Richard Begay interviewed Mrs. Salt at her home near Kayenta, Arizona. Summary translation is by Harris Francis, reproduced with Mrs. Salt's permission. Confidential details on places have been omitted.]

Every inch of ground, all vegetation and the fauna on it are considered sacred. There are no places that are holier than others. There are so many stories that go with the land that it would take more than twenty years to tell them.

[She informed us of some of the local landmarks around Kayenta.] The Water Monster, a Holy Being, made the [name] canyon and lived in there. [This is the same being whose baby Coyote stole and caused the flood in the creation story in chapter 1.] He used one of his horns to dig the channel where

[name] creek now flows. There is never supposed to be any dispute about the water, but like everything else, there are disputes
about the land on which the stream flows. The Holy People put
us here and the people considered all things sacred, the land,
plants, and animals—we are their children. When it is cold, we
burn the wood, which keeps us warm. We cook with it in order
to eat, to keep us from getting sick. We use the plants for medicine and to smoke. We pray with the smoke. Learn the prayers
for the plants, and you can use them to help yourself and other
people.

[The Black Mesa Mountains are another sacred area.] It is
said to be the body of the Female Pollen Range lying there. It is
there to protect the people. The Navajo people were told by the
Holy Ones to leave it alone. Now the coal companies who hire
Navajos have come in and are strip-mining the mesa, desecrating it. This coal is said to be the blood of the Female Pollen figure lying there. This coal is considered sacred.

Young Navajos help in digging up the coal today. They burn
the coal for heat, and use it for cooking, breathing in the fumes
from it. This causes many different kinds of sickness. You hear
about the people working in these mines become sick with can-
cer. The desecration of Black Mesa will burn out our souls one
day.

Today when we try to teach the young people about these
important things, they will not listen to us. We, the Navajo people, are travelling on the same road the Anasazi travelled. The
Anasazi [prehistoric inhabitants of Navajoland] were placed here
before us. They were a part of us also, only their language was
a little different. As time went on they stopped listening to the
Holy Ones and did everything they weren't supposed to. They
continued their bad ways, and in time they actually developed
wings and could fly. This made the immortal beings very angry,
angry enough that the immortals destroyed the Anasazis. They
had become too crazy. That is why they are gone now, only
their houses and graves remind us that they were here.

We Navajos were then put here by the immortals. The Anasazis were given corn and other necessities needed to sustain
life. This was not destroyed with them. This corn and other
foods were then given to us. The immortals let us keep these
things. Now the Navajo people are headed in the same direction
as the Anasazis. We as a people are becoming crazy. We do not
pray to the immortals anymore, we don't respect Mother Earth

and all things on her. We desecrate everything we touch. The immortals are going to destroy us as a people one day and re-place us with another people. We are put here on Mother Earth for only a short time. This is Changing Woman's land, only she can say, "It is my land." Only hell is everybody's land.

SYLVIA MANYGOATS

[In July 1988, we interviewed Sylvia Manygoats at the Navajo Mountain Chapter House, then five days later at her home nearby. Close translation by Harris Francis, omitting details about locations of places, reproduced here with Mrs. Manygoats's consent.]

A long time ago there were various enemies [pre-Fort Sum-ner times]. Navajos lived here and there and were always being hunted. They were captured and taken prisoners. Their sheep, livestock were gathered and with their belongings on their backs they were forced to march on foot behind the enemy. Some went with only the clothes on their backs, ragged and torn, oth-ers were forced to take off their shirts and march in front of the column. This is how they were force-marched to Fort Sumner. This is how my mother and father used to tell me about this. There were many captured, some died of starvation, because Fort Sumner is a long way off. There they stayed.

Those from here [Navajo Mountain], that didn't happen to them. People were taken from over at Huerfano Mountain and Mount Taylor [in eastern part of Navajoland] and further on. All along the way the people suffered. Those that were captured—the women, their children—for them those who were still here, the men, performed prayers. It's true that the Navajo stories and prayers are sacred. Now this mountain here [Navajo Mountain], this way, on this side, a long time ago, Monster Slayer and Born for Water [twin war deities] were put there. They were put there. It was declared that the images wouldn't be disturbed when they were put there. The people who were left behind be-gan to offer prayers with sacred stones over toward this way [New Mexico] and at the location of the Twins [shrine on Nava-jo Mountain]. Prayers were made there, prayers called repeating prayers. People who had relatives captured performed these ceremonies. The clothes, jewelry, bridles, and other belongings of those who went were gathered and prayers were performed over these. As captives they were confined and the objective was never to let them return to their homelands. But the men from here were doing ceremonies.

My maternal grandmother went over there. There was an old lady, an old white lady who guarded the young girls. She would sit at the door, watch the girls, even sleep there. Even as they got there, she [the grandmother] had already made up her mind she was going to go home. Ceremonies were being done for her here [by those who didn't go to Fort Sumner] already [to insure her safe return]. She kept what little possessions she had with her all the time, ready to go. Then the old lady became sick, coughing all the time, to where it laid her out. Back then they had tobacco called cigala [cigar]. She [the grandmother] gathered some of these cigars, some matches, a long knife, and an old, thin blanket. Now the guard was sick and went to sleep, so she tried to persuade another lady to escape and go with her, but she [the other lady] was reluctant and stayed. So she [the grandmother] left alone. The old lady said "My daughter ran off," so they began searching for her, yelling "Mother, please come back."

They were on horseback and were searching near the trails, back then there were no roads like today, no cars, they used horses for everything including warfare. She kept off the trails and kept walking, she spent the night somewhere and where there were streams. She walked in them to hide her tracks. All the while they were still hunting for her, shouting for her. They came so close to her a couple of times that she was able to smell the smoke from their cigars. Then she heard the sound of horses going away so she continued on for a long ways.

Back then there were wild animals, animals like the mountain lion, wolves, too, that used to eat humans. As she walked along she all of a sudden heard a wolf howl behind her. She wondered what to do. Then she saw a large pine tree that had been burned. The fire had burned it so that it had made a hole in it. Then she crawled inside of this hollow. Back then they used to wear shoes, moccasins that had leather leggings all the way up towards the knee. At this point she unwound her leggings, got the knife and with her leggings tied the knife on a stick to make a spear. Then the wolf came around, she could hear his footsteps and he's smelling around. All this time she was inside the burned-out tree. Then the wolf spotted her, with his teeth showing, snarling, he attacked her. At this point, with the spear she had made, she stabbed the spear down his throat and killed the wolf. After that she spent two days there and then continued to walk on again until she came home here. The men all the while had been performing prayers for her.

My mother and father both said we [people from Navajo Mountain] never went over there, just the people that are located on that side [east]. It was their prayers, their songs were sacred, holy. They used to perform prayers to the rain [at certain spots]. Back then there were sheep. Those that were captured were given some sheep as payment for them after peace was made.

Where there are mountains, at the top, that's where they pray. The people have come a long ways with these. Now the people tell of the Twins [Monster Slayer and Born for Water], they were born, they went to see their father, because there were monsters eating the people. Just like the monsters there were enemies that chased, captured, tortured and killed the people. Upon visiting their father, the Sun, they told of the monsters such as the Big God [giant], the Slicing Reeds, the Man-Eating Eagle. They were given lightning, live plumes [feathers taken ceremonially from live birds] too, that they used on their trip. The trip to the Sun's home was perilous. The live plume was used against the monsters. The monsters couldn't harm them because of it and the Twins used this to defeat and kill them.

Kicking Rock, Travelling Rock, Crushing Rocks, the Slicing Reeds, the Twelve Human-Eating Antelopes, that's why they went over there [to see their father]. The one that killed the monsters is called Monster Slayer. That's the way my mother and father used to tell me these things. I never really asked more about it.

[HF: Where's your home? Around your home are there places where they do prayers?]

Yes, they do them. Men offer sacred stones where there are springs, those that know how, that's why it rains. And then they pray to the mountain. A long time ago when we had live-stock, sheep, there were no controversies over them. There was no talk of stock reduction. Even with the large amount of sheep, we had rain and there was plenty of grass, feed. There was plenty of everything because of the large amount of stock. Now we have all this controversy about the sheep, livestock and the clouds, rains are gone. The ground is hard and there is nothing

that blooms now. The people used to make a good living with
the livestock back then. There would be a big cloud of dust
when we were herding sheep, then the white man and his stock
reduction came along. With it went the rains. [Implication is
that if you don't use the vegetation that the rains provide, the
Holy People will take both grass and rains away.]

[HF: They say you're an herbalist also. Can you tell us
about it?]

On the mountain [Navajo Mountain], that's where they are
found, all kinds. When a person would get shot, and gets really
bad, we would use Life Medicine, there are many different vari-
eties, you make that for the person, let him drink it and he will
get well. There were no hospitals then, even with serious internal illnesses, injuries, with these medicines they would recover. At the hospitals they tell you to take their type of medicines,
I don't think these work myself. The people's life medicine is
what works and helps the people get well. There are Lifeway
chants like Claw Way, where they are singing, the patient
drinks the medicine.

[HF: Can we come back to see you to tour the mountain to
pinpoint the locations of these places?]

There's Rainbow Bridge, they dammed it up at Page and the
water kept rising and now the water is under the Rainbow
Bridge. These things weren't supposed to happen when they
[places] were created. Now when Navajos want to go swimming
or wading they enter the water and the water kills them. This is
a very sacred place. Men offer sacred stones here and pray for
rain, today everyone and everything is going crazy. The mountains are being desecrated by drilling, digging, and other de-
structive activities. They are holy.

We are hearing that the commodities that we get like rice,
corn and so forth [U.S. Department of Agriculture commodities
distributed at the chapter houses, which was going on where
this interview was taking place] are getting no rain in these
other places. So they want to ask us to perform prayers for
them also, to help them, the white people. They are afraid of
running out of food.

[Second interview:]

[HF: Our work for the Navajo Nation that I told you a little
bit about last Friday, it's for preservation and protection, this
mountain that's here, I guess the Hopis also claim it's theirs.

Maybe prayers are done on its top, maybe there are springs, and Anasazi ruins, also, there's a lot of them. White people and Mexicans run off with things and tear them [ruins] up to get pots and bones. It's to protect, preserve, oversee these things, that's why we came to you and the other Navajos who are talking to us. This mountain, here, over there they say that prayers are done. We'll make a form for it and the information, and we'll keep an eye on it and take care, and it [the information] will be confidential.]

What about the land dispute issue, is that still being decided?

[HF: I'm from there [the disputed area], all our homes are affected and have been under dispute. I was born over there, my parents brought me back over there. But they [Navajo Nation programs working on the land dispute] are doing something different. Our work is preservation for all Navajos.]

These white people and Hopis, what's the place called, The Rock That's Propped Up [Chaco Canyon]? There's a pueblo [ruin], pueblos extend along the edge [description of prehistoric ruins at Chaco Canyon]. From Lukachukai back this way, from Ganado back this way, the Hopis say a long time ago it was their land. But around here there were only Navajos. The Hopis all lived at Old Oraibi, that's where their land was, they were a small band with no sheep. They'd come and trade with the Navajos for meat. That's the only way they subsisted. Then over at Tuba City [Moencopi] there were a few who lived there. Navajos of different clans lived all over this land, so the land they [Hopis] claim now was never theirs. It's Navajo land.

The white people also never lived here. They came from far away also. There were no trading posts [the first trading post wasn't built at Navajo Mountain until the 1920s]. Only at Tonalea there was a small trading post. There were no cars then, only horses. They had to use horses to haul supplies from Flagstaff. Navajo men used to help them. There weren't even clothes like this then. They had to weave rugs, thin rugs called *biil* that were used for clothes for both men and women, they would really weave back then. Then there was no white flour, our grandmothers and grandfathers would plant corn, squash, watermelons, and beans. They sometimes planted wheat. These are the foods they lived on. Then there was Indian rice grass, sumac berries, amaranth, beeweed. The people used these foods and have survived this long. It was only recently these things that the people are going crazy with appeared. That's what my mother used to tell me. She died some years ago.

They used to have the metate, and everything else, today the young people don't grind [corn] anymore, it's just the elderly ladies who have metates and other things like manos.

We were taught never to abandon the mano, stirring stick bundle, metate. The Anasazis used to live like us, they had metates, stone clubs. They did protection ceremonies. Ceremonies, prayers were used even back then. Today when it doesn't rain, people offer prayers with sacred stones at springs, even at Lake Powell they used to offer sacred stones. Back then everything was in harmony and it used to rain all the time. They never bothered the Anasazis, they are buried in the ground. Then they used to grow and harvest squash, peaches, that were used in winter, even up to spring. This is how they raised their children and brought them up. The people who live around here still plant corn, peaches, make mush, dumplings, kneel-down bread, and paper bread, the kind they make. Navajos still eat like that today. Now this way they say there are none of these things any more.

Now there's the mountains, they all have names, and when our elder men used to live, our fathers, grandfathers, great grandfathers, they used to offer sacred stones there, gather mountain soil, mountain soil was essential for a harmonious existence. Now the mountain soil bundle [essential for Blessingway ceremonies] and the arrowheads have all been left behind and are no longer used. It seems to have all ended there.

Long ago the women, men, our grandfathers used to tell us, some men have a leather-and-metal protective band around the wrist, this is called the bowguard, they used to wear it on this side [right]. Then there was the arrow and bow, they were all used together, we were instructed, in the future we should never lay aside these things and forget about them. Then there's also the g-string men used to wear. Today these things have been put aside and forgotten.

They say when we put down and forget our ceremonial paraphernalia, when the girls start cutting their hair and start to look like men, our enemies will attack us, and that will be it, we'll lose control of our lands. These things like the bow guard, bow and arrow, they are what keep our enemies away. There are wars going on today overseas. There are going to be sings also, when the people first come into being. The Navajos used to

say we are not to tell these stories in the summer, only in winter, because of the lightning, snakes, they are dangerous.

So back then, water, flood, the coyote, he was the one who
made the stupid mistake. There was a whirlpool [possible reference to confluence of Colorado and San Juan Rivers north of
Navajo Mountain, or to confluence of San Juan and Los Pinos
in northwest New Mexico, both now flooded because of dams;
this location, in the world below the present, was part of the
physiography replicated by the Holy People on the present
earth's surface], and a baby kept crying from there, so the
Coyote said, "I'm going to take that crying baby out." Everyone
kept telling him, "No, no," but they couldn't persuade him.
There's something called dark sky, dark cloud, he wrapped the
baby in this and was carrying it around. Everyone kept telling
him, "No, put it back in the water," but he wouldn't listen.
Then all of a sudden the skies began to grow dark, first from
this side, then this side, in all four directions. I don't know what
warned them, but they say that the breezes used to talk to people and tell them things. The Coyote, who was running around
carrying Water Monster's baby, was the cause of it all. It was
just to be left alone right where it was. The waters kept rising
and the people were in a state of panic. They kept trying to
plant everything like trees, ponderosa pine trees, but they just
grew so far. The people were scared because the water was near
them. Now when the clouds converged, the water will kill
everyone. The people were running around not knowing what
to do. Now there's these reeds, they grow where there's water.
They planted one of these and it began to grow, up through the
clouds. Then the locust was the first one to go up. There were
groups of people that the reed grew up with. The male and
female Water Monster followed also, as the water kept rising.
The turkey, it was the last to come up, the water came up to
the tip of its tail, that's why the tip of its tail feathers are white.
That's why its tail feathers are used at Enemy Way ceremonies.

The Water Monster kept following them and stuck its head
out at them. I don't know if they [the people] had their sacred
stones with them. Then they got an abalone basket [white (?)
shell used as a receptacle] and abalone shells [pieces] and put
this on the female Water Monster's head between her horns. For
the male Water Monster, they put white shell [turquoise?] and a
white shell basket in the same way. They used those because
white shell and turquoise represents the male. You know when
a man has sacred stones being offered on his behalf [by a

medicine person], he is always told to pick out white shell and turquoise, green and white.

Then they pleaded with the Water Monster to let them take the baby with them, so that in the future the people may have plenty of rain, so that the rains may come all the time. "We have made offerings in packets to you, this also will help provide us with plenty of rain." After that the monsters left. [This implicitly explains why people accompany prayers for rain at springs around Navajo Mountain and elsewhere with sacred stone offerings—they kept the baby, because taking the baby caused the Water Monster to bring rain, but made an offering as a fee to the Water Monster to compel it to control the force of rainstorms.]

Then when they [the people] came up on top, they discovered that there was water everywhere. They then used the horns of the bighorn sheep to dig arroyos where the water drained off the land. Then they requested the wind to come, which it did and blew until it dried the land. While it was still muddy the one they call Badger tried to help but just fell into the mud, that's why his underside, chest and down, is dark. That's the reason. That's the stories of my mothers, fathers, and grandfathers.

I guess after that the land dried and the people started living there. There's lots of stories regarding this. But a lot of people say you're not supposed to tell these stories until winter. Stories of the Emergence. It's dangerous from above.

Then the people started living here [at the whirlpool] again and soon enough they started going crazy again. They call it "The Separation of the Sexes." [In many versions, like those combined into the summary in chapter 1, this event comes before the Flood and Emergence.] There was one man who took another man's woman away. One's name was Hashké Na'ígai [White-streaked Warrior?], the other's Bįįh Hasááł [Deer Raiser?]. The one called White-streaked Warrior was a leader and each morning would be up and talking to the people. Suddenly there was no speaking, and everyone was asking, "Where is our leader, it's so quiet." It was learned that he had his wife taken away from him and was hurt about it. Then he wouldn't eat, people would put food in front of him but he left it alone. For ten days he doesn't eat. Then there's this transvestite, they had transvestites even then. He acted like a woman, so he was sent to take care of the headman. He cooked some corn mush for him and told him to eat. The transvestite told the headman, "I ground the corn on my metate, I used my own stirstick bundle, my mano, to cook this, so eat it." So finally the man ate what was prepared.

Then things were straightened out and the men started planning. "We men will live on this side of the river, the women will move to the other side and live there." So the women packed up their belongings and moved across the river. Then the women started killing themselves, going into the water and drowning or being swept away. Then they started missing the men and started having relations with one another. They used things like petrified wood, also the twelve antelopes' [monsters'] horns. You know the petrified wood, the way it's shaped, they say that is the bones of Big God [giant]. After a while they became pregnant. The men were also doing the same crazy things. Then it was said that the women are just killing themselves, if this continues, there will be no more women. It was the same for the men. So it was declared to go across and rejoin each other, that's what they call the Separation of the Sexes.

Upon rejoining and living together again, the waters started rising again. The fear and turmoil they experienced before came back again, and they went through the same things as the last world, so the land dried up again, and new dangers were in this world. Monsters that ate people. For this reason, Monster Slayer and Born for Water were born. Their mother was Changing Woman.

[Mrs. Manygoats then told the story of how they went to their father the Sun, to get weapons to kill the monsters. See chapter 5 for another version of this story.]

Results: Places Important to Navajos

Through stories and statements like those above, we learned about 164 important places in and near the thirteen chapters (as well as others, like Fort Sumner, which are far away and which we didn't include in our documentation). This is about one place for every 26 square miles. As our own experiences and other studies show, such places sit much more densely on the land than that. If we had interviewed more people and included all the places on which each family pegs the story of its past, each medicine person collects materials for ceremonial use and makes offerings to the immortals, and so forth, we would have learned about tens or even hundreds of thousands.

It is useful to describe these places according to both what they look like and why people consider them important. We can't offer a Navajo ("emic") "typology" of these places because no one offered an explicit typology and we didn't ask people to help us draw out typological distinctions that might be only implicit in (or even absent from) their statements. We describe the places in terms of what they look like because that seems most accessible to most readers. We describe them in terms of their significance because that is closest to the contexts in which the people themselves described the places.

In terms of what they look like, most important places are features of the natural landscape (on which evidence of human use is incidental to their significance): mountains, hills, rock outcrops, canyons, springs and other bodies of water, natural discolorations on rocks, areas where certain plants grow, mineral deposits, isolated trees, places where rocks produce echoes, air vents in rocks, sand dunes, flat open areas, lightning-struck trees and rocks. Another common type of significant place is one where Navajos have left evidence of customary Navajo activities— certain types of cairns, traps for ceremonial hunting of antelope, deer, and eagles. People gave particular locations of these sites.

Other sites—abandoned family homesites, locations of most ceremonies, graves, sweathouses, corrals, cornfields—are so widespread that we didn't ask for or record specific locations except for such sites where unusual uses or events occur.

People mentioned certain prehistoric Anasazi archaeological sites— usually ruined masonry pueblos, sometimes petroglyph panels. Still another large category of places consists of "historic" buildings, "historic" sites, or "historic" districts—places with public functions such as trading posts, missions, schools, government buildings—either standing or reduced to archaeological remains. Hereafter we will call these public buildings or central places.

Most significant places, especially the natural landscape features, Navajo archaeological sites, and some prehistoric Anasazi archaeological sites, are important because they are where people have performed the activities that keep Navajo life going and because stories go with them. At these places, people offer prayers or gather water, plants, minerals, and other natural materials for ceremonial use, food, medicine, or handicrafts, and so forth. The sites of daily life (dwellings, cornfields, and so forth) also have this significance. Often, people choose a place for customary activities because "a story goes with it." These locations are connected to Navajo origin stories, family stories, or stories about some other event that conferred some special power on the place. There are also certain basic tenets of Navajo cosmology (although most interviewees didn't explain these to us) that ascribe special power to certain events or processes in the natural world (for example, lightning strikes, first rays of dawn). Places on the landscape where these processes occur, especially where several occur together or are somehow aligned, are thought to have special power. Battlefields—sites of colonial (often intertribal) warfare—belong in this group because they have special, harmful power from the killings.

A few places, mainly public buildings and central places, are important because they are connected to the recent past of the local community as a whole. Some people consider these important because they might attract tourists and their money. A few natural landscape features might be called "natural wonders," places with unusual natural characteristics apparently unconnected to stories or customary practices.

It's important to note that many people mentioned customary activities at many natural locations without saying anything about a story, but we believe that most of these places do have stories. The same may be true of the "natural wonders."

It's also worth noting the multiple, synergistic significance of battle sites and refuges. Because warfare was an important part of Navajo life—from the killing of the monsters by the Hero Twins, to the early Spanish colonial period that began around A.D. 1600, to the U.S. Army's conquest of the Navajos in 1864—much Navajo ceremonial practice is also linked to warfare. Places where Navajos in recent generations successfully hid or defended themselves, especially mountains, became validated by those events as good places for ceremonial practices linked to warfare, and go back to the time of Navajo origins.

Certain prehistoric Anasazi archaeological sites are important because "a story goes with them" or because ceremonial materials are gathered from them. Others, however, are of concern mainly because they attract visitors for better or for worse—either tourists desired as patrons for future local businesses, or undesirable pothunters and tourists who trespass on one's grazing area. Other studies have recorded Navajos who believe that all such sites, even those without stories, are homes of certain immortals, Talking God and Calling God, and are therefore sacred (see part II).

Of the 164 places, fully three out of four are significant because they are linked to Navajo stories, Navajo customary activities, or both. We will hereafter call these "sacred places," a translation of the Navajo term (*dahodiyinii*) applied to places with these sources of significance. We remind the reader that "sacred" in the Navajo context embraces much more than it does in the national principle that separates "church and state." One could almost say that Navajo life and the stories and beliefs and customs that go with it *are* Navajo religion.

3.

Interpretation of Results

When we started our work in the thirteen chapters, we were aware that Navajo stories and ceremonies tie places together into large landscapes. But (perhaps because of too much time spent with most of our professional colleagues), we expected people to answer questions about what local places are important to them by providing lists of places. Instead, people told stories, or at least alluded to them, about Navajo origins, about Navajo encounters with colonialism, and about their own personal encounters with immortal beings. The names of places are embedded in these stories, which explicitly tie many places together into landscapes or allude to or imply other, related stories that involve other places and landscapes. The people we talked with simply do not think of these important places as isolated locations. A place is usually important because it is part of a larger landscape constituted by a story, customary activities, or both.

Clearly understanding that we saw our purpose as developing an "inventory" of "significant places," more than one interviewee tried to correct the "piecemeal" perception of the landscape they saw in this purpose by saying, like Mamie Salt, "the whole land is sacred." Since the same people told stories that refer to specific locations, they clearly implied that there are qualitative differences among places. But they were also trying to tell us that one cannot isolate a particular place as being more significant ("sacred") than another—places each draw their particular distinct significant qualities from their interrelations, from how each functions in the overall system ("the whole land") that sustains the Navajo people and way of life. We will return to this contrast between the "piecemeal" and what some scholars call the "holistic" view of the culturally significant land base after we review other studies in part II.

While some people gave us more, and more detailed, stories than we expected, many did not tell these stories in anything like the full detail that some scholars have recorded. Instead, many people we talked with only summarized or alluded to these stories, or even evoked them simply by naming a person (usually immortal) or incident in the story (compare Basso 1990 [1983])—partly because it was the wrong season for storytelling but also, more importantly, because of our approach to people—asking about protecting places, not "tell me a story" to record the most complete version that the teller is willing to give. Long narratives have come through other types of research, presumably to preserve these stories for posterity, and increasingly are being published by individual Navajos themselves (see, for example, Yazzie 1984, Clinton 1990). Examples of these long, previously published stories appear later in this work, edited to help keep this book to an affordable length but we hope not edited too much to keep the reader from seeing how detailed they are (see "The Origin of Horses" [chapter 5] and "The Origin of the Frenzy Way Ceremony" [chapter 7]).

Further encouraging people to tell only short versions of stories was their desire to tell their concerns about "economic development" and recent events as they are affecting the landscape and Navajo culture in general. The stories are subordinated to this larger context, as locations where many Navajos use ceremonial and other customary measures to cope with changes imposed from national, even global, society.

Culturally Significant Landscapes

Several ideas—sometimes explicit in people's statements, but more often implicit—seem to organize places into culturally significant landscapes. In part IV we will take two short statements and show specifically how, when someone doesn't make an idea explicit, the idea is still implicit in the surface meaning of the statement. We have already mentioned two such ideas: stories and customary (usually ceremonial) activities. The places where successive episodes of a particular story or set of interrelated stories occurred make up a culturally significant landscape just as the episodes make up the story. The places where activities related to a particular ceremony occur make up a landscape just as the activities make up the ceremony.

Places often make up landscapes that symbolize various important groups in Navajo social structure and their interrelations. In the words of Navajo teacher and writer Grace McNeley:

> The Navajo term *kétł'oot*—derived from *ké*, meaning "feet", and *tł'oot* meaning "root system"—expresses the concept of having a foundation for one's life in the earth, much as a plant is rooted in the earth. . . . Let us visualize the central root as extending all the way back to Asdzaan Nadleehi, "Changing Woman"—who is Earth Mother herself. Developing from this main root is the complex web of kinship relations extending back even to ancestors and including clan relations, the extended family and the immediate family. Tied to this system are material goods, familiar surroundings and livestock. This webbing of earth, of ancestors, of clan and familiar surroundings all constitute a Navajo home, enabling those within it to flourish, to thrive. (G. McNeley 1987:163–64)

These thoughts reflect the objective bonds between the land and the people who have customarily produced food and met other basic needs from the land. The flow of family labor into the land produces livestock and crops that each family member consumes. The land, water, air, and sunlight that go into the family's food become the people's flesh. Among these substances are also the essences of the immortal beings like Changing Woman. By consuming the products of the land, one also incorporates the essences of the immortal beings into one's flesh.

Particular spots or areas on the land bases of various groups within Navajo society symbolize this relationship of the land and the particular group. To symbolize the land base of the Navajo Nation as a whole, Navajos commonly mention the four sacred mountains associated with the cardinal directions and the outer limits of Navajoland, often together with two others in their midst, the birthplace and home of Changing Woman. These mountains symbolize also the largest social unit in pre-conquest times, the tribe. They figure prominently in the origin stories and have names. Other places named in the origin stories would also symbolize the tribe.

A landmark may also symbolize the loosely organized network of several extended families that occupy neighboring or interfingered patches of land surrounding the landmark. During raids and warfare in pre-conquest times, people living around a mountain massif would flee to its upper elevations. People still pray from the tops of these mountains for protection, especially when they are about to travel far from home (as during military service).

To symbolize the land base of individual extended families, the interviewees commonly mentioned particular homesites and grave sites of members, and also landmarks (such as rock outcroppings) around which generations of the family have built and abandoned and sometimes reoccupied homesites while they herded and farmed. These and other locations within an extended family's land base are where its members may offer prayers. These places symbolize and validate the family members' rights to use particular lands and embody the family story.

Some important places don't symbolize territories of social groups but do figure in the story of the Navajo people as a whole, or various social groups without territories. Therefore, in some sense, they symbolize the associated group. These places include locations of certain events in the creation story, clan origin and migration stories, and origin stories of ceremonies. They also include some public buildings and central places, which have a comparable significance in the hazy zone where Navajo culture and that of the colonizers meet. They symbolize the local communities where they provide the central public architecture. This seems to be one reason why people told us these buildings are significant.

Sacred places that are not connected with stories about social groups may still be connected to the activities of such groups. Many of these locations provide raw materials for ceremonies or are sites for ceremonial offerings. The use of sacred places helps keep alive ceremonial repertoires that contain Navajo stories. Extended families sponsor these ceremonies, and the larger ones may attract virtually all other families in a locality. The ceremonial performances therefore strengthen the ties that keep the social groups and networks alive, not to mention the social ties between the humans and the immortals with whom ceremonial acts are the proper form of social interaction.

In addition to being the symbolic focus of whole territories of various land-using social groups, many places are also points on larger landforms, or zones, which in turn are parts of still larger landforms, to form a nested series of land areas associated with progressively larger land-using social groups. They may be parts of systems of places interrelated by various stories (family histories, origin stories, and so forth) and associated sequences of activities (collection of materials for use in particular ceremonies, each of which has its own origin stories which are in turn related to the main-stalk creation stories).

People also identify zones and spots on the larger landforms and in the surrounding country (commonly entire hills, mountains, and canyons) that some people say have too much power for residence, grazing, and other everyday uses. These are the places where, in the origin stories of various ceremonies, the hero encounters a Holy Person in animal form who says, "Earth-surface people don't come around here." Everyday uses should therefore be limited in such places, if not forbidden entirely (many voiced dismay at neighbors who have moved into these preserves). Navajos consider these zones storehouses of medicinal plants and natural materials for ceremonial and other customary purposes. The power of the identified landforms makes people prefer them for gathering raw materials for religious use, even water, earth, and plants common everywhere, because the power of the zones gives extra strength to whatever comes from them.

Besides their connections with the landbases of various social groups and with events or figures in stories, many points where people offer prayers and do other ceremonial activities are chosen for ceremonial uses because certain important attributes of the larger underlying landform are most intensely evident at these spots, and especially because the essences of the immortals—moisture, earth, the air and light (Reichard 1963 [1950]:264; J. McNeley 1981:24–26; Farella 1984:30)—come together at these places. For example, the land's capacity to give water and various plants is most evident at springs and the confluences of drainages. Many other places are chosen because there the landform interacts with certain important natural forces. For example, besides being refuges for local communities, mountaintops are where the dawn's first rays strike, and they gather the rain for the surrounding country. The tops of mountains and mesas also seem to be favored for prayers that relate to the surrounding country within view and the growing things upon it, such as livestock. These places, then, are the focus of activities that benefit the surrounding landscape.

Certain types of sacred spots, such as gathering places for ceremonial raw materials and places for offering certain types of prayers, are more likely to occur in the sacred preserves. Other types of sacred spots more closely linked to daily life are more likely to occur in or near homesites, cornfields, and grazing areas. These places remind one of the extended family's past and present dependence on its customary land base. Although some types of sacred places are more likely to occur in the religious preserves and others are more likely to occur in the residential-grazing-farming zones, sacred places of all types can be found in both types of zone.

Illustrating Grace McNeley's statement about the physical processes that flow between the people and the land, many (probably most) of the sacred places on the land are where people give something back to the land (and the indwelling immortals who make the land alive) in exchange for the life-sustaining things that people take from the land. This is another reason why one cannot grasp the full significance of a place by considering it in isolation from the surrounding landscape. These places are not sacred in themselves. They concentrate power from the landforms on which they sit, whether those landforms are the powerful religious preserves or the lifegiving areas outside them where people have their homes, farms, and grazing lands.

Through these interrelated symbols, stories, and activities, people never forget that they exist within, and function as part of, a very large, complex world that includes other groups of Navajos, the earth and the different landforms upon it, the celestial bodies, the atmosphere, and the immortals who animate them. Navajos thereby see themselves as part of much larger living systems.

Preserving Navajo Ways and "Economic Development"

People in the thirteen chapters tended to identify places significant to them in the context of their fears about loss of Navajo land and culture in the face of "economic development." They said many places are being physically destroyed or damaged by "development," while others are associated with stories, ceremonies, and other customs that "young people" no longer know or care about. The reason that most people emphasized damage and loss is that we told them we were asking about such places to do a better job in protecting them. Some people also linked the places they mentioned to "economic development" in positive ways—mainly as lures for tourist money.

The two points of view on the relation of economic development and preservation of the Navajo cultural landscape correspond to two groups of people we interviewed—middle-aged educated chapter officials and old people deeply immersed in Navajo culture. (Like Sylvia Manygoats, a few could remember when their communities were so "undeveloped" that there wasn't even a trading post within less than a day's horseback ride.) The chapter officials seemed more concerned than the elders did with balancing community development and preserving Navajo culture. Presumably, at least in part, the officials' concern reflects their attempts to balance the concerns of their various constituents.

The types of places that people mentioned to us reflect this division among the people interviewed. Almost all the public buildings and central places (and the few natural wonders) were identified by chapter officials, as well as many prehistoric Anasazi sites without stories about them. These officials also identified some sacred places. Almost all the places that old people identified are sacred places.

The same pattern is evident in the specific places we asked about that people said they don't consider important. Of the twenty such places (in five chapter areas) that we asked about, most were public buildings or central places and the rest were particular prehistoric Anasazi ruins (although there is a widespread belief that all such sites, storied or not, should be left alone). Almost all the interviews in which we asked about less important specific places were with old people. One of the youngest chapter officials we interviewed, however, said that to him most public buildings and central places "are really more culturally degrading than historical." He evidently meant that they represent the intrusion of colonial powers that have undermined the once independent sovereign Navajo Nation both politically and culturally.

Do These Places Really Have the Importance That People Say?

Non-Navajos often ask this question, especially about sacred places. Yes, they do. Having talked with the people face-to-face, we are convinced of their sincerity. But, for the skeptic, we offer the following corroboration. We are still in the middle of compiling the many references to places scattered throughout published works on particular Navajo ceremonies and the stories that go with them. Having read through virtually all of this body of literature[1] and consulted more general (non-ceremonial) works about Navajo places,[2] we have found that places mentioned tend to be on cross-regional pilgrimage routes. More than half of the sacred places identified by residents of the thirteen chapters are either mentioned in this literature or are on the routes mentioned. The places that the general (non-ceremonial) works identify as sacred include three places identified to us as natural wonders. Three chapters (Navajo Mountain, Indian Wells, and Tuba City) were parts of larger districts where Walter Vannette and Reed Tso (1988) studied sacred places very intensively. They list 18 of the 20 sacred places mentioned to us. Moreover, of our 164 (sacred and other) places, 39 were mentioned by more than one person in separate interviews or, in a few cases, collectively by the chapter organization. Of these 39 places, 27 were sacred places mentioned by more than one person in separate interviews (one out of every five sacred places mentioned).

The general (non-ceremonial) literature (see note 2) supplemented our own field observations and revealed more cultural resources that people didn't mention spontaneously and that we didn't ask people about. These sources mention many Navajo sacred places as well as other locations more likely to be significant to the colonizers than to Navajos. For example, Vannette and Tso (1988), besides recording almost all the sacred places that people mentioned to us and many of those in the literature we consulted, list about 200 places in the Navajo Mountain chapter area and about 150–200 in the Tuba City chapter area (but only one in the Indian Wells chapter area). Why didn't people mention these other places to us? An adequate answer requires the comparison of purposes and field methods between our study and those of Vannette and Tso (and other similar studies). Reasons include differences in field methods, time spent, people (especially old people and medicine people) interviewed, and the purpose of each study as the people understood it.

How Do People Learn about These Places?

The answer to this question may help explain the difference between middle-aged, formally educated chapter officials and old people that is reflected in the officials' tendency to identify primarily public places and archaeological sites without Navajo stories and the elders' tendency to identify primarily sacred places. The difference suggests that people who know about sacred places were raised in the old Navajo ways, are most involved in customary activities, or have had the longest time to accumulate knowledge.

This statement assumes that the chapter officials didn't mention such places because they didn't know about them. Instead, however, they may not have mentioned them because they wanted to identify possible tourist attractions and buildings to be restored for community use. Sacred places aren't appropriate for these purposes. Or they may have known something about such places but felt that their elderly constituents wouldn't want that information released, or that we should talk to old people who would know more.

This last possibility is evident in the chapter official who gave us a list of named places in the chapter area together with the names of medicine people and other old people who would know about them. He indicated that he didn't necessarily know whether each one had any special importance, but thought it might because it had a name.

The Importance of Place Names

The above incident suggests, first of all, that sacred places, or at least some types of them, tend to be named, although one can't assume either that all sacred places have names or that all named places are sacred. Secondly, the incident suggests that place names are a vehicle for conveying knowledge about places from one person to another.

The way people use place names in telling us about locations illustrates this process. A place name helps people talk about the place without either being there or identifying it with a cumbersome description every time they mention it (most Navajo place names are compressed descriptions). If the listener doesn't know the location of the place when hearing the story, he or she can ask someone else later, especially someone in the vicinity who can point it out. Probably the larger the number of people who need to talk about a place, or the larger the geographical area over which the people are spread, the more likely the place is to have a proper name.

Navajo elders customarily have told stories within the family at home on winter nights and during long ceremonial performances in periods of rest between procedures, whereas people probably have been taught the names of places when passing by them with someone who already knows the name. People therefore are likely to learn the locations that go with particular place names and the stories and songs that go with those place names at different times. The name bridges the time gap, which may be years.

Even middle-aged people, then, may know a place name without having been in the home of, or at a ceremony with, someone who will tell the associated story. If only one person in a learner's social network knows the story, and that person follows the common Navajo practice of not telling the story until he or she feels about to die, the learner, too, may be old before he or she hears the story. Many Navajos today, furthermore, don't attend ceremonies as often as Navajos did in the past. They therefore won't accumulate information conveyed during ceremonial storytelling as fast as their forebears did.

We suggest that widely known places tend to have names, whereas places without names tend to be known and used only by a single person or family. The unnamed places, being in the family's customary land base, are near at hand, often within view. Activities at unnamed places need not be planned at distant times or locations. Such sites tend to have common descriptive designations rather than proper names, such as "the spring," "the wash," "the confluence," because there may be only one such place in the family's area and such labels are specific enough for the small group of people who talk about them. Some families, however, seem to make up their own place names that they use only within the family. Some proper names are duplicated in various localities, suggesting that mainly the residents of a particular locality use them. Still others, like those of the six sacred mountains, which all Navajos know about, are unique. This doesn't mean that the least-known places are also the least important, however. A medicine person who performs a ceremonial repertoire all over Navajoland may use certain sacred places shrouded in secrecy but essential for the effectiveness of the performances.

Conclusion

Our study of thirteen Navajo chapters resulted in various types of statements from 81 people and a list of 164 places significant to those people for various reasons. The great majority of the places are natural features of the landscape, some are structures built by Navajos for hunting and other customary Navajo activities, some are prehistoric Anasazi ruins and petroglyphs, and some are public buildings that have housed the schools, trading posts, and government offices of colonialism.

The most important lessons that we learned are as follows. First, these places derive their significance from their position in larger, culturally "constructed" landscapes. Second, places may have different qualities that make them significant, but none can be ranked above another or singled out for preservation while the surrounding landscape which the place both gives significance (power) to and takes significance from is destroyed. Third, to old people, "economic development" is destroying such places and luring youth away from the old ways at such a rate that the survival of the culturally significant landscape, and not incidentally, Navajo culture itself, is at stake.

PART TWO

PLACES

IMPORTANT

OTHER STUDIES

TO NAVAJO

PEOPLE

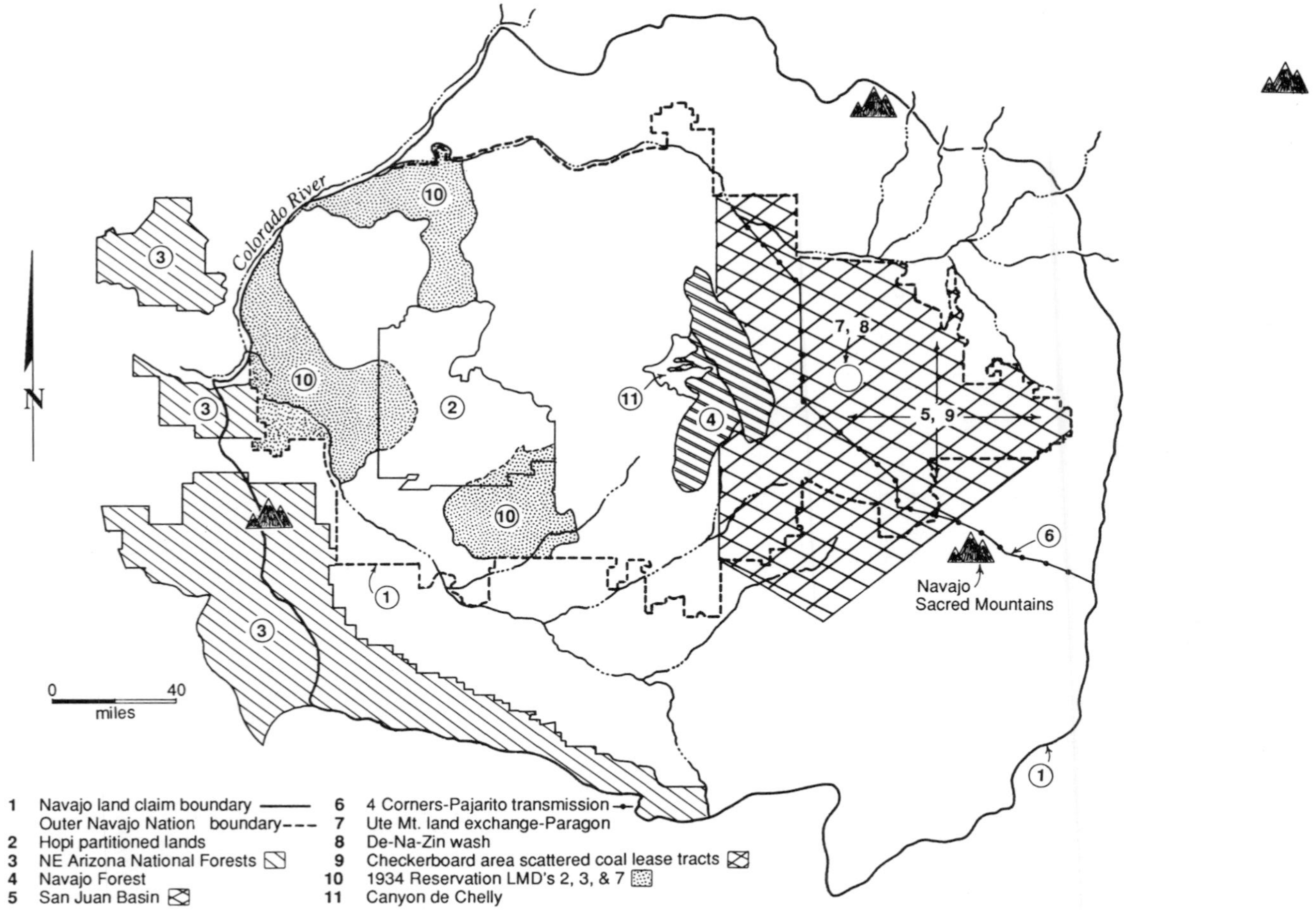

Figure 2. Locations of other projects.

1 Navajo land claim boundary ——
  Outer Navajo Nation boundary ---
2 Hopi partitioned lands
3 NE Arizona National Forests ▨
4 Navajo Forest
5 San Juan Basin ▨

6 4 Corners-Pajarito transmission →
7 Ute Mt. land exchange-Paragon
8 De-Na-Zin wash
9 Checkerboard area scattered coal lease tracts ▨
10 1934 Reservation LMD's 2, 3, & 7 ▨
11 Canyon de Chelly

Navajo
Sacred Mountains

Colorado River

0   40
 miles

N

4.

Other Studies: What They Did and How They Did It

The purpose of part II is to compare the results of our study of thirteen chapters (part I) with the results of similar field studies in Navajoland. Developers during the last fifteen years have sponsored most of these studies to meet federal and Navajo Nation legal requirements for rights-of-way, leases, and other land-use permits. A few other compilations of Navajo sacred and historical places exist (Van Valkenburgh 1941, Watson 1964, for example), but we have excluded them because they seem to be based on literature more than on interviews. We chose the studies discussed here for comparison with our thirteen-chapter study because only these studies both focused on "inventories" of large numbers of places important in Navajo culture and used interviews as the main method for getting these "inventories." When we started writing this book, these were all the studies like ours that we could identify (although a few have been completed since then, and are not covered here). Taken together, all these field studies illuminate one another. They also give one a more detailed understanding of the relationships between Navajo ways and the landscape, particularly the relationships that development threatens to disrupt.

The technical appendix gives statistical information on the field methods and results of these studies. Figure 2 shows their locations. We intend to show what other field studies, together with our own study of thirteen chapters, tell about places and landscapes important to Navajo people. Chapter 4 describes the different historical contexts and purposes of the studies, the geographical areas they cover, and field methods.[1] Chapter 5 covers the stories and types of places that these studies reveal. Chapter 6 discusses more general Navajo concerns about culture and landscape preservation made known by the various field studies and relates these to the professional debate about "landscape" versus "piecemeal" approaches to protecting culturally significant places. Chapter 7 suggests some things we should learn more about.

Purposes and Areas Covered

Studies connected with land claims. The earliest of these studies (Van Valkenburgh 1974), appropriately enough, covers the largest area. It was part of the documentation for the Navajo "aboriginal" (pre-conquest) land claim before the Indian Claims Commission, the area that the Navajo Nation claims to have used "exclusively" at the time of the Treaty of 1868. According to the principle of tribal sovereignty in federal Indian law, by signing that treaty, Navajos relinquished to the United States their claims to exclusive use of the pre-conquest area in exchange for a much smaller reservation inside that area. Beginning in 1946, the Indian Claims Commission decided claims that Indian tribes made against the U.S. government for monetary compensation for aboriginal acreage that they gave up through such instruments as the 1868 Treaty. Van Valkenburgh, whose research dates to the 1930s and early 1950s, gives information on 88 sacred places throughout the Navajo Land Claim, which extends from a few miles west of the Rio Grande in New Mexico westward beyond the Little Colorado River in Arizona, and from the Mogollon rim in Arizona northward past the San Juan River in Colorado and Utah (shown on Figures 2–4).

Not until the 1970s were there more efforts to record many Navajo sacred places. Again, the purpose was related to land claims, this time in the 1882 Executive Order Reservation, a 55-by-70 mile rectangle in Arizona originally set aside, by executive order, for the Hopi Indians "and other such Indians as the Secretary of Interior may see fit to settle thereon," at the request of an Indian agent who wanted authority over a large district to compel boarding school attendance (Indian Law Resource Center 1979:10–13; Kammer 1980:27). The south-central part encompasses the Hopi villages and surrounding lands that the Hopis use for farming and grazing, which the U.S. government has considered exclusively Hopi since 1936 (expanded in 1943) (Indian Law Resource Center 1979:56–64; Kammer 1980:38–41). Since before 1882, Navajos have inhabited the rest of the area, which is the object of the so-called Navajo-Hopi land dispute (Van Valkenburgh 1956:70–73; Stokes and Smiley 1964).

In 1974, forty years of efforts by oil and coal companies, the Bureau of Indian Affairs, and the Hopi tribal government (but with opposition from significant "traditionalist" segments of Hopi society who do not recognize the authority of the Hopi tribal government) paid off when Congress passed the Navajo-Hopi Land Settlement Act (U.S. Congress 1974). Among other things, this law eliminated the joint and undivided surface ownership (outside the exclusively Hopi area) established by a previous lawsuit of the Hopi government against the Navajo government, *Healing v. Jones* (1963). These interests evidently found joint, undivided surface ownership an obstacle to mineral leasing. Although Navajos occupied most of the land, the law divided the surface acreage equally between the two tribes, while keeping the mineral rights undivided. A federal mediator finished drawing the partition line in 1977 (Redhouse 1985a:9–32; Indian Law Resource Center 1979:74–79; see Whitson 1985:377–78, 392–96, for a critical comment on the role of mineral development in this dispute). Anywhere from 2,500 to 4,000 Navajo families and about 30 Hopi families found themselves on the "wrong side" of the line and therefore were required to move, most (but not all) with federal assistance. An estimated third or more Navajo families are still on the land (Whitson 1985:372n; Colby, Aberle, and Clemmer 1991). According to the 1974 law, members of each tribe have sacred places on lands partitioned to the other and retain the right to use those places (*Attakai v. United States* 1991:9).

Because the court has needed to know the locations of sacred places, and because Navajos who resist relocation have invoked those rights to justify their refusal to move, several studies have been made. When the federal court asked the two tribes to identify sacred places in 1977, the Navajo Nation (1977) documented eighty such places. Two years later, when Navajos living on lands partitioned to the Hopis (Hopi Partitioned Lands, or HPL) around Big Mountain refused to move, the Navajo-Hopi Indian Relocation Commission (NHIRC), the federal agency responsible for removing families from the "wrong" side of the line, sponsored a study (Wood and Vannette 1979) about possible special religious significance of the Big Mountain locality.

And finally, in 1990 and 1991, these and the other estimated third of all Navajo families on HPL in 1977 who had still refused to move got two new chances to plead their cause. One was an investigation by a federal-court-appointed mediator who is to help the Navajo Nation and Hopi Tribal governments reach out-of-court settlements in two lawsuits relating to Navajo use of HPL. The other was hearings by a U.S. Senate committee to oversee the recently reorganized NHIRC (now Office of Navajo and Hopi Indian Relocation, ONHIR). In a report intended for both of these initiatives (Kelley, Francis, and Scott 1991) we described 222 Navajo sacred places in HPL.[2]

We know about one other inventory of Navajo sacred places connected with a land claim: the study of Vannette and Tso (1988) of Navajo "religious uses" of the Navajo Reservation in Arizona, the external boundary of which Congress confirmed in 1934. Forty years later, as part of the Navajo-Hopi Settlement Act (U.S. Congress 1974), Congress allowed the Hopi Tribal government to file a claim against the Navajo Nation for land within that area, excluding the 1882 Executive Order Reservation (Whitson 1985:381). As part of the documentation of various Navajo uses of that area for the resulting lawsuit (*Masayesva v. Zah* 1991), the Navajo Nation engaged Vannette and Tso to record religious uses. They focused on areas northwest and southeast of the 1882 Reservation rather than cover the entire Arizona Navajo Reservation of 1934, probably because time didn't permit close coverage of so huge an area. Even in the smaller areas they recorded 689 sacred places.

Studies in the eastern Navajo country. After the 1974 so-called Arab Oil Crisis, the Carter administration's energy policy threatened to make the San Juan River Basin of northwestern New Mexico a "national sacrifice area" for the federally-owned coal it could contribute to the domestic fuel supply (Radford 1986:43–44, 62–63, 137–63; York 1990:176–86; Reno 1981:106–14; Kelley 1982:82–86). According to some (perhaps highly speculative, in both senses of the word) estimates, the Basin holds 25% of U.S. coal and 17% of the world's uranium supply (Holt 1981:46). Most of this area is called "the checkerboard" because of the pattern of land ownership there. Navajos occupy most of the land and have done so for centuries (Stokes and Smiley 1969; Kelley and Whiteley 1989:5–30). Early-twentieth-century federal efforts to place the land in trust for the Navajo Nation as a whole failed because of opposition from non-Navajo ranchers and their influence in Congress. The federal government did, however, allot quarter-section tracts to individual Navajos in the early twentieth century (Brugge 1980:204–

205 and ff.; Kelley 1982:49–63). The federal government administers most of the surrounding land through the Bureau of Land Management, and also asserts ownership of the coal under the Navajo allotments, although Navajos are contesting that ownership in court (Kelley and Whiteley 1989:147). The studies described here were done for energy development projects that the Carter and Reagan energy policies encouraged. The centerpiece was a power plant that Public Service Company of New Mexico (PNM) and a shifting group of partners proposed, and the coal mines to fuel the plant (Kelley and Whiteley 1989:146–47; Radford 1986:137–63; York 1990:176–86).

As archaeologists swarmed over the San Juan Basin to study the famous prehistoric Anasazi "Chacoan" ruins that might be in the way of the new mines and power plants (Radford 1986a:59–61), Fransted (1979) tried to find out which large Anasazi pueblos have stories or other significance to Navajos (his report doesn't identify the sponsor). He found 44 such sites. PNM and related interests also sponsored several studies of overlapping areas in the general vicinity of the proposed power plant site near Bisti (Carroll 1982, 1983; York 1984; there were other, smaller studies not reviewed here because the work of Carroll and York incorporates their results) and the many widely scattered tracts of federal land that the U.S. Bureau of Land Management was considering leasing to supply coal, mainly to the PNM plant (York and Winter 1988; this study incorporates most information from an earlier inventory [York 1982 in Condie and Knudson, eds., 1982] which is therefore not covered here). The number of places recorded by these studies ranges from 16 to 156 (see Technical Appendix).

The recently passed AIRFA apparently prompted these studies, although the federal government had not issued "implementing regulations." PNM and related interests reportedly expected that various federal agencies would soon make up their own internal procedures to do what AIRFA told them to do, namely try to avoid approving leases and rights-of-way and permits to mine and generate power that would prevent American Indians from freely practicing their religions (Carroll 1982). Compliance with the National Environmental Policy Act (U.S. Congress 1966 as amended) and the National Historic Preservation Act (U.S. Congress 1969 as amended) was also a factor.

Other studies sponsored by federal agencies with an eye toward AIRFA. AIRFA seems to have prompted federal agencies also to sponsor studies of how Navajos use lands under the agencies' jurisdiction for customary purposes, and how Navajos think agency plans might affect cultural resources important to Navajos. These studies were heavily weighted toward getting "inventories" of places on lands under agency jurisdiction. Perhaps the studies of the early 1980s, at least, were prompted by fears of a lawsuit like the one that Navajo medicine people, together with members of other tribes, brought against the U.S. Forest Service for ignoring AIRFA in allowing a ski resort to expand on the San Francisco Peaks (*Wilson v. Block* 1983; see part III).

The first of these studies (Vannette and Feary 1981) covered the Coconino, Kaibab, and Apache-Sitgreaves National Forests (the San Francisco Peaks are in the Coconino). Through interviews, the authors identified 42 places. The Bureau of Indian Affairs (BIA), as trustee, also sponsored similar studies about timber sales and a ten-year plan in the Navajo Forest on the Navajo Reservation (Kemrer and Lord 1984, incorporating information from earlier studies by Bartlett [1982] and Cleeland and Doyel [1982]), which identified 15 places (not counting a large number of homesites, grave sites, and sweathouses identified categorically but not individually as significant to Navajos). This flurry in the early years of AIRFA soon died down, however. Federal agencies quit sponsoring so many studies, probably because courts decided the dreaded lawsuits (again, including *Wilson v. Block*) in the agencies' favor (see part III). Also, perhaps seeing that neither Congress nor the courts would put the much noted missing teeth in AIRFA, the agencies' sense of urgency about developing their own procedures to follow their responsibility under AIRFA was eliminated.

No more sacred places inventories were done in the Navajo Forest until after 1989, when the Navajo Nation government invoked the American Indian Self-Determination Act (U.S. Congress 1975) to contract with the BIA for all that agency's cultural resource management responsibilities on the Navajo Reservation. By this time, the Navajo Nation had its own requirement that all developers make good-faith efforts to identify such places and related Navajo concerns. The Navajo Nation furthermore insisted on such efforts under the National Historic Preservation Act (see part III). The result in the Navajo Forest was Mitchell's (1991) inventory of 27 sacred places (not counting homesites, grave sites, sweathouses, identified archaeologically but not by interviews as significant) in a proposed timber sale area. Many other similar inventories have been done on Navajo land since then but we don't include them here because all were in progress when we started writing this book and because most cover rather small areas.

The last study in this group is our own in Canyon de Chelly for the National Park Service (Francis and Kelley 1990, 1992). This study was one result of a new "joint management plan" between the Navajo Nation, which owns the land, and the National Park Service, which has administered the Monument since Congress created it in 1931 (National

Park Service and Navajo Nation 1990). Tourists of sixty years ago and more saw in this landscape a pristine, garden-of-Eden quality that non-Navajo entrepreneurs who have dominated Navajo Nation commerce since the nineteenth century were quick to exploit and thereby undermine. After 1931, the National Park Service licensed these early entrepreneurs to feed and lodge the tourists and haul them into the canyons (Brugge and Wilson 1976).

In recent years, local Navajos have tried to gain more direct benefits from the tourist trade besides low-paying jobs with the concessioner by forming an association of guides to take more tourists into the canyons. Monument staff have worked closely with the guides, but the non-Navajo concessioner still gets most of the business. As a result, in summer, tourists overrun the canyons, where about sixty Navajo families are living (Andrews 1991). The joint management plan is supposed to help the NPS and the Navajo Nation cope better with, among other things, these disruptions, including tourist intrusions on places important in Navajo culture, of which we recorded 154.

Place name studies. Finally, several studies have focused on places with names, regardless of whatever other significance they might have. Most of these studies have a more scholarly motivation than the others we have described. They include a collection of 170 place names by Fransted and Werner (n.d.) in a large region with Chaco Canyon at its center; a project of the Alamo Navajo School Board in which high school students collected 126 place names and stories about them (Walt and others 1987); Christensen's (1990) list of 54 place names in and around Tsegi Canyon, which he collected as a sideline during archaeological field work there; and the collection of place names and stories that go with them by Jett, Neboyia, and Morgan (1992) in Canyon de Chelly, which started as an inventory of trails and has enumerated at least 153 places (not including Canyon del Muerto).

We include these studies because, as we learned from our work in the thirteen chapters, place names are vehicles for older people to teach younger ones about the landscape. They are therefore a clue to which places people distinguish and link together into landscapes, and how those places function in the landscape. By analyzing the lists of names in these studies and the others covered here for patterns of association with landforms, stories, and so forth, we might learn what clues are in a place name.

Summary. All these studies have as their main purpose "inventories" of places with cultural significance to Navajos. Some studies aren't restricted to places with specific visible characteristics or reasons for significance, while others are—the studies limited to big Anasazi ruins, to places with names, and to sacred places. These studies also differ in the purposes of their inventories—most are either to establish land rights or to minimize potential damage from development. Except for the place name studies (and maybe the Anasazi ruins study), however, all (including our thirteen-chapter study) came about directly or indirectly at the behest of some governmental authority.

Field Methods

The studies discussed here are like our thirteen-chapter study in focusing on "inventories" of culturally important places and seeking such information mainly through interviews. The studies differ mainly in what groups of people they focused on, how they chose people to interview from within the group, how structured were the interviews, and whether they verified the locations of places with maps, field visits with or without interviewees, and so forth. It is important to look at these methods because they account for many differences in the results.

Probably the main contrast in interview methods is between studies that defined the group to be consulted as all families living in or near the lands of interest, and studies that used what Vannette and Wood (1979:5) call "the snowballing, non-random technique"—start with a list of knowledgeable people, get them to refer you to others, interview the others, get more referrals, and so on until most of the referrals are to people you already know about.

Carroll's (1982, 1983) work for PNM electrical generation and transmission projects used the first approach. Carroll says that this type of survey should be analogous to archaeological inventory of 100 percent of the ground surface, "but what the investigator is attempting to sample 100 percent of is much harder to define . . ." (1983:45). The first step, he suggests, is "100 percent coverage of Native American landholders to be directly affected or in close proximity to the proposed action." By coverage he means "opportunity for 100 percent of all primary landholders or their representatives to express their perceptions of significance or sensitive locations on the lands with which they were most familiar" and recommend other knowledgeable people (1983:5). Carroll's perception of his goal as making sure everybody has a chance to comment on how the proposed development might affect sacred places, rather than as getting an inventory of sacred places, shows a rare and welcome sophistication. Carroll's second step was to try to identify 100 percent of all significant places. For complex reasons, it is hard to tell how far he was from reaching this goal. Carroll wanted to visit medicine people and others whom land users recommended, no matter where they lived (1983:6) but apparently didn't succeed in this.

One of the most interesting things about Carroll's work is that it suggests the scope of knowledge of land users who are not religious specialists.

> . . . even local grazing committee members [chapter-level officials] who have some direct knowledge of the land in question, claimed no knowledge of sensitive locations and deferred comment to the local residents. A similar inclination was found among residents at a short distance from study area lands. . . . It was found that at about three miles from the central study area, residents claimed only second-hand knowledge of major locations and no specific knowledge of lesser locations such as grave sites. (1983:64)

As Carroll interprets this pattern, "People have been told about significant locations in their own grazing areas by parents and kin but know only major locations in the surrounding region" (1983:64).

Because most residents knew about only limited geographical areas, even Carroll's attempts to ask all local residents for their opinions didn't guarantee that he would always have more than one opinion about every place, or prevent contradictory opinions from surfacing later.

> The primary informant [in the 1982 project] was questioned from several perspectives on the effect of the existing AF line and the proposed 500kV line on these features [sacred cairns associated with rain requesting and other ceremonies]. He maintained that there was no effect from the existing line and he anticipated none from the proposed line—presumably so long as the actual sacred features [the cairns] are not disturbed. (1982:52)

Later, in connection with the 1983 project, Carroll (1983:78) reported the reaction of another local resident to construction in this same area: "Speaking as a medicine man for the Navajo people, this informant said he does not want . . . [the mesa] disturbed in any way."

Most of the other studies probably tried to approximate the second, "snowballing" approach, although few probably reached the point where most referrals were to people already known. Probably many studies (certainly our work in Canyon de Chelly) were more like the Big Mountain study of Vannette and Wood (1979): as time ran out, the researchers used their contacts from an earlier, large-scale land-use study (Wood, Vannette, and Andrews 1982)—or sought out chapter officials (Vannette and Feary 1981)—"to contact key informants"—people most likely to have the type of knowledge sought, and representing different parts of the geographical area and its social networks. At one extreme, Navajo Forest researchers (Bartlett 1980, Cleeland and Doyel 1982; information incorporated in Kemrer and Lord 1984) who relied on one "key informant" described the selection process (and the limits of confidence) this way:

> On behalf of the Navajo Medicine Men's Association, Mr. Eddie Tso of the Navajo Health Authority directed a letter to the [Navajo Nation government's] Cultural Resource Management Program expressing concern over planned timbering operations by Navajo Forest Products Industry. The association felt that such operations might damage sacred areas or objects in the project areas, and requested that an attempt be made to protect them. Accordingly, [BIA] Branch of Forestry specified that the services of a medicine man be acquired as part of the contract for a cultural resources inventory survey, and Mr. Tom Watson Sr. of Fort Defiance, Arizona was hired as consultant to the project.
>
>   . . . The rapid economic development of the Navajo people, a high priority of the tribe, is juxtaposed with the traditional lifeway and the objects and places associated with it. The data gathered by the archaeologist and his recommendations, applied early in the planning process, can aid the continued economic growth while helping preserve elements of the traditional way of life. Thus, Navajo Forest Products Industry will be able to accommodate the concerns of the medicine men who in turn can cooperate with the logging industry. [This statement has turned out to be overly optimistic, as part III will show.]
>
>   The drawback to the application of information provided by Mr. Watson is that it represents the viewpoint of only one medicine man. . . . (Bartlett 1980:33)

Mr. Watson also consulted on a later survey of an area overlapping Bartlett's, and the information he provided wasn't just "the viewpoint of one medicine man."

> Mr. Watson stated that his comments on these sites reflect the official policy of the Medicine Men's Association and not just his own opinion. Confirmation of his evaluations was sought from Mr. Eddie Tso, Director of the Native Healing Science program, who stated that while all of the medicine men agree that sacred shrines, graves, and ceremonial sites should be protected, they had not yet fully discussed other sites, such as habitations and herding camps. (Cleeland and Doyel 1982:237)

Mr. Watson's personal opinion, according to this source, was that homesites, herding camps, sweathouses, and the like are also likely to have absorbed some sorts of power from the ceremonial performances and other activities there, and therefore should be respected and avoided.

Trying to interview all residents in and near a project area is usually possible only when one is working in a rather small area, and even then may be hard with limited time and money. Also, one runs the risk of missing medicine people who have esoteric knowledge of the area but live elsewhere. The "snowballing non-random" technique to reach most of the knowledgeable people is better suited for large areas, and even then only researchers with the most time (Vannette and Feary 1981, Vannette and Tso 1988) seem to have come near the end of the snowballing referrals.

Virtually all researchers who describe how they structured their interviews say they were "open-ended." Only Fransted (1979) even mentions an interview schedule, which he says was a checklist to organize information, not a questionnaire used to structure the interview itself. We believe this testifies to the cultural sensitivity of these researchers. To use questionnaires gives the interviewer the superior, controlling role in the discourse and is therefore disrespectful of the elders and medicine people, as well as inconsistent with the way requesting the gift of valuable knowledge subordinates the interviewer.

Most studies are somewhat vague about how the researchers verified locations with the interviewees. Most evidently relied on a combination of visits to the places with interviewees, having the interviewee point out locations visible from the homesite, and using place names already on maps. One variant is our study of sacred places on HPL, during which we met with local residents in several parts of the HPL to identify sacred places by having people point out their locations on maps (at the same time tape-recording any stories and other information about the places). This resulted in a very large number of places being identified by a relatively large number of people in a short time. We also believe the locations are accurate because most are places with names given on maps in English translation, and people who couldn't read the labeling on the maps nevertheless pinpointed places with Navajo names right where the map showed the same name in English. (Field verification is still desirable to validate the results for future reference, but it was not necessary for the essentially educational purposes of the report.) This approach only worked, however, because the interviewees were squarely behind the project and the meetings had been organized by community liaisons with the Navajo Nation government who had already been consulting the same people on related matters for years.

5.

Stories and Types of Places in the Other Studies

Stories

Some studies give a few very detailed stories and others present none at all. Presumably all researchers were given at least a few short stories, but some chose not to reproduce them in deference to the wishes of the storytellers.

> When I learned [the stories] I was told to keep them to myself until a year before I die. At that time I can give them to one of my grandsons. I cannot tell them to a white man. (Vannette and Feary 1981:31)

Fransted (1979) was all set to tape-record long narratives, but no one told him one (one reason may be that he was working in the fall, too early for storytelling, as Sylvia Manygoats says in part I).

The stories reproduced here are among the most detailed that other studies presented. Two of those from our own work (stories of Teddy Draper Sr. and Reginald Nabahe) are not reproduced in the reports. The tellers gave us permission to publish them in this book, and they show the riches that researchers may receive but withhold from their reports. We also have added a long story that Edward Sapir recorded decades ago for linguistic study. It belongs here because it is probably a version of the story that the person who told Carroll about White Rock refers to but wouldn't tell. Also, although we have edited it here, it shows how people tell stories fully when they are telling them for the stories' own sakes in something more like a proper setting for storytelling—right place, time of day, time of year, and situation.

REGINALD NABAHE

[In May 1990, we interviewed Mr. Nabahe at his home near Crystal, New Mexico. After we explained the purpose of our work in Canyon de Chelly, he made this statement. Close translation is by Harris Francis, reproduced with Mr. Nabahe's consent.]

Monster Slayer and Born for Water. War God Twins story. They were born on top of Huerfano Mountain. After they were born and were small they only had a mother. Their father was the Sun. Have you heard of this?

[HF: Yes.]

That was their father, and they asked, "Make us a bow," they asked their mother, "a bow and arrows." This is all they did, practice with the bow and arrows every day, learning how to handle and shoot them. That's the way it happened.

Then they started asking their mother who their father is. She replied that their father was that thing that shines, the light, the Sun. So they asked, "How do we get to the Sun?" After that they left. Only one left, they were twins, the older one. Then their mother said, "Why don't you go visit your father?" [Implication seems to be that the younger one followed the older.]

Then the Sun lived at this place, his wife was home also, "When does our father come home?" "When the Sun goes down and it gets dark, that's when he returns," she replied. Their in-law, another wife of their father, that's how it happened, they say. Then the Sun went over the horizon and it became dark, and he came home. "Your children, calling you father, have come to you," he was told. Then he asked, "Why have you come to me?"

And then, they had a sister, they say. The Sun told their sister, "Fire up the sweathouse," which she did. She got the rocks very hot so that they were glowing. I don't know how big the sweathouse was, it was just a sweathouse. Then their sister brought the hot rocks into the sweathouse for them. Then she poured water on the hot rocks, cold water, they were already inside. Hot steam filled the sweathouse. Their sister had a fawn for a pet. Then they went outside, nothing had happened to them.

Then their mother, at their home, had some tobacco, some kind of tobacco. It was hanging up and it would light up. When it would light up it was telling her that her children were in danger. The breeze was what was telling her. And when the tobacco would light up she would put it out, and the Twins would be all right again.

"Why have you come to me?" the Sun asked again. Again the sweathouse was fired up, the rocks heated and cold water poured on them. Hot steam filled the sweathouse and again they emerged unscathed. This was the second time. Again, this procedure was repeated. Then again, making it four times. People associate with the number four, that's what happened. Every time they emerged from the sweathouse the fawn would come to them. At first it came just to the entrance, then closer, then eventually up to them. When the fawn did finally come up to them it licked them. At this point the Sun admitted that they must be his children because the fawn came to them and licked them. He said, "Thank you for coming to see me, and why have you come to me?"

The Sun then said, "To the east there are white horses, this way yellow horses [south?], this way to the west, black horses, and then to the north, there are horses of all colors, white, black, horses of mixed colors. Maybe this is what you're after."

"No, this is not why we're here, not for horses. We're here for only one thing," they replied. You see that bow hanging there? [points above doorway].

[HF: Yes.]

Maybe you're wondering what I'm talking about. "We came for a bow and arrows," they replied. That's the way it goes.

"What's it for? The bow and arrow?" There at this place called Black Lake, this way towards Hawk's Nest [general vicinity of the crane petroglyphs in the story below, several dozen miles east of Mr. Nabahe's home], and then this way, that's where I go, it's about two miles there, this way. There's a dam there, Black Lake [implication may be that the Black Lake in the story isn't the same as the one near his home, but some kind of connection seems implied—at least, they have the same name]. There used to be a lake there, when there used to be rain, now there's none. It's all dried up. And when you go to the lake, it would be walking around it, Big God [giant]. When you look into a mirror, you see yourself. The giant while looking into the lake saw them. "Earth surface people don't come around here." [Implication is that then he would eat them up.]

Then the Sun asked, "Why do you want the bow and arrow?" The Twins replied, "This giant, our brother, Big God [the Sun was his father too], we want to kill him, that's why we want the bow and arrows, that's why we come here to you." Then he said, "All right, here it is," and gave them the weapons. They were told that they were not to shoot first, but let the giant take the first shot.

Then he [Giant] took a shot at them, then they took the bow and arrow, aimed, shot, and killed the giant instantly. He was killing humans, that's why there were no earth-surface people around. That's how he was killing people.

Then they asked their mother, "Where is this thing called The One That Lies in the Middle of the Flats, where is he?" Over at Black Lake. It was like a bull, it was huge and really mean. "We are going to kill that one also," they said. Then there was a gopher, who said, "I go to where the One That Lies in the Middle of the Flats is." A huge bull which was very mean. When he came after you he would scoop you up.

Then the gopher said, "I visit this bull where he lies, I burrow to where he is at and chew off some of his hair and use it for my children. My children keep warm with his hair." Then the Twins went into the burrow that the gopher had dug and came up on the monster. They had their bows and arrows with them. Then one of them went up to the monster while the other waited a little ways back. He was lying there close and he shot an arrow into the heart and killed—they killed the One That Sits in the Middle of the Flats this way.

By the way, this person you're with, does she understand Navajo?

[HF: She understands a little.]

After they killed the bull and the giant, his intestines, big intestines, they cleaned it out and filled it up with his blood and took it back to their mother. "This is the blood of the giant," they told her. Again they did the same with the bull, filled his intestines with his blood and told their mother, "We have killed the bull, here is his blood." That's how it happened. These stories are truly savory.

Shicheii [polite term of address, man-to-man], if you really want to hear stories, we should get a sweathouse ready, then you must bring the wood for the next two to four days. Then we'll spend the next four days in the sweathouse telling one another these stories like this.

[HF: That would be fine.]

It was said back then, when a boy went to visit his grandfather, the grandfather said, "Grandson, what are you doing?" Grandson said, "I just come to visit you." Grandfather said, "Grandson, there's a sweathouse over there, go and get firewood enough for four days and four nights." The grandson did as he was told and gathered a large pile of firewood. At this point the grandfather might just have [walked off and] left him! [A mean trick by the grandfather is implied.] That's the way it goes, shicheii.

Then, after killing the bull, there was the Travelling Rock. I don't know how big it was, but it was called the Travelling Rock. They [the Twins] chipped the rock and it came after them here. Now that mountain that is there [pointing], Star Mountain, you probably saw it when you were coming here. There's a gap in between the two buttes, there, I didn't see it myself, big star, like a crystal, this big, was there in the gap. [Implication is that this was a chip off Travelling Rock.] Then the Mormons [probably local traders or missionaries] stole the big star, they took it and hauled it away. That's the way it happened. Then they [the Twins] started chasing the Travelling Rock again. Now, it was the Mormons who stole the big star. Now, they [Twins] started chasing the Travelling Rock again, from there where the big star was, from where they hit him and chipped a piece off. That's why it's called Star Mountain. From there they chased it to a place called Big Waterfall and chased it off the waterfall there. There's big cliffs there, Chinle and up this way there's big cliffs [Canyon de Chelly] down there. They chased it off there.

Now they had food, there's a place called Blue Corn Dumpling Rock, it's up at the pass. Now this pass is sacred too, shicheii.

[HF: Yes, we know about that place, people have told us about it.]

That's sacred, Enemy Way ceremony, there's the road up the pass, the highway up. To take the rattle stick [a ceremonial object that the family sponsoring the Enemy Way sends on horseback to another family many miles away to invite them to the performance at the inviting family's place] up and over through there is prohibited, strictly prohibited! If that should happen, big enemies will appear and there will be war, the people will go to war. That's how it is. Only to the south [around the south end of the mountains] do the people carry the rattle stick, and behind them [the mountains] like [names of several places]. They carry the rattle stick around that way, that's how they go about it. Then also around [place name to the north], they bring the stick over that way. That's the way they bring the rattle sticks to one another, because big enemies will appear if the stick is brought over the pass. That's the way it is, shicheii. That's the way people are probably telling you of these things. [The implication may be that the mountains are a defensive barrier and carrying paraphernalia of a war-related performance over them might invite enemies to breach them as well, or that the particular route over the pass is used for ceremonial activities that restore peace and harmony. Ironically, this is the route that Col. John M. Washington of the U.S. Army and his troops used in 1849 to move westward through Navajoland right after having "accidentally" killed Narbona, the most prominent Navajo headman of the time to advocate peaceful coexistence with the United States.]

[HF: Yes.]

That's the way it happened, now after that there was the One That Would Turn to Stone. Now this One That Would Turn to Stone was also killing people. Now that Shiprock Pinnacle that's over there, that's where she had her offspring. She had two offspring, one was a boy and the other a girl. Now this One That Would Turn to Stone was an eagle, a very large one. Back then there were Navajos present, also Zunis and Pueblo Indians, they were present in that area. Now this large eagle would pick up these people and take them back to Shiprock, where her offspring would eat these people. That's how it happened. And then they [Twins] asked [the eaglets], "When does your father come home?" "When it rains, my father will come home, when the rain comes from the west, at dusk." The eagle would come home with the rain.

Now, they had their bows and arrows ready when the eagle

came back with a woman, a Zuni woman. It landed and they talked to it. If it understood, I don't know. Then they put an arrow through its heart, killing it. And then they had no way of getting back down to the ground. I don't know how they got up. Then there was a bat, who only travels at night and never in the daytime. It was this bat that lowered them down. Then the feathers of the eagle, they gave to the bat's children. They [bat's children] then were told of a place where there were lots of sunflowers and were told not to go in that direction for there were also lots of birds without feathers there. They [birds] could fly, but didn't have any feathers. After being told not to go in that direction where the sunflowers grew, the bats went anyway. When they reached that place the birds attacked the bat and took the feathers, that's where birds got their feathers. That's the way they tell the story. You've heard of this.

[HF: Yes, we've heard a little of it.]

Those are my stories. That's how it happened. There are places people don't go to, there's this hill that's sitting here. [name] it's called. You don't go on there either. I'm afraid to go up on it myself. There was a man from [place] named [name], he used to go on top of the hill, and offer sacred stones there. It's a sacred place. There's also [place name] that you don't go on top of. Then there's Star Mountain.

[HF: Do they still perform ceremonies on this mountain? Star Mountain?]

Yes, I'm sure they still do. This one here no one uses it for ceremonies anymore.

[HF: Do people still conduct ceremonies on top today?]

I don't know, they say it's a dangerous place. You don't go on it, even though it's there. I only travel beside it where the cattle and horses wander. My goats wander there also near that hill. I started putting salt there for them to lick. Instead, deer started licking the salt and now my goats have become wary and afraid. When they lick the salt they also lick the saliva of the deer on the salt. That's why these goats I have around here are all very afraid.

[HF: On top of the mountain [Star Mountain], do they still collect crystals? Medicine men who perform the proper ceremonies?]

Yes, I'm sure they do. They say there's crystals on there. That's probably the chips of that rock where it was hit. How many people have you asked now about it?

[HF: You're the only one right now but we plan to visit others.]

T E D D Y   D R A P E R ,   S R .

[In April 1990, Mr. Draper took us into Canyon de Chelly and Canyon del Muerto, where he pointed out dozens of places important in the Navajo past. During that trip he summarized in English the Navajo past in the following way as background for what he was telling us about the places in the canyon. Klara Kelley transcribed this statement from the tape, reproduced here with Mr. Draper's consent. We emphasize that this statement was made in very informal circumstances. Interested readers are referred to Mr. Draper's published work (Draper 1973).]

When those Anasazis were here, there's some power by the same group, a man named Náhwiiłbįįhí [the Great Gambler]. That man had the power as a gambler. So all these Anasazis were kicked out and taken back to Chaco Canyon. And they were slaves.

But the Navajos were still somewhere in the La Plata Mountains [Navajo sacred mountain of the north; place of emergence onto the present earth's surface is said by some to be in this vicinity]. Then they start moving to the east, where there's a canyon that they call Tséyi', too [same name as Canyon de Chelly, meaning Rock Canyon], that's Largo Canyon [in Old Navajoland, Dinétah, area around Huerfano Mountain, home of Changing Woman and the Twins before she moved to the west; see chapters 1 and 10]. And that's where the Navajos had their government. They teach people how to do ceremonies, and there's pictographs there, too.

Then they started coming west, and they met some Spaniards, around sixteen something, there was a new group [Spaniards] from the south, and then they had trouble. They learned how to slave, then how to trade people. Then later, the white person from the East came. They got guns, and the peaceful people started killing, they learned how to use guns.

But there were still some Anasazis at Tall House in Chaco Canyon—they [Navajos] met some part of the Anasazis. And finally they were down here, and they met the first Hopis on east side of Flagstaff. There's a [National] Monument [Wupatki] that's where the wind comes out of the hole [refers to Navajo and Hopi names for this place]. That's where the Hopi were, then they moved across. But the main population was there.

They call it Oozéí [Oraibi, western Hopi village]. They [Hopis] had a different pictograph and these people [Anasazis of Canyon de Chelly] had a different pictograph [implies that they are of different ethnic groups].

So Navajos moved everywhere, up to Page [Arizona, northwest part of Navajoland], all the way out there, my great-great-grandmother told me about the Utes. She was about ninety-seven, she lived about five more years. She said the only trouble was the white people gave guns to the Utes. They sent the Utes from that area to the canyon [Canyon de Chelly]. Utes tried to hunt down and kill Navajos.

WHITE ROCK

[Story of unidentified person retold by Carroll (1982:51–54). Bracketed material is our interpolation; parenthetical material is Carroll's. Deletions indicated are details of location.]

On top of White Rock . . . there are sacred rock piles. In the old days there was a "Hadahoniye' " [banded calcareous aragonite—translucent "mirage stone"—symbolizes both invisible and thus safe travel and also the lifegiving combination of air-light-moisture and may be considered a solid concentration, or essence, of this combination; see story of the origin of horses below] inserted vertically in one of the rock piles. (The Hadahoniye' was a 5-to 6-inch long, cylindrical stone, approximately 1.5 inches in diameter, of a rock, "like marble.") This was a place to hold ceremonies to pray for rain and good weather. White Rock Butte is a good place for this because it has ridges that run out in the four cardinal directions, and ceremonies held on top can therefore benefit the areas and people in all directions. The cylindrical rock is gone now—someone took it or moved it [compare this story to those of Reginald Nabahe above and Rose Francis below]. If this was a Navajo who took it, he will have trouble from it (the informant did not believe that it would bother an Anglo). Now that it is gone, they still have ceremonies there, but they do not work very well. Ceremonies still take place on top, but in June (1981), there was a ceremony . . . (also a weather-related ceremony).

[Here Carroll injects his understanding that the teller doesn't expect powerline construction to affect the landmark.]

Origin of the White Rock Topography: According to the informant, his grandfather told him that the White Rock formation was not always rough like it is now. Once it was all a smooth rise. Then the Ram (desert bighorn, by the description) and Lightning began to argue about who was the "toughest." They argued back and forth, until finally they decided to fight. They butted heads and fought back and forth across the rise until it got so hot the rise caught on fire. It burned out the rough formations, hills, and valleys that are there now. Somewhere on the southwest slope of the formation (west of the AF power line) there is a "place where steam comes out." This is probably the last remnants of the fire. (Note that the White Rock formation includes layers and eroded piles of bright red and orange burned shale, the result of underground coal fires.)

Also mentioned was the fact that some formations east of [name] (still part of what I am calling the "White Rock formation") resemble houses (hogans). There seemed to be an implied significance to this, but information was not available in this one, long interview. Information will be requested in later phases of the project. It may be notable, however, that similar features—two small knobs on top of Huerfano Mesa [home of Changing Woman and the Twins—see chapter 1]—which resemble cribbed-roof hogans are believed by many to be symbols used by supernatural personalities to show the people how to make houses.

White Rock Affinity to Horses: Throughout the stories and answers to specific questions by the primary informant, there was a theme of the presence of horses.

THE ORIGIN OF HORSES

[If Carroll had later been told the story that connects White Rock with horses, it might have been a version of the story below, recorded by linguist Edward Sapir (1942:109–27). White Rock is similar geologically to the place in the story from which the makings of horses came. Sapir's explanatory interpolations are in parenthesis, and ours are in brackets.]

Now he who was the son of Changing Woman, what place is there that he did not go to? He being the Turquoise Boy [Monster Slayer; Sapir calls him Enemy Slayer], (he went everywhere) so that things should be created.

[He asks his mother, Changing Woman, how the means by which people get their livelihood will be created.]

"You may go to the holy places for your purpose, my son. . . . Go to the summit of Pelado Peak [this is how Sapir identified the Navajo name for the sacred mountain of the east]. There twelve of the Talking Gods live. [For more on these beings, see Frank Mitchell statement below.] It seems to be a place in which holy things take place. You may go there, that for which you travel about is known there, perhaps," she said to him. . . .

Then he started off over there. . . . At the entrance, a big ear of corn was standing. . . . He entered. . . .

"For what reason are you travelling about, my grandchild? [the Talking God] said, . . . "Yes, my [grandfather]. In order that things be created I am travelling about. . . .

"Yes. All right, just look! What is it for which you travel about? Now, you see, there are all the soft goods. There are white shells. . . . There is turquoise. . . . There are buckskins. . . . And there are mountain lion skins. . . . And there are quite all of the blankets," [Talking God] said.

"That is not what I am travelling about for, my [grandfather]. All right! I am travelling about for this. . . . In order that we may have a means of travel I go about," he said to him. . . .

"That is not in existence here, my grandchild," [said Talking God].

[Monster Slayer visits each of the other sacred mountains of the cardinal directions in turn, where he has similar experiences. At the last one, the sacred mountain of the north, the Calling Gods tell him,]

"That for which you say you are travelling, my grandchild, surely your mother has it, White Shell Woman, Changing Woman, surely she has it, my grandson," he was told. . . . "That for which you say you are travelling, surely your father has it, the Sun. . . . Go back to your mother. . . ."

[He returns to his mother's home at Huerfano Mesa.]

So she counted the four (baskets) [filled with sacred stones of the four directions] . . . Now these will be my offering," she said to him. . . . She spoke as if these were to be used as a payment for something here. ". . . you shall now go to your father, my son." . . .

[He starts out toward his father's home but his father

encounters him on the way and sends him back home to his
mother.]

. . . "There is just one thing left (for you to do), my
son," she said. . . . "You shall now go to the place called
[name]." . . .

So then he started off again. . . . When he got to the place
called [name], a step-ladder was sticking out of the undisturbed
soil. . . . Here, when he did so, a certain person was sitting
down below. . . . An old man, a very fat one, was sitting there
[along with his wife, son, and daughter]. . . .

And then that old man arose. . . . It was indeed the Mirage
Man. . . . He looked up there at (Enemy Slayer). . . . "Come in,
my grandchild," he said. . . .

[Monster Slayer tells the man his purpose.]

And then (Enemy Slayer) started off with that old man.
"Here they are: those with which in time to come (people)
will live," he said to him. . . . He opened a door toward
the east. . . . The place was so large that it extended as far as
one could see. . . . At the entrance, white shell was pranc-
ing about . . . in the likeness of a horse. Even its rope was
of white shell. . . . A great amount of mist-like rain was fall-
ing on them continuously, they extended off in great numbers. . . .

[Mirage Man opens doors in each of the other directions in
turn to expose a similar view.]

So he had opened doors to all four directions, it happened. . . . "You who are earth people keep nothing holy, I
shall just shake (the pollen) off (the horses) for you," he said to
him. . . .

That happened so. . . . He just shook (the pollen) off (the
white shell horse) for him . . . [put pollen over the horse and
let the horse shake it off]. [He does the same to the horses of
the other three directions each in turn.]

He went with him again to the (horse) standing on the east
side. He moved a white bead in and out of its mouth for him.
[He repeats the same procedure with the appropriate sacred
stone for the horses of each of the other three directions, each
in turn.]

At that point, he tied up (in a bag) all that (pollen) which
had been shaken off (the horses) for him. He put in (the bag)
those (beads) which he had put into the horses' mouths for
him. He tied (the bag) up with (the beads in it). "Now that is

all, my grandchild," he said. . . . "Now you may start back to your mother," he said to him. . . .

[Monster Slayer returns to his mother and gives her the bundle, which she takes and does the following with:]

. . . From over yonder the Holy People assembled, they say . . . the Sun, the Moon, the Mirage people, the Mist people, the Sun people, the Moon people, (and) all the Holy people [light plus air and moisture, in combination the life stuff.]

[An unwounded buckskin] was spread out. On its surface, that which had been shaken off the horses was placed. . . . It was placed with the white beads. . . . [Repeated for the sacred stones of each of the other directions/colors.] Twelve [unwounded buckskins] were placed over it. . . .

And then the people [Holy People who had assembled for the performance] sat down comfortably. . . . And then the singing started . . . [Blessingway songs]. When the singing was about half-finished, those things which had been put down rose up to this (height). . . . That which had been shaken off the horses had begun to move. . . .

So, while the songs . . . had been sung, the dawn broke all around, they say. On the horses' side, they kicked the covering off themselves. . . . They began to get up. . . . Just as the singing was finished, they stood up. . . . These, the turquoise horse and the white shell horse, they called to each other. . . . On this side, the abalone shell horse and the black jewel horse, they called to each other. . . . [Thus] horses were created (and) the naming took place. . . .

CRANE PETROGLYPHS AND MASSACRE SITE

[According to Carroll (1983:70–72), the Crane Petroglyphs site "is associated by some with the Coal Creek Massacre site" a few miles away because "enemy tribes" camped at the cranes during raids in Navajo country. The two places are therefore parts of a landscape defined by related stories. According to Carroll (1983:79), "several informants believed that in addition to a great many unburied Navajo dead in the area, the location also contains the sacred contents of medicine bags and other sacred material buried by the victims before they were killed." York (1984:42–43, Appendix A) relates previously published information to what interviewees told him about the crane petroglyphs, and retells what two local residents told him about the massacre site. Bracketed material is our interpolation and parenthetical material is York's.]

Interviews with local Navajos concerning the origin of the petroglyphs have produced two different accounts. One informant has stated that he believes the petroglyph may have been done by the Ute Indians when they were travelling around the San Juan Basin and fighting Navajos. The water at the base of the bluff may have encouraged the Utes to camp in the area, and it was hypothesized that the petroglyphs were done on such an occasion. There is sufficient information concerning Ute raiding in the San Juan Basin as recently as the 1850s–1860s to make such a hypothesis plausible (Judd 1954:350; Schroeder 1965).

More recent interviews have acquired information about another possible origin for the crane petroglyph. According to an informant, who also supplied information about a nearby site where a historic raid took place, it is possible that the petroglyph was made long ago by either the Anasazi or the Navajo Holy People (Dine Diyinii). It was also said that the locality has been utilized for rain rituals. A reference by Neil Judd (1954:345) to an unpublished version of the story of Noqoilpi (variant, Noqolipi), the Great Gambler of Chaco Canyon in the origin legend, provided to him by a personal communication, suggests the possible ceremonial significance of the crane petroglyph: "Noqoilpi was banished to Tiz-na-zinde, 'where the cranes stand up' (referring to birds pictured on the rocks [specifies number of] miles west of Pueblo Bonito), died and was buried there."

Sandhill cranes had both medicinal uses and ceremonial uses according to W. W. Hill:

> The dung of the sandhill crane (de'l) was drunk with water to cure diarrhea. The dirt from its track was placed in the patient's moccasin during the Flintway chant to assist in the cure. Its bill and parts of its flesh and viscera were put in its neck and head to form part of the Flintway shaman's bundle.
>
> Hunters often hid near water and when the cranes alighted, rushed them on foot or horseback and clubbed them before they could take to the air. (1938:175)
>
> · · ·

The raid [that led to the massacre near the crane petroglyphs, an ironic juxtaposition in view of the power of cranes used through Flintway procedures for emergencies like serious wounds] took place in the period following the return of the Navajos from Fort Sumner or Hweeldi in 1868. The raiders were Beehai, Jicarilla Apaches, not [Utes].

A woman lived in the vicinity of [place name]. The Tlaaschii
clan woman asked her brother, Naakaiisneez, to get salt for her
from another family. (Naakaiisneez was born shortly after the
return from Fort Sumner.) Naakaiisneez and two other boys
went on a rabbit hunt on horseback, which took them to
[several named places]. During this hunting trip, the [Jicarillas]
saw the three mounted hunters and began to follow them.
Naakaiisneez and the two boys may have had extra horses with
them that attracted the attention and interest of the [Jicarillas].

On the way home, Naakaiisneez and the others stopped to
visit his sister, also of the Tl'aaschii clan, who lived at [location]
in a settlement consisting of numerous brush structures.
Naakaiisneez stayed overnight, and the next morning after starting a campfire he heard what sounded like a mule and then a
noise like the mule had been slapped. After this he heard horses
riding toward the settlement and he went inside a structure to
warn the people of the approach of the raiders.

The people panicked, grabbed anything they could get their
hands on to fight off the raiders. The raid lasted from early in
the morning at sunrise to the end of the day at sunset. Many
Navajo people were killed and scalps were taken and then
loaded into sacks that were placed on a mule. The [Jicarillas]
did not kill all of the people, but gathered some women and
children to take as captives. Although the [Jicarillas] tried to kill
and scalp all of the Navajo men, one man [name] escaped
death. Pretending to be dead, he was lying face down on the
ground when a [Jicarilla] came up to him to take his scalp.
When the Apache saw lots of lice on [the man's] hair, he just
kicked the body and left. All the other men were scalped. The
[Jicarillas] used rifles.

The [Jicarillas] then burned down the settlement and took
Navajo women and children, and horses and sheep away toward
their homeland [name]. Among the captives were the boy,
Naakaiisneez, one of his brothers, and a sister. Shortly after the
[Jicarillas] had left the settlement with their captives and booty,
a man [name], whose family lived in the vicinity of some ridges
near [place name], visited the area with a friend. They saw
many dead bodies and the remains of the settlement.

Another man named Nabahe then began to follow the tracks
of the [Jicarillas]. The first night the [Jicarillas] camped and did
not sleep, as they were watching their captives, the Navajo. One
[Jicarilla] had a Navajo woman on his horse and he was going

to rape her. However, they struggled and fell off the horse. Then the woman revealed a pistol and threatened to shoot the [Jicarilla]. She took the horse and escaped. The [Jicarilla] then walked back to camp.

The [Jicarillas] did not sleep at all the first night, and the next morning they continued to travel. The second night they let the horses loose to rest and the [Jicarillas] went to sleep. Nabahe and a friend had followed the raiders and took all but three or four horses from them during the second night. In the morning of the third day, the [Jicarillas] left the [place] and continued to head east. That day they travelled to the vicinity of [places].

On the third night the sister of Naakaiisneez killed the leader of the [Jicarillas] and was killed in turn. The next morning the raiders proceeded toward [Jicarilla land] and completed their journey. They stayed there for a long time, and then went somewhere else to sell their Navajo slaves.

Naakaiisneez was sold to Mexicans and then raised among them. A girl of the [Ute] clan was also taken in a raid and sold to the Mexicans. Naakaiisneez and the girl married and returned to the eastern Navajo region of northwestern New Mexico. He and his wife had no children, but they adopted a girl of the [Ute] clan and raised her as their own. That girl grew up, married, and had a child who became [name], the mother of a woman who currently uses the project area. In 1917, Naakaiisneez visited this woman's family and told them the story of the raid. He was in his fifties or sixties at the time.

R O S E   F R A N C I S

[The following stories by Rose Francis were written by her daughter, Peggy Scott, and given to us to use in the report on Navajo places in Hopi Partitioned Lands (Kelley, Francis, and Scott 1991:23ff.).]

During the migrations of various groups of Navajo clan members [see chapter 1, one of the later episodes of the creation story], cairns were established to inform other travellers that people passed through the location previously and have made prayers and offerings there. Each then became a holy place for all people. This is so with Star Mountain. When the Navajo people [the newly created original Navajo clans] were coming back from the west, after visiting White Shell Woman [often identified as Changing Woman or her sister], they drank from a lake nearby [location], Lake That Takes Pity on Others. There they saw a glow of light shining from the top of Star Mountain and creating a clear reflection in the lake. At the same time they saw a big star with a long tail. As this star travelled towards the mountain, the tail aligned with the glow from the mountain and the light reflection in the lake. The people knew that this was a true phenomenon and should not be ignored.

The people investigated the top of Star Mountain to see what produced the first glow from the mountain. They found a long crystal rock there [compare stories of White Rock and Reginald Nabahe above]. They gathered to discuss the particular event that happened the night before. As they watched the star with the tail, they noticed that it did not appear several days later. One group remained behind to determine the cause of the incident. They put sticks around the crystal rock on top of Star Mountain and began marking exactly where the sun's shadow hit the crystal rock at sunrise. During the midsummer, the sun rose in one position for four days and then it began its journey back. The fourth day, a special Blessing ceremony was performed. From that time on this has been observed as the "end of the journey for the sun in the summer and in the winter." This is known as the summer and winter solstice. It is during this time of the four days in the two seasons that the Blessingway ceremony was done for the sun. It is the only time of the year that sacred stories were told. This was the time young men were initiated to become medicine men. During these four days a small cornmeal mush made into a cake was offered to the sun by a young female virgin. She went to the top of Star Mountain to await the rising sun, and when the sun came up she would offer the cake with special prayers and songs. This time of the year was very special and sacred.

As the years passed, one stone was laid aside to signify that one year had passed by. When there were fifty to sixty stones the star with the tail reappeared. Again a very special Blessingway ceremony was performed when the light from the tail of the star, the glow from Star Mountain, and the reflection in the lake aligned themselves in a straight row. These special observances are still practiced today.

Types of Places

Except for Fransted's study, which was limited to Anasazi sites, all the studies revealed similar types of places as ours in terms of both what they look like and why they are important. The main differences are between studies that focused on relatively small geographical areas, like the works of Carroll (1983) and York (1984), and studies of larger areas. Because the studies of small areas occurred farther along in the development process, when specific pieces of land had been singled out, these studies were supposed to locate all significant places, large and small. They couldn't afford to ignore specific places related to the stories of particular families. The studies of larger areas, however, didn't have the time and funds to identify and record the large number of important places. They therefore note that people consider these types of places significant but leave the recording of specific places for a later time, when developers decide exactly where they want to locate.

The inventory of eighty Navajo sacred places on HPL recorded by the Navajo Nation in 1977 fairly accurately represents the range of places in all the other studies combined, both in terms of what the places look like and why they are significant. The descriptions tend to combine the observable characteristics of each place and its function. The specific types of places characterized by their observable features include: mesas, hills, clay sources for Navajo pottery, springs, flat areas, "wind homes" (probably air vents in volcanic rocks and cracks or holes in rocks the narrowness of which magnifies the force of air currents that pass through), rock outcrops, waterfalls, dinosaur remains, place where an unusual sound (probably from water or air) occurs, eagle nests, and a big tree. Functions include offering unspecified types of prayers with the precious stones of the four directions (whiteshell, turquoise, abalone, and jet), and prayers from specific ceremonial repertoires, the most common of which are those to ward off misfortune predicted by bad dreams, prayers for protection, rain-requesting, well-being of livestock (on hilltops used for spotting wandering livestock), and prayers of Blessingway and Windway (the latter usually at Wind Homes). Other functions are gathering medicinal plants for unspecified uses or for basketry or for specified ceremonial repertoires (the most common of which are Lifeway and Blessingway; areas under lightning-struck trees are often specified), getting minerals and soils (sand and pigments for sandpaintings, clays for ceremonial body painting, pottery clay), and securing ceremonial paraphernalia (sealed in a canyon).

Medicine people use all places, often alone, otherwise together with their patients. "Any Navajo" may use some places, mostly those for offering unspecified prayers with precious stones. Descriptions imply that some places are more widely known than others. Widely known places are "major sources of medicine," those used by "any Navajo," those used by "medicine men from all over the reservation." Most, but not all, are large landforms. The descriptions of users also suggest that the people who know about these places tend to be medicine people, their patients, and the patients' families. Time of use for most is year-round, and for all but one of the remainder, summer. The one, an eagle nest, is used in April-May-June.[1] Access to most places is from any direction rather than from a specific approach route. Several separate large landforms are also associated with each other in some way (through a story and possibly ceremonial procedures chartered by the story).

Other studies add the following to the list of repertoires associated with recorded Navajo sacred places: hunting repertoires, Enemy Way, Bead Way, Upward Reaching Way, Evil Way, Coyote Way, Night Way, and Mountaintop Way. The stories most commonly associated with places, according to the various studies, are those about the Twins going to their father, Changing Woman going to the west, the eastward migration of the Western Water Clans, and the Great Gambler.

Fransted's observations on the significance of Anasazi ruins in general (those that are not settings of events in the origins of Navajo clans or ceremonial repertoires) are worth amplifying.

> Anasazi ruins are part of the scheme of things, of the way this world was made to be after the emergence from the previous world. As such, they are part of the balance of beauty and harmony which constitutes right living (for all things) and, therefore, they should be preserved.
>
> To balance the picture it should be stated that not everybody believes the above, though the attitudes are very strong. . . .
>
> [I] wonder, again, if ruins are not basically considered as much a part of this world's landscape as [they are considered] previously inhabited places. (1979:6–7)

For many Navajos, Anasazi ruins are the homes of the haashch'ééh, a group of Navajo immortals whom masked dancers impersonate at different ceremonies and of whom the pre-eminent one is Talking God, also called the Grandfather of the Gods. These immortals are all involved in the creation of the Navajo people and their homeland, and thus are in a sense ancestral. Blessingway singer Frank Mitchell explained the importance of these places.

> The people in those [Anasazi] villages got to multiplying so fast they were crowding each other. And they were getting so closely populated that

there was a discussion about what to do for a solution. They were ordered to move to various places like the mountains, to the holy places in the mountains, holy places in the rocks, holy places where the waters are, where the springs are. They were told that they would disappear into those locations and would live there without dying off. They would just continue on with no births and no deaths. Those people who went to live in all those holy places would have everlasting life, it seems.

But it was said, "Some of you who are left here behind, after all these other people have gone into these holy places out of sight, you will still have death, and you will have to have births to replace the dead. . . .

I do not know what killed those early people off, what kind of epidemic might have come among them and wiped them off the earth. I asked Curly Hair, and he said he had an answer for it. He said that a big cyclone, a tornado, got them. . . . At the present time all we see is the ruins, the remains of their homes. . . . We do not know what happened to them at all. . . . My father told me this different story, that they vanished because of water or rain. He thought it must be water because you see all those water marks in Canyon de Chelly and it is below the water marks that you see some of their ruins.

Now all these different chants, like Male Shootingway, Female Shootingway, the Navajo Windway, and in fact all of them down to the small rituals, all these originated with these people and holy beings who used to live in the ruins. This is my late father's account of it. (1978:178–79)

Fransted notes that Navajos collect materials from Anasazi ruins for customary, including ceremonial, purposes—potsherds for pottery temper, projectile points, manos and metates, as well as plants, presumably certain species like wolfberry that tend to grow on Anasazi sites (the Navajo word for wolfberry means "the food of the haashch'ééh").

Some of the ruins also have specific Navajo stories that go with them. "[S]ome ruins, usually the larger and/or better preserved ones, seem more important in the thought and knowledge of the Navajo people living around them" (Fransted 1979:5). The implication is that these sites are more significant in some sense than are Anasazi sites that don't have specific stories that go with them. We suggest that these sites, like certain other spots on the landscape, are points with specific powers within a generally sacred landscape. The stories that Fransted mentions include origins of two Navajo clans. According to one story, "these people lived at [a particular ruin] before joining Laguna and Jemez Pueblos. They later became clans among the Navajo" (Fransted 1979:139). They also cover more recent incidents, such as people hiding in ruins to escape capture by the U.S. Army and internment at Fort Sumner.[2]

Some researchers impose their own schemes to classify places according to their significance (Carroll 1982, 1983; Vannette and Wood 1979; Vannette and Feary 1981; Vannette and Tso 1988—the last three use Watson's [1964] typology). All these schemes are based on various types of stories about the Navajo past, Navajo customary activities, and immortals associated with places. All recognize that many places have multiple associations and can fit into more than one category.

Overlapping Lists of Places

Some of the studies discussed here and our own study of the thirteen chapters overlap geographically, and so do the lists of places that these studies identify. We have already mentioned overlap between the thirteen-chapter study and the work of Vannette and Tso (1988) in the 1934 Navajo Reservation, in which they identified 18 of the 20 places we identified in the area of overlap (they also recorded ten times as many as we did in the chapters where we worked). Other studies that overlap are our study of HPL (Kelley, Francis, and Scott 1991) with the Navajo Nation (1977) study and with the Vannette and Tso (1988) study of the 1934 Reservation, and our Canyon de Chelly study (Francis and Kelley 1990, 1992) with that of Jett, Neboyia, and Morgan (1992). The studies that recorded the largest number of places in each area of overlap duplicated respectively 90%, 37%, 50%, and 94% of the places recorded in the smaller studies of the same area. Proportions that each smaller study identified of the corresponding larger study's inventory are 10%, 14%, 20%, and 40%. These are to us surprisingly high proportions of places in common, given the differences in the studies—time spent, purpose, methods—and the private way that Navajos pass down stories.

Place Names and Their Cultural Significance

Neither the studies that had inventories of place names as their central purpose (Fransted and Werner n.d., Walt and others 1987; Christensen 1990; Jett, Neboyia, and Morgan 1992) nor the other studies that consistently indicate the names of the places that they recorded for other reasons (Vannette and Feary 1981, Fransted 1979, Mitchell 1991, Francis and Kelley 1990, 1992, Kelley, Francis, and Scott 1991) offer any analysis of the place names. We have analyzed these lists of place names to see what names might reveal about the significance of a place. Places get names because people need to talk about them when they are far from the place. One might therefore expect that places with cultural significance, especially to people other than those living near the place, would have proper names. But the cultural significance of any named place may be no more than that it is a prominent landmark useful for orienting people.

Technical Appendix Table 6 compares information from the various lists of place names. Some of the studies are limited to named places (Chaco Canyon, Tsegi Canyon). Others are based on lists of places that Navajos identified as noteworthy for one reason or another, the reason depending on the purpose of the study. If one excludes locations (mostly places with Navajo cultural features) significant mainly in individual family histories, most of the places that Navajos call significant seem to have names. Studies in which interviewees identified places on maps, not on the ground itself, tend to have the highest proportions of places with names. But even studies that involved tours of the locations have names for a large majority of the places (75% or more).

The names tend to describe the physical appearance of the place and offer few clues to why the place is noteworthy—the story or activity that might go with it. Only very low proportions of the names even hint at a particular story or use. There are two categories of place names, proper and generic. When someone mentions a place using a descriptive phrase, one can tell when it is a proper name because it is followed by the word "a-place-called." Generic names, as discussed above, are simply translated as "the canyon," "the wash," and so forth, and aren't followed by "a-place-called." Proper place names help people talk about distant places. Navajos use generic names for nearby places and proper names for those at a distance. A generic name may indicate that only the few families that live near the place talk about it, but not necessarily. People farther away may also talk about the place, using a proper name (Chaco Canyon is an example). Just as one might say "I'm going to the store" to refer to the only store nearby, others living farther away would call it by its proper name.

No study has made a systematic effort to see how many places with names are associated with stories and customary Navajo activities, especially ceremonial repertoires, or how many places have cultural significance only as locally orienting landmarks. Our impression is that most places named in the most detailed recorded versions of stories that go with ceremonial repertoires are landmarks that people can see from long distances or are less conspicuous places on a line between two such landmarks. The reason is that these stories tell how the hero or heroine of each story puts together the ceremonial repertoire, mainly by travelling from place to place learning (first by accident and later by design) various procedures and paraphernalia from the holy people who inhabit each place. Medicine people and others may replicate segments of these journeys to gather materials and make offerings. Place names that describe the appearance of the landmark, especially from a great distance, help the modern people identify places named in the stories and songs of a ceremonial repertoire.

As one person told us during our work in Canyon de Chelly, "The two immortals travelled around, saying, 'This is the name of this place,' and telling the story about each place. And I guess those place names came from them." But, while we can say that most places with cultural significance (at least to groups larger than the families that live near the place) have names, we still can't say whether most named places have stories or customary activities associated with them.

Results Reflect Methods and Purposes

It is clear when one compares the results of the various studies (including our own survey of thirteen chapters covered in part I) that each one shows only part of a picture of places important to Navajos. The results are conditioned by the purpose and methods of the study. A crude way to compare studies is by taking their quantifiable aspects and comparing the figures, then trying to account for differences with other, often unquantifiable, aspects of the studies.

The figures in Technical Appendix Table 4 indicate variations among the studies. They vary in scale, from 14 to 60,000 square miles and 16 to 689 places identified. They differ in how intensive and systematic efforts were to canvass people whose knowledge covered the whole area, as roughly indicated by the ratio of the project area to number of people interviewed. This ratio ranges from 1 square mile per person to 72 square miles per person. The studies also vary in how much effort was used to locate places on the ground, roughly indicated by the number of places identified per week and number of people interviewed per week. For the most part, the higher these figures, the less the field workers were visiting the places either with the interviewees or on their own to verify and record the places. For the most part, the smaller the area, the more intensive and systematic the coverage, both of knowledgeable people and of the land itself.

The figures also suggest that, if one visits places with people to identify them, or visits places to record them, one will only be able to interview three or four people per week along with field recording. One could average ten or more interviews without site visits. Omitting site visits, one also learns about more places in a week (dozens, as opposed to about ten with site visits). Without site visits, the average number of places that each person mentions won't necessarily be larger, however. In fact, visiting places with willing, knowledgeable people in a restricted area, one will probably learn about more places from each person than one will by discussing the same area at home over a map. People remember places as they pass them by that they might not remember at home. This may be the reason for the high ratio of significant places to number of people interviewed in Canyon de Chelly, although the very density of places owing to the long and intensive use also might explain the figure. We expect that the average would have been lower if we had interviewed more people.

Other reasons for low ratios of places identified to number of people interviewed exist. In some areas, like the northeastern Arizona forests, which are far from Navajo settlement and which Navajos use selectively for limited purposes, most people tend to mention the same few places, which also tend to be very large. In Canyon de Chelly, the opposite type of area (densely settled, intensively used), overlap between our study and that of Jett, Neboyia, and Morgan suggests that we would have started getting the same kind of repetition (although of small places) if we had interviewed more people, since people share so much of the landscape because they all must use the same routes into and out of the canyon. A study also might show a low ratio of number of places to number of people interviewed if many people consulted are not knowledgeable or oppose the purpose of the study. Lack of knowledge among many interviewees seems to explain the low figure for the Four Corners power line project.

Finally, the more intensive the interviewing, the more dense the places are on the land (fewer square miles per place), but not if one concentrates on people with little knowledge.

While any one study gives an incomplete picture of places important to Navajos, the results of the studies combined give a more complete picture. In terms of their observable characteristics (Technical Appendix Table 5), the types of places that are important to Navajos are mostly natural features if one excludes places important only in the histories of particular extended families. The more systematically and completely one tries to interview the people whose families have lived in a particular area for a long time, however (surface users of record so intensively consulted for the Four Corners power line [Carroll 1982], Ute Mountain land exchange [Carroll 1983], and De-Na-Zin Wash [York 1984] projects), the more places with Navajo cultural features will outnumber natural places. Not surprisingly, Navajo cultural features always predominate over other cultural features.

Large natural areas tend to outnumber small ones, especially in distant outlying places where Navajos don't live (Arizona forests). In intensively studied small areas where Navajos live (Ute Mountain land exchange, De-Na-Zin Wash) or in culturally dense landscapes (Canyon de Chelly), however, people identify not just the large area but small features within it. Then small natural localities outnumber large areas.

One can relate differences in the inventories of places to differences in purposes and methods with more confidence than one can understand differences in the stories reported, since the inventories of places were more essential to the purposes of these studies than knowing the stories that go with them. Vannette and Tso (1988) avoid retelling stories because they consider them the "intellectual property" of the teller. That is why we avoided reproducing stories in our original report on the thirteen chapters and on Canyon de Chelly.

Carroll suggests that factors relating to methods and purposes might limit the stories that people give the researcher, and thereby the number and type of places identified as well. In his 1982 study, the number of places identified seems very low for the size of the area. At first, Carroll thought he was getting so little information because people were withholding it, and also because spring, when he started working, is the wrong season for storytelling. But with the same results in late fall, when stories can be told, he decided that people really didn't have much information—for example, the area where he did the first interviews has few plants, and people mentioned few gathering areas; when he moved on to more vegetated places, people identified more gathering areas.

> While I believe all informants . . . did disclose areas of general concern, the time and context of such discussions may still have had effect. All information provided on ceremonial plant use came after the first frost. (1982:49)

One might ask whether the reason that interviewees mentioned relatively few places is because most were land users of record, since these people would expect right-of-way payments that might, in their view, ameliorate the possible disturbance. However,

> in general, no one—even those most favorable—wants the line across his or her personal grazing area. All, however, are willing to put up with it if they receive equitable monetary compensation. (1982:48)

And the line could have been shifted without jeopardizing the payments. Another possible explanation for the low number of places identified is that religious uses of the landscape and the associated stories may be more esoteric then we think, and surface users of record aren't necessarily aware of these things. The fact that surface users were willing to identify other sensitive locations like graves supports this possibility.

In trying to identify sacred places on lands considered for coal leasing, York and Norberto (York and Winter 1988:10) found that many people refused to talk with them because these people opposed the mining. For the medicine people whom they contacted but failed to interview, "it is clear that being unavailable was a convenient excuse for not divulging information regarded as too sensitive to reveal to an outsider."

In our work in Canyon de Chelly (Francis and Kelley 1990, 1992) we inadvertently discovered how the setting of the interview affects what people tell, especially how they convey cultural geography. On a tour, the route itself dictates the sequence in which the person identifies particular places. At home, the person is more likely to mention places by telling a story or ceremonial sequence that interconnects a group of places. Actually travelling on the land, then, ironically, minimizes the conceptual connections among places that bind them into culturally constructed landscapes. The home interviews are more likely to bring these landscapes out. Tours are essential, though, to pin down exact locations of many places, to help people recall more places than they would at home, and to prompt visualized, and thus more detailed, accounts of what happened at certain places.

Talking about places in these two types of settings, it turns out, approximates how the people themselves learned about many places: first by hearing the place named and described in a story at home, then by visiting the place with an older person who knew about it. It also approximates the form of instruction in sacred geography as idealized in stories that go with various ceremonial repertoires: the teacher (usually an immortal) first gives the learner an overview of the landscape from some central viewpoint, telling about the various alignments of places and the holy people who live there. Only then does the new initiate visit the places, in sequences that may be replicated in a series of songs during a performance from the repertoire.

We noticed another interesting pattern. The residents of Canyon de Chelly whom we interviewed, not surprisingly, emphasized places within their own customary use areas. More surprisingly, they told different stories about widely known sacred places in those areas than non-residents told about those same places. The non-residents referred to stories known all over Navajoland about the origin of particular Navajo ceremonial repertoires, beliefs, and customs. They referred specifically to the episodes of these stories that occurred at particular places in the

Canyon. The residents told about encounters between family members and immortals or unusual manifestations of power that go with these places according to the widely known origin stories. The residents' stories linked the family through personal experiences with the forces of Navajo creation. The customary use areas are geographical zones that embody a family's history. At these places history articulates with larger, more extensive landscapes relating to Navajo origins. The different emphases of residents and non-residents are necessary to see the various culturally constructed landscapes and how they overlap and intersect. There seems to be a comparable difference in perspectives of residents and non-residents on the relation of the Canyon to more recent Navajo chronicles, especially those of the eighteenth and nineteenth centuries when the canyon was a major Navajo refuge from Spanish, Mexican, and U.S. armies and slave raiders, both non-Indian and Indian.

We have discussed how the different results of the various studies, including our own work in the thirteen chapters, reflect differences in methods and purposes. The results we are concerned with are the stories and the inventories of places. Many of the studies also show, usually through anecdotes, that people have more general concerns about "historic" and cultural preservation. These are the same concerns we discovered in our study of the thirteen chapters: that "historic preservation" efforts focus excessively on isolated places and fail to recognize the significance of whole landscapes, that those same efforts are wrong to view the significance of places quantitatively so as to rate places according to their "preservation-worthiness" when instead the places differ qualitatively; and that Navajo culture is in danger of being eliminated by the forces of "economic development" and the apathy of young people.

6.

Preserving the Culture by Preserving the Land: The "Landscape" and "Piecemeal" Approaches

This chapter covers the general "historic preservation" concerns that Navajos expressed in both our thirteen-chapter study and many other studies. In the thirteen-chapter study, many people, like Sylvia Manygoats, named places by telling stories in which the places figure. Like Mamie Salt, many gave their statements about places in the context of more general ideas, including some that we interpret as guidance for our use of the place names and stories. These ideas are: That Navajo culture is in danger of dying out, that whole landscapes are significant, and that no one place is more significant than any other. We will first show that the other studies encountered these same three concerns, then interpret the logical connections among the concerns and what we see as the root issue of all three. Finally, we discuss the implications for the practice of "historic preservation" of Navajo cultural resources.

General "Historic Preservation" Concerns in the Other Studies

The evidence of historic preservation concerns in various studies is usually indirect. Many studies mention these concerns in discussions aimed at "historic preservation" bureaucrats about how to draw a boundary around each place (isolate it from its relevant landscape) and how to classify the places in ways that also might allow ranking them according to their significance. Studies by Vannette and Wood (1979) on Big Mountain, Vannette and Feary (1981) on the northern Arizona National Forests, and Carroll (1982, 1983) on Public Service Company of New Mexico projects as well as our work in Canyon de Chelly and Hopi Partitioned Lands (Francis and Kelley 1990, 1992; Kelley, Francis, and Scott 1991) deal with these questions. (See also Holt [1981] for a bureaucrat's policy orientation specific to Navajo cultural resources.)

Vannette and Wood (1979) broach the question whether places differ in terms of their sacredness or significance. The authors note that some places are mentioned by everyone in a local community, while knowledge of others seems confined within a particular "kin-territorial unit" (p. 9). The authors also quote Wyman (1975) to show that one must not assume that this phenomenon indicates that Navajos recognize different levels of significance:

> Animals, plants, mountains, and many natural phenomena are endowed with power. Even the seemingly most insignificant of these are indispensable; all are interdependent, being complementary parts of the whole. (Wyman 1975:8–9)

While recognizing that Navajos may not rank places by their sacred significance, Vannette and Wood offer a framework for non-Navajos to do so. It is a list of indicators of level of significance from questions and testimony in the Taos Blue Lake case: (a) is there a symbiotic relationship among land, religion, people; are sacred places used today that symbolize that relationship? (b) is the place important in the "origin myth" of the people? (c) can shrines or offering places be moved? (d) is the area used for a long time, continuously, often? (e) do people today feel the same as in the past toward sacred places? (f) does the area symbolize the unity and continuity of the people? (g) do ceremonies and rituals bind people to specific locations? and (h) can those ceremonies and rituals be carried out elsewhere?

The most sacred or significant places are those about which one must answer yes to all but questions c and h, to which the answer must be no. Vannette and Wood apply these indicators to Big Mountain and find that it fits the profile of a most significant place. But we believe that one cannot answer some of these questions with an unqualified yes or no for Navajo sacred places without some oversimplified assumptions about Navajo beliefs.

Vannette and Wood also approach the question of "boundaries" or "zones" around each sacred place.

> The relationship among occupancy, land use, and sacred places at the local level may be seen in several ways. First, ritual at sacred places may define traditional land use boundaries for the kin-territorial units. . . . The boundaries appear to have meaning for use-rights as well as for "protection"; . . . one's ancestors could be thought of as having "secured" the land through proper prayers and offerings. To leave the land might be potentialiy dangerous, and it might be a violation of the stewardship and reciprocity with the Holy People. (1979:24)

The authors suggest a relationship between certain sacred places where people offer protection prayers and the boundaries of "kin-territorial unit" land-use areas. The implication seems to be that the area covered by a protection prayer site is an entire family land base.

We applaud Vannette and Wood's attempt to show that even what seems to be a small sacred location is actually a point for engaging special powers to cover a much larger area, so that the extent of the sacred area around the prayer offering spot is very great. We also suggest a couple of refinements. First, "boundary" is probably not the best word for the outer limits of the land base of the "kin-territorial unit." We assume that this "unit" is a group of interrelated extended families that may share one homesite but are more likely dispersed among several homesites with their own associated grazing areas into which the whole land base is informally and expediently partitioned and repartitioned as time passes and family circumstances change. In our experience, some "kin-territorial units" may fence or otherwise mark the outer limits of their areas, but most don't. They simply range the stock within various distances in different directions of particular homesites, so that neighbors often argue about where one's area ends and the other's begins. Second, we think this notion is most likely to apply to the cairns on top of Big Mountain, where members of the "kin-territorial units" whose lands extend onto the mountain's flanks offer protection prayers. Thus the area associated with the cairn consists of the lands of all those "units," in other words, what might be called the Big Mountain Community.

Like Vannette and Wood (1979), Vannette and Feary (1981) tackle the thorny question whether and how places differ in their level of significance. The authors imply that one basis for establishing relative significance is the proportion of interviewees who mention a particular place. On this basis, their 42 places form three distinct ranks. At the top, each mentioned 29–35 times, are four places: San Francisco Peaks and three other large landforms. In the middle are 9 places, each mentioned 6–11 times. At the bottom are the other 29 places, 11 of which were mentioned only once (p. 32). However, in response to the question "'Are the San Francisco Peaks a place of Holy People more than others,' " only 7 percent of the interviewees said yes.

> It is likely the nature of these responses reflects a reluctance of Navajo specialists to differentiate too specifically as to significant differences between sacred places, or perhaps [what seems to be the same thing] due to the omnipresent character of the gods, they are somewhat uncertain about how best to answer such a question. One procedure to obtain the Navajo view of the degree of sacredness of specific places would involve collection of the stories associated with these places. (1981:29)

But Vannette and Feary recognize the "difficulties and obligations" in doing so. The authors seem reluctant to give up their quest for a Navajo system of ranking places according to their significance. "'Are there some sacred places that are more significant than others?' . . . A judgmental answer to this question is yes," based on the number of times people mention a place and the tendency of the most frequently mentioned places also to have the greatest variety of uses. But "quality of a place is not directly indicated" (p. 32).

Why Vannette and Feary keep looking for a Navajo basis for ranking places becomes evident when they discuss which Forest Service activities the interviewees found acceptable in various locations. Interviewees were most favorable toward range management and least favorable toward mineral extraction. In between these extremes were recreation, watershed management, wildlife management, and timber management. Concerning "what may and may not be done on the San Francisco Peaks. . . . Harvesting timber is permissible . . . because the area is able to return to an acceptable state, but mining cinders is not because it means the permanent alteration or virtual destruction of an area" (p. 72). "The implication is that with moderation and respect, activities not permissible at the most significant places (e.g., Peaks) may be tolerated and even appropriate at these lesser locations" (p. 88).

The question of "boundaries" around sacred places is another that forest managers wanted Vannette and Feary to address. But since "boundaries . . . are largely conceptual and physically not well defined" (p. 88), people evidently found that notion alien, as they did the notion of levels of significance.

Yes, sacred places do have boundaries so long as the term is not restricted to a physical line surrounding a particular place. . . . these boundaries are zones. . . . boundaries . . . may be identified in part by the kinds of relationships and activities that are internally appropriate within an area. (1981:86)

Activities appropriate at sacred places are praying, gathering plants, conducting ceremonies; also gathering food and fuel wood in some places, but not mining, grazing livestock, or building roads in the upper elevations of sacred places (one example of which, according to Vannette and Feary, is the San Francisco Peaks).

The purposes of Carroll's work for PNM (1982, 1983) also forced him to address the vexing questions of levels of significance and boundaries around places. Carroll uses the relation of a place to origin traditions to determine the relative significance of a place. He also suggests that how widely known the place is might be another criterion for significance, then immediately undercuts this suggestion.

The first order of Navajo sacred places, then, could be defined as: I. Origin-Related Locations: places perceived by a significant percentage of the Navajo population to be the location or result of events or settings described in widely accepted versions of the Navajo origin story. . . . In my opinion, there is no utility in attempting to carry this category of "sacredness" further in degrees of significance. But, whether this category of site is recognized by the entire Navajo population, or one singer who employs the place in the practice of ceremonies for his clients, it is a category of primary concern for studies seeking to identify potential impacts upon sites of traditional religious importance. (1982:39)

In the next order, locations acquire significance

because of actions of people in our time (in this world) as opposed to human or supernatural beings in mythological times. This type of significance may be known to only a limited number of local people, but would be recognized by "all" Navajos as a traditional cultural concept. (1982:39)

Carroll makes this point even more strongly in his 1983 report: even a particular site "known to only one person . . . would be recognized [in principle] by 'all Navajos' as 'sacred.' "

Carroll, then, seems more uncomfortable than Vannette and his co-authors with basing degree of significance on how widespread the knowledge about a place is. In fact, he seems uncomfortable with the whole idea of levels of significance: "A hierarchy of Navajo sacred places is probably a dangerous precedent to attempt to establish. But the first few steps are probably relatively uncontroversial" (1982:36).

The "historic preservation" decision maker for the BIA with jurisdiction over Navajoland at the time showed the same discomfort. "It would be inappropriate for the United States government to rank Native American sacred places according to their perceived relative religious values" (Holt 1981:51). And about boundaries, he says only,

> Interviews with Navajo practitioners have yielded limited suggestions for avoidance, including prohibition of projects within 15 miles of sacred mountains. . . . Because of the disposal of ceremonial objects and the placement of offerings near hogans, a one mile buffer zone has been suggested between any project and every home. . . . (Holt 1981:51)

The regional planners of the National Park Service who sponsored our study in Canyon de Chelly (Francis and Kelley 1990, 1992) hoped that we would find out what culturally important places residents would allow the Park Service to "interpret" for tourists and how close tourists could come to such places without compromising their special qualities. Before we even started asking these questions, however, statements by residents about their general concerns made it clear that the questions would be meaningless to them. The questions assume that Navajos see the landscape as a surface on which are scattered small places physically isolated from each other. But instead, residents see the landscape as an integrated system of locations for the various activities that make up the customary Navajo way of life. And the system is what the tourists (and other outsiders—including non-resident Navajos) disrupt—visibly and audibly as well as by physically intruding on residents' activities. Navajo residents do not necessarily want to ban all outsiders from the canyons, since many residents make a living from the tourist trade. But clearly tourist traffic needs to be reduced and restructured so that it intrudes less on Navajo life in the canyons and so that more tourist money comes to canyon residents, especially to finance erosion control and irrigation systems and other improvements that sustain customary life in the canyons.

Finally, in our inventory of sacred places on HPL (Kelley, Francis and Scott 1991), people kept calling our attention to how the places they were plotting on our maps related to each other and to their various other customary uses of the surrounding landscape to which they are clinging. There are pilgrimage routes to sacred places on the edge of or outside the pre-conquest Navajo homeland (including mountains that Vannette and Feary [1981] identified on outlying forest lands) that interconnect strings of sacred places. There are large areas—certain canyons and mountains—that they consider sacred preserves, with daily activities of residence, herding, and farming to be restricted to adjoining lands outside these preserves. People—families, communities—use large landscapes with zones of both types, and both have places of special power within them.

The studies and our own experiences also leave us with the dismaying impression that many young and middle-aged Navajos have prematurely stopped building their knowledge of Navajo culture. Chapter officials and surface users of record (or a family member who speaks for them) tend to be in this age group. According to Vannette and Feary (1981:32), "one person expressed concern about young people and implied they no longer are carrying on cultural traditions." Fransted (1979:9) found that old people are worried by younger Navajos' lack of interest in old Navajo ways and that many express "bitterness and demoralization" as a result of centrally planned "culture change" from "Window Rock." The various studies suggest several reasons. Circumstances in which older people instructed younger ones are becoming less common: ceremonies, the sweatbath (once a common domestic ritual several times a month where the men of an extended family would share stories and songs, and the women, separately, might do so too), evening storytelling at home in winter (replaced by television and the VCR), and travel (especially on horseback) in remote places.

We also believe that this concern is underreported. We have heard it a lot and often it doesn't find its way into our own reports, both because it is somewhat removed from our focus—the cultural significance of certain places and whole landscapes—and also, frankly, because we're afraid that opponents of the landscape and cultural preservation that we advocate (not to mention the protection of the individual places identified) will abuse these statements to undermine the protection of sacred places. Opponents may try to portray the concerns we document and the preservation we advocate as of interest only to a cranky minority of old people. Part III will show that active concern with Navajo land and cultural preservation is much more widespread than that. Concerns about lack of interest in Navajo culture only seem to be limited to old people because interviews concentrate on the elderly, who know the most about the places that are the focus of the studies. This is another reason why one must allow for the purpose and methods of a study before one can make generalizations about its results.

The Underlying Issue:
The Land and the People Are One

Economic development is undermining Navajo culture by disturbing or destroying particular important places on the land, by disrupting the customary activities on the landscape through which people integrate the various places on their landbase into the system of Navajo life, and by seducing younger people away from living in the Navajo way. (Not the least insidious is the pickup truck, an even more labor saving device than Monster Slayer considered horses to be in the story in chapter 5. People of all generations use them liberally not just to make customary life on the land easier but for trips to "town" for consumerism and entertainment.) Preserving places important to Navajo people can help preserve Navajo culture, but to be most effective, preservation efforts must widen their focus from the specific place to the culturally significant landscape within which each place functions and from which it gets power (significance) and to which it gives power. A focus on places isolated from their landscape contexts also allows preservation bureaucrats to try to assign different levels of significance to each place to justify not preserving certain places. Preservation efforts that focus on places but ignore their associated landscapes that provide the material basis of the Navajo way of life run the risk of saving the places while letting the living context be destroyed, as in a strip mine that "islands" or "pedestals" the family graves that people won't consent to have moved but evicts the living people and turns the land into an uninhabitable moonscape. Without Navajos living the customary life on the land, the places will no longer be part of a living cultural system and the landscape that it animates. They will only commemorate the past existence of a dead culture.

In a nutshell, most of the people whose ideas are expressed in these studies don't want "historic preservation" efforts to preserve mementos of "traditional" Navajo culture. They want those efforts to help keep the Navajo way of life itself alive. And the Navajo way can't survive unless its practitioners have some control over the whole landscape that they need to live. This is why they insist on "landscape" preservation as opposed to "place" preservation.

Navajo statements about the Anasazis relate to the threats to the Navajo ways. Although some people, like Mamie Salt and Frank Mitchell, see them as "part of us" or originators of some Navajo ceremonies, the Anasazis lived badly and therefore the immortals swept them from the land, breaking the bond between the people, culture, and land (see also Wyman 1970:58–59). The ruins commemorate a living relationship between the land (or its immortal inhabitants) and the mortal Anasazis, a relationship that died when the bond was broken (although a few immortal Anasazis in the form of haashch'ééh inhabit the ruins, according to Mitchell, and help Navajos to live). Anasazi ruins to some Navajos are a "memento mori" or a warning. Navajos don't want their own places to be like that.

This discourse is an example of a much more general, repeated, never yet resolved discourse that Gill (1987) finds between Indians and "European Americans."

> Here [in the discourse of the late nineteenth century], as throughout the history of contact, the issue is land, the earth. This issue continues the imagery of savagism versus civilization. American policy centers upon the transformation of native hunters (gatherers and fishers) into cultivators (miners and builders). It is an issue of property and ownership. In the native lifeways the land is not divided and owned as personal property, while this division, settlement, and personal ownership is essential to European-American ways of life. The issues, the contrasting imagery, changed little as the United States spread across the continent. (1987:63–64)

Various Indian statements in this late nineteenth-century discourse involved

> the notion of the chieftainship of the land. This is a political and legal extension of the creation doctrine. That is, . . . native peoples have the creator-given charge to maintain certain responsibilities toward land, heritage, and lifeways. Furthermore, this is a basis for the inherited rights to the lands. All this amounts to law whose authority is none other than the creator of the world. No other authority can supersede this, not even that of the President of the United States. (1987:65)

The discourse involved references to "Mother Earth" by members of various tribes, each of which had its own distinct stories, beliefs, and pantheon. Many "European Americans" have thought these references indicate a pan-Indian religion centered on an Earth Goddess, but Gill disagrees.

> These references to the earth are metaphorical, not theological [they do not make the earth an immortal personification]. The Native Americans [sought] in the metaphor of motherhood some commonality with their oppressors by which to communicate effectively their reluctance to be severed from their lands. They say simply that their traditions, cultures, heritages, and very existence depend on their land as a child depends on its mother. (1987:66)

By the mid-twentieth century, however, Gill thinks that "these [European-American] misinterpretations [mistaking metaphorical portrayal of the earth as a mother for a pan-Indian deity] were appropriated by Native Americans who transformed metaphor into divinity" (p. 66)—Mother Earth has become a divinity in a modern, emerging, pan-Indian religion. According to Gill, Indians have constructed "an

Indian tradition out of a huge variety of tribal traditions, and in turn, [there is] the reflection of aspects of this common tradition in the respective tribal traditions" (p. 150). Gill sees this recent construction as an aspect of "[n]atavism [which] indicates the rejection of the oppressing culture and the assertion of native or indigenous values and ways in response to the experience of cultural deprivation" (p. 138). Much political discourse between Indians and "European-Americans" emphasizes "the differences between cultures . . . [and] the superiority of Indian culture over white European-American culture," especially since the latter has degraded the environment so much as to jeopardize life on the earth.

We aren't so sure that a lot of Indians who refer to "Mother Earth" in their public statements even today actually see the earth as a divinity. Many may still use the phrase as a metaphor (and a veil) for their own particular tribal beliefs. Others, especially those with much formal education, may have trouble believing literally in any kind of earth-inhabiting, humanlike deities, including the immortals of their own particular tribal beliefs. They may think of Mother Earth and the other immortals as metaphors for an all-pervading power. Such people may not have adopted the "European-American" construction, as Gill suggests, so much as shared with "European-Americans" the difficulty of squaring a secularized formal education that emphasizes scientific routes to knowledge with a literal belief in anthropomorphic immortal beings immanent in the land. Figurative language is the way out—its ambiguity allows one to keep two seemingly contradictory frames of reference.

Gill quotes Navajo Tribal Chairman (now Navajo Nation President) Peterson Zah (p. 144) and Asdzáán Bázhnoodaa'í (Woman for Whom They Held an Enemy Way Ceremony) of Black Mesa, both of whom criticize strip mining by asking rhetorically how Navajos can allow their "Mother" to be so damaged (pp. 143, 144). We suggest that these statements, like that of Mamie Salt in chapter 2, continue the "Mother Earth" imagery of the nineteenth century, and for the same reasons—to get their bonds with the land across to non-Navajos by using imagery more accessible to non-Navajos than mentioning Navajo immortals would be (and also probably because there is a widespread reticence to invoke the immortals in non-Navajo contexts). There is also, in statements like that of Mamie Salt, the idea of an apocalyptic catastrophe, cultural annihilation, in store for Navajos who give up their responsibility for the land. These are the ideas behind the statement we and other researchers have heard so often, "the whole land is sacred."

Implications for "Historic Preservation"
Decision Making

Our own study of thirteen chapters and the various other studies reveal a tension between the historic preservation bureaucrats' need to set "management priorities," on the one hand, and, on the other, the Navajo cultural aversion to hierarchies, especially in connection with Navajo customs. In the other studies, the researchers reveal a sense of being caught between the go-ahead interests of developers that shape the "realpolitik" of "historic preservation" decision making and their professional responsibility to convey the concerns of the people they consulted. They compromise by focusing on places—not on whole landscapes, as the people want, but not on nothing, either, as many developers wish.

This focus on isolated "historic properties" lets preservation decision makers recommend the relatively easy protection measure of resituating the development to avoid these places. This is one reason that they want to know where the boundaries of such places are (documentation for compliance with the National Historic Preservation Act also requires such boundaries). Establishing different ranks of significance gives decision makers a loophole to justify the disturbance or destruction of some places.

It should be clear by now that these "piecemeal" approaches focused on "preserving" isolated places with "cultural significance" to Navajos from the inroads of economic development are at odds with the Navajo approach to preservation. The goal of the Navajo approach is to keep entire, interacting cultural landscapes intact by keeping economic development from disrupting the full range of customary activities that keep these landscapes alive. The preservation decision maker's goal in Navajoland therefore should not be to rank isolated places according to their "level of significance" and then to single out the high-ranking places for protection efforts such as setting boundaries within which development is forbidden. Instead, the goal should be to find out how each place functions in the physical, social, and conceptual landscapes of which it is part, and how (or whether) a proposed development can be integrated into these landscapes, among these interrelated places, with the least disruption to the lives of the people (including the immortals) whose activities tie them together.

An obvious way to practice this "landscape" approach is through meetings between project planners and overseers (including preservation bureaucrats) and representatives of the interested communities.

Such meetings may then lead to more detailed information gathering about the various parts of the landscape, including particular places, through private interviews. But such place-focused, individual interviews should not occur until the larger landscape context has been established. The landscape approach basically asks that cultural landscape preservation be integrated more thoroughly into overall planning, a political process that ordinarily fails to realize cultural landscape planning because it doesn't involve "grass roots" people whom the plan will affect. The project planners must include those who might want jobs in the project as well as those who want landscape and culture protected—too often, developers succeed in pitting people who need jobs against preservationists, blinding them to their common interests—curbs on superexploitation of both land and workers.

There is another reason that people emphasize landscapes and sacred places when they address "historic preservation" questions. For a long time, one of us, to avoid being a non-Indian prying into Indian "religious" matters, tried to show long and continued Navajo relationships with the land by focusing on family land-use patterns for residence, farming, and grazing. This approach, although necessary, has turned out to be insufficient, and not only for the obvious reason that it offers only part of the picture. It is also inadequate because a story that validates the land rights of local people by emphasizing the land rights of each family separately may be easy for people to support in principle but inevitably contains details that neighboring families with land disputes can't agree on. A story that validates residents' relationship to the land by relating that relationship to things that all Navajos have access to—ceremonialism, stories about Navajo origins and customs, and so forth, is easier for local people to drop their differences and unite around. Similarly, it is easier for people to unite around a story about a landscape that covers everybody's land than the story about a small place on one family's land.

Seemingly among the critics of the "landscape" approach are Richard Stoffle and his colleagues (Stoffle and others 1990; Stoffle and Evans 1990), who call the approach "holistic" and its advocates self-defeating in light of all the evidence that the approach is politically unworkable. Their conception of the "holistic" approach isn't entirely like our "landscape" approach, however. Stoffle sometimes suggests that "holism," based on the idea that "the whole land is sacred," implies opposition to all land-disturbing development. But this is not quite the message that we get from the Navajos we've talked with.

Like Sylvia Manygoats in chapter 2, they say, for example, that if people don't use the livestock forage and medicinal plants that the immortals put out for them, the plants will disappear. This statement may seem backward from the omniscient viewpoint claimed by "Western Science." From the holistic Navajo viewpoint, "Western Science" seems to claim omniscience, yet its practitioners dismember things analytically and then often forget to reassemble them analytically to see if they still work together in the natural world as they seemed to in experimental isolation. But the statement's truth depends on the magnitude of disturbance and of time and space. Older Navajos have seen land once well-vegetated, where farming in small drainages checked erosion and maintained commensal plants, become gullied and bare after people quit farming to buy food at the store. The land undisturbed by humans won't necessarily support humans as well as land that people tend, at least in certain ways. In fact, an example of scientifically grooming a place so natural species won't disappear is no less a national "sacred place" than the Grand Canyon National Park. Scientists are diligently working to tame the river flow even more than the hydroelectric dams have already done (by evening out the flow from Glen Canyon Dam) to save endangered species and promote species diversity, including hikers, boaters, and even Navajo and other Indian medicine people (Begay and others 1992).

Developments that don't disrupt these relations, especially those that help the land sustain the people and their customs (windmills, for example) without depleting the land, are fine. Everyone realizes that the land can no longer support most Navajos with the old ways of herding and farming, and most people must work for large-scale productive enterprises or government. Other developments that deplete the land, do nothing for the people or disrupt their lives, displace them, exploit workers and run away with the profits, are less acceptable. Of course, not everyone will evaluate a given project the same way (for example, electric line extensions to people's houses that bring power generated with coal mined on Navajo land).

Stoffle and his colleagues have refined an approach to preservation decision making that they call "triage." It resembles what we call the "piecemeal" approach in its focus on places without explicit reference to their relation to the landscape. In practical terms, the "triage" approach requires the bureaucrat (usually through a researcher) to ask concerned community members to pick which places are most important to preserve and which can be sacrificed to development if necessary. Unlike most practitioners of the "piecemeal" approach, however, Stoffle and his associates have often worked with community members in groups early in the planning process, as we advocate for our landscape approach.

In fact, we believe that the contrast between our "landscape" approach and the "triage" of Stoffle and colleagues is more apparent than real. Community representatives talking with researchers in the framework of "triage" may actually base their decisions on an unspoken (at least to the researchers) analysis of how the project can best fit into the landscape with the least damage to its interconnectedness. The "landscape" approach simply tries to make this framework explicit. This explication is important because (assuming that it's voluntary) it can lead to better understanding between community people and planners.

7.

The Hidden Reservoir

The old people say that stories and knowledge of Navajo culture (not to mention language) are being lost. But there still seems to be a reservoir of stories and customary activities relating to the land beyond the reach of studies like ours. Several studies discussed here, including our own, indicate that people know more stories than they told. Several studies have turned to the literature on Navajo stories and there found references to certain places, although the people interviewed for these studies did not themselves mention such stories when talking about those places. Fewer people may know these stories now than when the stories were recorded, but interviews reported in several of the studies (including our own) show that some people still know them.

For example, the study of Chaco Canyon place names (Fransted and Werner n.d.) indicates that people around Chaco Canyon use the English phrase "The Great Gambler" to identify a previously recorded creation story that is also among the origin stories of the supposedly

extinct Frenzyway and Waterway repertoires. The people cited by Fransted and Werner didn't tell the story. Of other previously recorded
stories, the ones most often mentioned (if not told) in connection with
places in the studies described above are the Great Gambler story, stories
about the Nightway ceremony, and stories about the emergence and
origin of things on the present earth surface—specifically the placement
of the sacred mountains and other features of the land, the journey of
the Twins to their father the Sun, the Twins' using the weapons from the
Sun to kill the monsters, and Changing Woman's journey to her home
at the western ocean where she created Navajo clan progenitors, who
then travelled eastward back across Navajoland. Each story interconnects several places identified in the various studies discussed.

People still do tell stories, even to researchers. Some have never
been recorded, others are versions of stories previously recorded (but
even then, often including references to places with no previously
recorded connection to the story). For example, we learned of the
cluster of places connected with the annihilation of the Monster Travelling Rock around the head of Canyon de Chelly. We also learned about
part of Canyon de Chelly where the Great Gambler story is set. Furthermore, regional landscapes emerge when one combines the various
versions of a story—landscapes which in their entirety no one teller may
be aware of. For example, by putting together all the places various
people separately have connected with the story of the travels of the
Twins, Changing Woman, and the clans, one can see east-west routes
across Navajoland that may correspond to trails of religious pilgrimages
to sacred places on the edges of or outside Navajoland. One person we
interviewed even explicitly identified several points on a very long
segment of one of these trails, including a place that someone else years
before had told us was a sacred place with a trail shrine but wouldn't tell
(or didn't know) what the place was connected with. Combined information from these various studies also suggests an east-west series of
hills that oral traditions, or the place names themselves, indicate once
had shrines on their summits that contained crystals or mirage stone (or
whose summits themselves were considered shrines and verbally
adorned). Some (or all) of these places are associated with Changing
Woman's trip west and with other stories that mention giant white shell
"baskets" (receptacles) that were to be offered to the Sun. A cryptic
comment in one interview makes us wonder if these were locations for
the reportedly no-longer-performed rain-requesting version of the
Blessingway ceremony; the fact that most are also on an east-west line
and references to sun, moon, and midpoints in the associated stories
suggests some relation to the equinoxes.[1]

Finally, other works not reviewed here (because inventories of sacred places are not their main focus) do suggest something more about the untapped reservoir of stories. One type of study consists of stories of past land use of particular families, a common addition to archaeological survey reports about large areas proposed for development, like coal-mine leaseholds. These studies commonly identified sites such as abandoned homesites, sweathouses, corrals, fields, graves, and water sources important in reconstructing the land-use story of each extended family that has used the area of interest.

In one such study (Kelley 1985a), one of us interviewed representatives, mostly elderly, of almost every family that had used a 21-square-mile coal mine leasehold. She asked all of them about place names and sacred places as well as about their past (archaeological) homesites and other land-use sites. These people identified 106 archaeological sites in the 16-square-mile area that had not already been strip-mined, as well as water sources, cornfield locations, and named landmarks in and just outside the leasehold. Altogether, in about a 25-square-mile area in and near the leasehold, these places significant to local Navajos averaged 11 per square mile, including about one named place per square mile.

The only sacred places these people identified other than family-related archaeological sites, however, were three hills, all just outside the leasehold (they mentioned several more places well outside the leasehold). The interviewees explicitly denied sacred significance to the other named places. Continued residence in the area and more work on sacred places elsewhere since then has convinced Kelley that residents probably had in fact used several of the named places inside the leasehold for offering prayers, and that some of the people interviewed (including children of a medicine man) would have known that. Maybe they felt that reporting these places would serve no useful purpose, since the mining company had already removed the people and fenced off the leasehold. The landscape was no longer alive, and they perhaps saw no use in commemorating its former sacred uses. But none of these residents may have known about another sacred place, a ceremonial plant-gathering area destroyed during the first round of mining, that a non-local ceremonialist later told Kelley about. He used this example to show that asking local residents about sacred places isn't enough.

The late Ninibah Cahn (1982) showed what such a landscape looks like when one does include sacred places that only a single family may use. She illustrated the area around her own family's customary use area with locations of ceremonial materials and activities in addition to places related to the family's past.

Finally, ceremonialist Alvin Clinton (1990) has recently provided a story about the origins of gathering ceremonies for certain medicinal herbs that integrates a large landform southeast of the Hopi villages and many smaller places within it. A story similar to Mr. Clinton's is included in the stories of the origin of the Waterway and Frenzyway ceremonies recorded a couple of generations ago (Haile 1979; Kluckhohn 1967 [1944]).[2] The previously recorded stories also contain episodes set in Canyon de Chelly and Chaco Canyon, and include the Great Gambler story. One previously published group of stories excerpted below shows how the stories tie together areas covered by studies of sacred places discussed here.

Mr. Clinton's knowledge of at least the stories set in the area south of the Hopi villages and Canyon de Chelly, and the stories in part II that suggest that Navajos around Chaco Canyon and Canyon de Chelly know at least the stories from this group that are associated with their area, suggest that long, complex narratives besides those of the widely told Navajo creation stories still survive. The survival of these stories is especially noteworthy because they tell about the origins of ceremonial repertoires that are no longer practiced (or rarely so). Mr. Clinton's version seems to be an herbalist's version, associated with ceremonial gathering of certain plants. Possibly stories of other ceremonial repertoires no longer practiced (at least not in their entirety) have been carried on by herbalists who know how to gather plants once used in those repertoires that continue to be used in fragments of the repertoire that have survived, or in other related repertoires. The following story is also typical in how it features large numbers of places.

THE ORIGIN OF THE FRENZY WAY CEREMONY

[Told by Old Soldier of Stony Butte and translated in Kluckhohn (1967 [1944]:158-76).]

The boy was living there in Coyote Pass Canyon [near the Pueblo of Jemez] with his grandmother. They were hungry and poor, trying to get some way to live. The boy hunted rats and cottontails. . . .[H]e went up on top of a hill where there was a spring. He found that the Pueblo people had put some prayer-sticks away there. . . . And so he broke them up. . . . The Jemez people found out about this and got very angry. They wanted to find the boy and his grandmother and kill them. . . .

The boy and his grandmother started off to the west. . . .

They came to Rock Way Up In The Air. From there they went to Rock With Willows and from there west to Water Runs On. They started from there west again but changed their minds and walked back quite a ways to Bee Weed Rises Up. Then they started again and got to Blue Rock Canyon. . . . Then they went northwest—not straight west as they had been going. They got to Stinging Water. Then to Snake Water. Then to Little Water. Then to Tall House. Then down to House on the Rock. Then they walked to Two Rocks Lay. Then to Many Notched Hills.

. . . They came to another place called Water Resounds. This was a cave and there was a spruce tree in front. When someone walked in the cave to get a drink, they would always hear a noise, "don, don, don." (That noise was still there for many years, but it no longer makes a noise that way now.) . . .

. . . [T]hey started to walk to another place called Red Willow. Then from there to another place called Pinyon Needle Water. Then there is a big valley across called Red Valley. Then another place called Black Water. Then . . . Coyote Box Canyon . . . Choke Cherries Spread Out . . . Mark On Rock . . . Black Weeds Stand Up . . . Hill Spreads Out . . . Picking Up Rock (where they used to have contests to see who could lift the rock). . . . Water Carries Wood Out . . . Hill Stands . . . Bands of Green Grass . . . Long Side of Hill . . . Grass Green Again . . . Water Moves Clockwise . . . Hill Like Man's Face . . . Gray Cottonwoods Spread Out . . . Red Flint Notch . . . Rock Breaks Off. . . .

. . . Round Stick Lies . . . Dry Around Water . . . Shooting Water . . . Black Rock . . .

. . . Then they started to walking from there towards the west to Hole In The Ground. They kept walking to Swallow's Nest. . . . Cool Water . . . Green In The Mountain. . . . Horse Falls In The Arroyo . . . House Under The Rock Spreads Out . . . Mistletoe Hangs . . . Dead Tree Stands Up . . . Possessing Fish . . . Red House . . . Lake With Weeds on Surface . . . Rock For Making Paper Bread . . . Rock Points Toward the Valley . . . Wide Reeds . . . In The Middle White Top . . . Hill Where Water Cuts In . . . Water Comes Together. . . . Water Afraid. . . . Big Willow Juts Out and Droops. Then to Keams Canyon. Then to Walpi [Hopi village].

It had taken them four years to get from Coyote Pass Canyon to Keams Canyon. They got to Walpi in the spring and they stayed there four years. By that time the boy was a full grown man. . . .

. . . After four years he got tired of walking around that place and he said he wanted to go down near San Francisco Peaks. [On the way, he encounters Talking God and the two of them stop at a hill called Cone Towards Water (Woodruff Butte).] . . .

Inside were Cone Towards Water Man [the inner form of the hill, who has a humanlike form] and his wife and seven children. [They don't like the hero's human smell and bathe him for four days.] . . .

Right after that they put up Blessing Way for this man. They sang all night for him. And in the daytime of Its Day [last day] they shaped him up [like Navajo girls' puberty ceremony]. . . .

[Cone Towards Water Man said] ". . . You must pay me for the singing I have done for you with antelope." . . .

Cone Towards Water Man had given him black gum and blue gum [Datura and another plant]. . . . when he needs something, he must take a little bite, chew it, and blow it and it will turn into whatever he needs. . . .

Next he started off for Walpi. He looked around for his grandmother. . . .

. . . [S]ome girls in the town [were] living in a house which was like a basement down in the ground [Puebloan ceremonial kiva]. These two girls had only lived inside where it is dark. They never get out into the light. . . . this man . . . wants to get them. . . . So he got the two. . . .

[The father of the two girls finds out and demands a bride price of antelope.] The next day, [the young man] started out west over to the first place where he had shot antelope for Cone Towards Water Man. . . . [He kills dozens over the next four days.] . . .

Each of these four days, his father-in-law gave him a new girl. That makes six wives for him altogether. . . .

The next morning he went back to his grandmother. She had been getting all the young boys. When he came to his home, he wanted to leave that place. . . . [T]hey walked from there to Canyon de Chelly. They started to live there. . . .

[They travel through a succession of places in Canyon de Chelly, then to the head of the canyon, then through the mountains and on to villages around Chaco Canyon inhabited by Anasazis.]

At the time when Cone Towards Water Man had sung for him, Cone Towards Water Man had taught him how to use

Cone Towards Water Plant pollen. Just take a little and mix it with the dew from the plant and touch the girls and they will come. He did that to the girls in all those towns.

. . . He then went to Dark Lake [near the crane petroglyphs mentioned in chapter 6, scene of killing Big God in Reginald Nabahe's account in chapter 5] where there were a lot of birds called Prairie Dog Legs [rainbirds]. . . .

He lived there and made his bed with the feathers of those birds. . . . When the Pueblo Indians saw him using the feathers this way, they started in to call him Downy Home Man. . . .

. . . [T]here is a man there called Earth Winner [Great Gambler]. He beats everyone at gambling and wins girls. Downy Home Man wants to meet this man and so he starts off.

On the way he stopped in Chaco Canyon. They were having a big meeting there. . . .

The crowd was talking about Wide House [Anasazi pueblo near Aztec, New Mexico]. Some people were living way down there in the basement [kiva], they said. . . . Earth Winner had been trying himself to get those girls out at Wide House, but he couldn't.

In the evening when Downy Home Man was starting for home he just spoke one word and then left. The people just laughed—they didn't get the word the first day. Next day he came back, and that evening when he left again he said, "Eat my brain." . . . He did that four days. . . .

[The young man turns himself into a butterfly and flies into the girls' underground home.] So the two girls followed the butterfly, trying to catch it as it went up the ladder. And that was the way he got these girls out.

[Then Earth Winner decides he doesn't want the girls because he can't support them, so the young man takes them and chews and blows out the blue gum to make home and food for them. But later Earth Winner decides to take them and himself changes into a white butterfly to lure them away from the young man. The young man goes in pursuit, encountering Spider Woman.]

She told him White Butterfly had twelve wives. . . . The woman said she would loan him her twelve daughters. "That man down there, he is going to ask you to bet twelve wives, so I am going to loan you my daughters." . . .

White Butterfly came outside and they met him there just in front of his door. . . .

. . . Then White Butterfly said that he wanted to play a ball game. Downy Home Man asked for time to think but then agreed. . . . While he had pretended to be thinking, he had fixed up a ball and gotten Big Snake to help him by promising shell and pollen [valuable materials to make offerings to immortals to enlist their power to help]. Everybody had said they would help Downy Home Man so he could win.

. . . White Butterfly . . . hit the ball, and it didn't go through that hole. . . . Then Downy Home Man used his ball with a mouse inside. . . . [I]t just went through. . . .

There were supposed to be four games. The next was the hoop and pole game. . . . Downy Home Man had Big Snake in his hoop. . . . There was an argument again, but White Butterfly finally admitted he had lost.

Next was "pushing the posts." . . . Downy Home Man had the Wind People fix White Butterfly's post so that White Butterfly couldn't move it at all. On his own post he put the worms that eat wood. . . . He won again.

Now three times he has won. One remains: a footrace. They bet everything: the earth, what is on the earth, flowers and trees and themselves. . . . [White Butterfly shoots at Downy Home Man's foot, but the Winds warned Downy Home Man.] But Downy Home Man jumped aside and grabbed up the shot as he passed by. Then he threw it into White Butterfly's body. . . .

. . . Downy Home Man crossed the line and beat White Butterfly. . . .

White Butterfly said Downy Home Man might as well kill him. He had nothing left. . . . White Butterfly had an axe called "Reversing Axe." White Butterfly said, "Use my own axe and chop my head off with that." . . . He put his head down again and then Downy Home Man quickly substituted his own axe. So White Butterfly was killed, and when the head was chopped off all colors of butterfly flew out of his head. . . .

White Butterfly got all his girls from the Pueblo Indians. These were his ten wives. Downy Home Man sent all these girls back where they belonged. . . . And his two wives he took back home.

Mr. Nevy Jensen is at Fort Sumner (February 1992) telling the story that ends this book. Mr. Jensen's specialities include Blessingway ceremonial repertoire, which immortals developed as they gave order to the present earth surface. Many Navajos consider it the "main stalk" from which all other ceremonial repertoires extend. Stories relate the origins of these ceremonies to specific places in Navajoland. Here, far east of Navajoland, Mr. Jensen tells a television crew about how the U.S. Army conquered the Navajos in 1864 and held them here for four years. Many Navajos surrendered to get relief from slave raiders and from the U.S. Army, knowing that relatives still hiding in their homeland would pray from the mountaintops for their safe return. In 1868 the Navajos signed a treaty with the United States that established in the middle of their homeland a reservation to which surrounding parts of the homeland have since been added. To Mr. Jensen, the Treaty is the good that came out of the suffering at Fort Sumner. Much of the original homeland and its sacred places have stayed outside Navajo jurisdiction, however.

The four mountains that symbolize the outer limits of the Navajo homeland (and even the known earth surface) were the first geographical places created. Before people came to live on the surface of the present earth, they moved up through a series of lower worlds. By most accounts, the four mountains were created in the lowest world. Every time the people moved up they took pinches of soil from these mountains, from which they recreated the mountains in the new world they had just entered. Each of the four mountains is associated with a cardinal direction, the first and most important of which is east. This picture shows the eastern part of the large massif that makes up the sacred mountain of the north, "Big Sheep," west of Durango, Colorado, on National Forest land outside Navajo jurisdiction. Roads are for jeep touring and gold mining, which began on the mountain before the turn of the century and continues (a little bit) today. Many Navajos locate the place where people emerged onto the present earth's surface somewhere north of this mountain. Every one of the four directional mountains, as well as two that symbolize the center of the Navajo homeland, is outside Navajo Nation jurisdiction, mainly on land administered by federal and state governments.

This old-style hogan is part of a homesite with more modern dwellings. Navajo dwellings of all types customarily face east, as prescribed by Blessingway, which includes detailed instructions for building and blessing the hogan. Another old-style hogan is a cone-shaped earth-covered log structure based on a frame of forked poles, one in each of the four cardinal directions. The frame orients the dwelling to the four sacred mountains and thereby to the entire Navajo homeland. After the people emerged from the lower worlds, they conducted the first Blessingway to make the first hogan. They then went inside to continue planning the earth's surface (beginning with the four sacred mountains and the two in the middle).

This hogan's lack of a stove pipe suggests its use for storage when not needed for ceremonies. Such hogans are among the main customary places for storytelling both during ceremonies and in the family's daily life. Families living in the hogans needed for ceremonies may move their belongings elsewhere temporarily, including the stove, to make way for the customary ceremonial open fire in the middle of the floor below the smokehole, and to make room for sandpaintings on the floor at the back (west side) of the hogan.

The sweathouse (steam bath) is another place for storytelling. In the old days, every family had one, tucked out of sight of the dwellings for privacy, and many still do. Some extended families have separate sweathouses for men and women (otherwise the two use the same sweathouse at different times). The conical wood superstructure a few feet in diameter is covered with earth and heated with rocks brought in from a fire outside and steam from water poured on the rocks. Many ceremonial procedures also require a sweathouse, the prototype of which was designed by First Man right after the Emergence. This sweathouse lacks the earth covering because it has been abandoned, and is considered a sacred place. Like abandoned homesites and graves, it is to be left alone once its former users have salvaged building materials.

This rural Navajo homesite is atypical only in the willingness of its residents to tolerate one of the authors (with intrusive camera) as a neighbor. Dwellings face the rising sun. The dwelling at right is a typical modern version of the hogan. Corrals and storage buildings are visible, but not the cornfield, behind the rock at right. The family may conduct daily and weekly prayers and other private ceremonies in the hogan, sweathouse, corrals, and cornfield, as well as from outcropping rocks nearby. Less often, the homesite may accommodate more elaborate ceremonial performances lasting from one to nine nights and conducted by specialists (medicine people, chanters). These are attended by anywhere from a few family members to dozens or even hundreds of relatives and friends from the surrounding region.

This peak marks the edge of what some Navajos
consider a sacred preserve extending several miles in all
directions from the home of First Man and First
Woman, a mesa where they moved from the
Emergence Place and raised the miraculously born
Changing Woman. She then gave birth to the War
Hero Twins, superseded the First Pair in creating things
on the present earth surface, and (after moving to the
western ocean) taught humans the Blessingway. This
peak is on a direct line of sight between the home of
Changing Woman and the sacred mountain of the
north. This boundary peak stands within sparsely
vegetated "badlands," banded clays that resemble
mirage or heat waves. The combined air, moisture, and
light permeate other matter and make it appear alive,
animating the immortals who populate the earth and
sky of Navajoland. The state government, which has
jurisdiction over the area, evidently authorized the sign,
which refers to the lone tree (branch on left) and
expresses an intrusive landscape esthetic that fails to
recognize the symbolism of "badlands" to Navajos.

These petroglyphs are near the confluence of a main canyon in Dinetah and the San Juan River. Together with the Colorado, the San Juan forms a perennial river across the northern part of the Navajo customary homeland. Dinetah is the home of Changing Woman and the Twins, as well as the earliest archaeological remains (A.D. 1400s) that archaeologists consider Navajo. The corn image may refer to Blessingway (although many other ceremonial repertoires include procedures to make crops flourish). The small bow image (right and below the circle) is a symbol of the older Twin, Monster Slayer, and the hourglass-like figure behind the corn (left of the circle) is the hair bun symbol of the younger Twin, Born for Water. The circle may represent a shield, another symbol of the Twins. Blessingway now (and perhaps since the middle 1700s) enjoins Navajos from making petroglyphs of sacred symbols, allowing only ephemeral representations during ceremonial performances in sandpaintings and paintings on the body of the person over whom a performance is held to cure or prevent illness or misfortune and promote well-being.

Trail shrines consist of rocks and twigs that travellers place with prayers for safety and success, especially (now) on pilgrimages to gather materials for ceremonial use. They occur along routes described in stories of the origins of various ceremonial repertoires as the hero or heroine travelled around learning the various parts of the repertoire from immortals who inhabit different places. This shrine is at or near one of several places from the far west to the east of Navajoland where Monster Slayer chipped pieces off the monster Travelling Rock as it fled eastward, and is also on or near the route that Changing Woman took to her permanent home in the western ocean, after the Twins killed all the monsters.

After they had killed the monsters and their mother
had moved west to the ocean, the Twins moved to the
confluence of the San Juan and Los Pinos rivers in the
northern part of Dinetah. At their home (petroglyphs)
here, the Twins may have helped protect the Navajos
of Dinetah from the Ute slave raiders who swept down
from the north during the 1700s and ultimately forced
the Navajos to move away, although they continued to
make pilgrimages to this sacred place. A more recent
onslaught was from the U.S. Bureau of Reclamation,
which built Navajo Dam just below the confluence
(shown here) to store water diverted eastward over the
Continental Divide into the Rio Grande, thus insuring
plenty of water for the growth of Albuquerque. Now
the main visitors are well-heeled pleasure boaters, few
of them Navajos.

Another place on Changing Woman's route westward, the rock in the foreground is the remains of food she left behind, and she also left the spring in the background (rock outcrop on the right). People offer prayers here to insure the basic necessities, but road construction moved the rock away from the spring, making privacy a problem. This location is similar to the place that is the subject of the story in chapter 12, "Where Whiteshell Woman Stopped for Lunch."

The Little Colorado River in southwestern Navajoland isn't perennial, but it flows most of the time. The falls here are a prayer offering place upstream from the canyon (background left) that Changing Woman visited on her trip westward to the ocean. After she created the original western water clan people there, they returned east to Dinetah. Some stories say that at the sacred mountain of the west, the gateway to Navajoland from that side, they split into two groups. The southern group crossed the canyon in the vicinity of this place on its way back to Dinetah.

This is a Navajo fortified site in Dinetah, where the Navajo clans from the west came together with survivors of the monsters in the east. Like nearly all such sites, this one, Hooded Fireplace, dates to the 1700s and was evidently a refuge from Utes, who took Navajo captives and sold them as slaves to the Spanish colonists of the Rio Grande Valley. Navajo inhabitants of Dinetah included descendants of Pueblo Indians who in the 1690s had taken refuge here from the Spanish reconquest of the upper Rio Grande Valley after the 1689 revolt, in which Puebloans and their Navajo and other allies had ousted the Spanish. In the foreground before the masonry refuge on the point, with its six or seven rooms, are the remains of hogans, probably the forked-stick type. Swarming over all are visiting anthropologists (include one of the authors after she took this picture), whose well-intentioned zeal for self-education can't diminish their impact on the structure, although (unlike most such sites) it has been stabilized. Worse are vandal curio-seekers who can easily find the site over the network of roads (background) to gas wells on U.S. Bureau of Land Management land.

Craters like this collapsed volcano are important in the songs, prayers, and stories of many ceremonial repertoires that involve the power of thunder and lightning (which seeks depressions and lava rock) and wind. These powers are also associated with the Great Snake, whose body is the curving hill in the foreground and head the mountain in the middle. Like many craters, this place is also a home of Salt Woman, who emerged from the lower worlds with First Man and First Woman and moved around with her salt deposits, which are interconnected by pilgrimage routes described in ceremonial stories. In the old days Navajos travelled long distances to gather salt ceremonially for both everyday and (still today) ceremonial use. Despite its dangerous powers, this valley contains a few Navajo homesites. Even in the 1850s, wealthy Navajo headmen and the U.S. Army quarreled over whose livestock would be pastured here.

White House Ruin in Canyon de Chelly National Monument is a
central place in the larger sacred landscape that encompasses the
whole canyon system. Both the ruin and the surrounding canyon
dominate the origin stories of several Navajo ceremonial
repertoires, including the nine-night Nightway, the all-night-long
masked dance performance on the last night, which is popularly
known as the Ye'ii Bicheii dance. Construction may have begun on
the lower house around A.D. 1050. The site was abandoned by
A.D. 1300. Wherever its Anasazi occupants moved, their
descendants, intermarried with Athabaskans and now considering
themselves Navajos, may have been among the Navajos who
resettled the Canyons and perhaps contributed their surviving
stories about the place to the evolving Nightway repertoire. The
man in the center is a local resident who sells jewelry (on the
white cloth in front of him) to tourists who drive up the canyons
or hike down the trail.

Like Canyon de Chelly, Monument Valley is another Navajo sacred landscape where Navajos trying to live in a customary way are overrun by tourists. The jewelry sellers here, like the man at White House, exemplify the dilemma for Navajos posed by tourists, who may intrude on daily life and ceremonialism but also pay for goods and services that employ local people. A third factor often ignored by boosters of tourism consists of non-Navajo concessions, more heavily capitalized than the Navajo entrepreneurs and therefore able to get most of what tourists spend. An obvious (if politically problematical) way to limit the number of tourists without reducing what Navajos earn from them is to cut back these concessions, although that would force the Navajos who now work for them into the insecurity of self-employment.

This gravel pit was once a volcanic hill on a pilgrimage route in the origin stories of several ceremonies. A generation ago, local elders reportedly stopped gravel mining for road construction here because of its use as an offering place. A couple of years ago, the BIA again sought a permit to mine gravel for much-needed local road improvement. Despite recommendations of some Navajo Nation government staff to avoid the hill, extraction proceeded because local people evidently expressed no such concerns to the project's cultural resource consultants. Why such concerns failed to surface is unclear. People in the foreground are packing up after handing out trophies for a 10-km run.

Strip mining for coal is a large-scale and irreversible disruption of customary landscapes. It also pays royalties to the Navajo Nation government and employs many Navajos at union scale, making them among the best-paid in Navajoland. This dragline, poised on a former Navajo homesite, is in view (and earshot) of domestic prayer offering places of remaining residents nearby. Better integration of cultural resource inventories and post-mine land use planning, especially earlier in the mine plan than is now the case and with the guidance of the families who theoretically can return to their land after reclamation, could perhaps lessen devastation of sacred places and customary land-use patterns.

Local people donated labor and a local trader donated lumber and roofing paper to build the original White Rock Chapter House in 1930, when the BIA was beginning to promote political organization of local communities into chapters so that it could more easily propound administrative changes. (The BIA's effort backfired when many chapters became centers for opposition to a federal stock reduction program later in the 1930s.) In the 1950s or 1960s, the Navajo Nation government built the community another chapter house, still used today (in background on ridgetop, left). Around 1980, the chapter restored the building, which now houses a preschool. A well and pumphouse (outside frame to right) offer water and showers to the many local families without running water. The present chapter compound also includes a hogan (on ridge above old chapter house chimney) for various chapter functions. Chapter compounds are meeting places and social centers for the interrelated and intermarried extended families that make up rural Navajo communities. Because they symbolize these communities, many residents care about preserving the buildings.

Not an outdoor bistro, but an example of the anthropological
cliché, the technological adaptiveness of Navajos (contrasted with
conservatism in belief) is evident. At one of the many "flea
markets" that have sprung up in the last decade in larger
communities and heavily travelled road intersections around
Navajoland, one of the authors buys corn for lunch during field
work, but it could just as easily be for ceremonial use. Corn,
livestock, even medicinal herbs and other ceremonial materials are
available at these markets.

Mr. Nevy Jensen makes an offering at the travel shrine at Fort
Sumner after telling the story at the end of this book. In 1970,
many medicine people travelled from Navajoland several hundred
miles eastward to this place when the State of New Mexico
established it as a monument. To commemorate the detention of
Navajos there after the U.S. Army had conquered them, and the
return of (part of) the Navajo homeland through the 1868 Treaty,
the medicine people placed the first rocks at this trail shrine.
Monument staff attest that many Navajos visit the monument and
offer rocks with prayers here.

PART THREE

NAVAJO

CUSTOMARY

LANDSCAPES

AND

DEVELOPMENT

LANDSCAPES

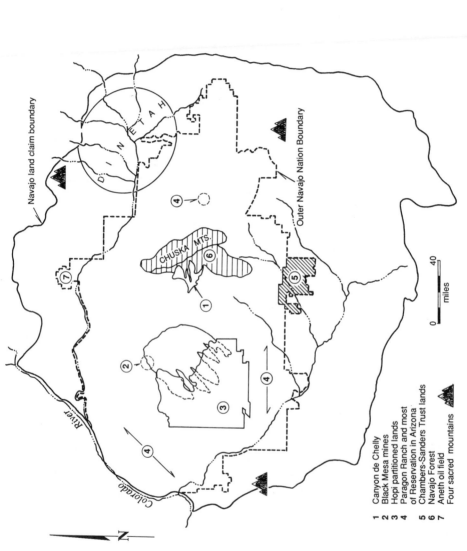

Figure 3. Areas needing extraordinary preservation measures wholly or partly within Navajo jurisdiction.

1 Canyon de Chelly
2 Black Mesa mines
3 Hopi partitioned lands
4 Paragon Ranch and most of Reservation in Arizona
5 Chambers-Sanders Trust lands
6 Navajo Forest
7 Aneth oil field
   Four sacred mountains

Navajo land claim boundary

Outer Navajo Nation Boundary

D I N E T A H

CHUSKA MTS.

River

Colorado RIVER

N

0   40
    miles

8.

What Navajos Say about Cultural Preservation

As Navajo ways of life converge with ways of life in the United States as a whole, Navajo customs, stories, and language symbolize the ethnic distinctiveness of the Navajo people. At the same time, this convergence means that fewer young Navajos learn Navajo ways at home from their elders. It also means that the once natural process of accumulating more and more such knowledge throughout a lifetime has been cut short for many young and middle-aged Navajos. And it means that many have lost interest in Navajo ways.

In parts I and II we have emphasized preserving places and landscapes. We've treated keeping alive the stories and activities that go with them as a much-desired indirect result (although preserving the places is only a necessary condition, not, unfortunately, a sufficient one). Through conversations and interviews with the old people who know and care most about these places (and with younger people who at least knew and cared enough to send us to the old people), we and other researchers have found that these people do indeed want places, stories, and landscapes preserved, but specifically by keeping Navajo culture and its land uses alive in the face of competition with "economic development" projects both for land and for the interest of young people. Much, they say, has been lost, but there's still a lot left.

In part III, we widen our focus to the Navajo public discourse on cultural preservation in general, although we continue to put in the foreground what people say about places and landscapes. In chapter 8 we look at what Navajo institutions have done, then at the opinions of "grass roots" Navajos, individually and through various organizations. Like the interviewees in the studies covered in parts I and II, the people who have the most to say about cultural preservation are overwhelmingly advocates of cultural preservation. Navajo opinions are divided not so much over the merits of cultural preservation in general but over how it is to happen without depriving people of "benefits" of economic development (not to mention what aspects of development are beneficial) and what roles, if any, new social and political institutions should have. Chapters 9 and 10 cover "grass roots" discourse about the development assault on sacred landscapes in the parts of Navajoland most threatened, and offer specific examples of landscape preservation methods.

This part contains stories and other statements about the land and cultural preservation, but most of the statements were written by young and middle-aged Navajos. They testify that cultural and landscape preservation is important to younger Navajos as well as to the old people interviewed, although it is not expressed in the same way.

Cultural Preservation Efforts
of Navajo Institutions

The Navajo Nation government and other institutions have actively tried to preserve significant Navajo places and landscapes, not to mention those of other Indian communities. By 1961, the Navajo Nation government had set up the Navajo Tribal Museum and a research program (mainly for researching the Navajo pre-conquest land claim before the Indian Claims Commission, including the sacred places report mentioned in part II) (Begay 1991). Between 1955 and 1962, the Navajo Nation government helped support the Navajo-Cornell University Field Health Research Project at Many Farms, Arizona, which, among other things, consulted Navajo medicine people to bring Navajo ceremonial healing practices into U.S. Indian Health Service programs. Between 1967 and 1969, the Navajo Nation government, with money from the federal Office of Economic Opportunity, ran the Office of Navajo Economic Opportunity (ONEO) Culture Project, which deployed young Navajos to record stories of medicine people and other storytellers. Funding ran out before material from the 1,000 tapes that this effort produced could be compiled into a high school textbook (Greenberg and Greenberg 1984:123–25; Frisbie 1987:258–59).

In 1972, the Navajo Nation government created the Navajo Health Authority (NHA), which included the Office of Navajo Healing Sciences (ONHS). These programs researched Navajo ceremonialism and curing practices, combed Navajoland for medicine people to list in a "Navajo Ceremonial Practitioners Registry," and helped organize the Navajo Medicine Men's Association, which adopted Articles of Incorporation in 1978. These programs fell by the wayside after 1981, when Reagan-administration cutbacks in federal funds (and other factors) forced bureaucratic reorganization within the Navajo Nation government. The Medicine Men's Association nevertheless continues to meet regularly (Frisbie 1987:256–320; Frisbie and Tso 1993; Greenberg and Greenberg 1984:123–25, 150–52; Navajo Times, Feb. 7, 1991, and July 18, 1991).

Navajo Nation laws and policies since the mid–1970s have also encouraged such preservation. Just about all proposed developments in Navajoland (other than a family's construction with its own funds) require archaeological surveys beforehand, as well as efforts to find out if development will affect culturally important places. By 1977, the Tribal Museum's archaeological research section had become a separate program, which, in turn, split in 1986 into the Archaeology and Historic Preservation departments to widen the scope of planning, policy formulation, and seeing that developers follow the historic preservation laws (Begay 1991).

Between 1972 and 1988, the Navajo Nation government also set forth its official position on historic preservation in a series of legislative council resolutions (Navajo Nation Council 1958, 1972, 1977, 1978, 1986, 1987, 1988). These culminated in (and were superseded by) the 1988 Cultural Resources Protection Act, which states,

(1) The spirit and direction of the Navajo Nation are founded upon and reflected in its cultural heritage;

(2) The cultural heritage of the Navajo Nation should be preserved as a living part of our community life and development in order to give a sense of orientation to the Navajo People;

(3) Cultural properties of the Navajo Nation are being lost or substantially altered, often inadvertently, with increasing frequency;

(4) The preservation of this irreplaceable cultural heritage is in the interest of the Navajo Nation and its people so that its vital legacy of

cultural, educational, esthetic, inspirational, economic and energy benefits will be maintained and enriched for future generations of Navajos;

(5) In the face of ever increasing energy development, economic
development, sanitation and public health developments, the present
Tribal governmental and non-tribal governmental programs to preserve
the Navajo Nation's cultural resources are inadequate to ensure future
generations a genuine opportunity to appreciate and enjoy the rich
heritage of the Navajo Nation;

(6) Increased knowledge of our cultural resources, the establishment
of better means of identifying and administering them, and fostering their
preservation will improve the planning of federal, Tribal, state and other
projects and will assist economic growth and development and ex-
peditious project implementation; and

(7) Although the major role in cultural resource preservation has been
borne by the federal and state governments, and both must continue to
play a role, it is nevertheless essential that the Navajo Nation expand and
accelerate its cultural resource preservation programs and activities.
(Navajo Nation Council 1988)

The Navajo Nation government and other Navajo organizations,
especially the Navajo Health Authority working with the Medicine
Men's Association, have also tried to use federal laws passed during the
1960s and 1970s to protect sacred places and Navajo customs. In hind-
sight, the most important federal laws for sacred places have been the
National Historic Preservation Act (U.S. Congress 1966) and its amendments and guidelines (mainly *National Register Bulletin* 38 [Parker and
King 1990], which explains how the Act covers sacred places), and the
American Indian Religious Freedom Act (U.S. Congress 1978). (The
National Environmental Policy Act [U.S. Congress 1969] hasn't been
used as much but seems to have potential for the future with increased
focus on preserving sacred landscapes.) As Frisbie (1987:369) points
out, there were hopes for the Archaeological Resources Protection Act
(U.S. Congress 1979), but that law hasn't proved very helpful. The
various efforts of the Medicine Men's Association and other Navajos to
use these laws to protect Navajo sacred places and traditions are described below. See also Frisbie (1987:365–400).

Since the late 1960s, Navajo educational institutions have also tried
to keep various old ways alive. For example, the community of Rough
Rock in 1966 opened its own school, funded through the BIA, as the
first Indian-controlled school in the United States. The next year, the
school set up the Navajo Curriculum Center, which produces books and
other classroom materials based on Navajo history and culture. In 1968,
this school also started a program in which medicine people trained
other Navajos to be medicine people. Reagan-administration budget
cuts closed the program in 1983, but not before it had trained more than

one hundred students in at least twenty-three different ceremonies. Training occurred with customary methods in customary settings (teacher's hogan and at ceremonial performances). The program paid stipends to teachers and students, rather than the student paying the teacher as is the custom. Most students were middle-aged and were descendants of medicine people. Some were relearning ceremonial repertoires (Frisbie 1987:259–68; Shebala 1992).

Navajo Community College, a two-year college that the Navajo Nation government established in 1968, offers a curriculum in Navajo language and culture, trains teachers to teach the Navajo language in primary and secondary schools, and has sponsored various projects to record Navajo oral history. It also houses the Ned Hatathle Museum, which opened in 1977 and has operated, among other innovative programs, a repository of jish—bundles or "kits" of paraphernalia needed for particular ceremonial repertoires—not for exhibit but for lending to medicine people who lack complete jish themselves. Most of the jish have come from museums outside Navajoland, notably the Wheelwright Museum in Santa Fe. Others have come from heirs of medicine people who haven't been trained in the relevant ceremonial repertoires themselves (Frisbie 1987:315–20).

Many elementary and secondary schools also offer varying amounts of instruction in and about Navajo language and culture. Among them are schools at Ramah and Rock Point, which came under community control soon after the Rough Rock school, and the Window Rock Elementary School, which has recently started a total immersion Navajo-as-a-second-language program.

The foregoing is a brief summary of complex recent actions by the Navajo Nation government and other Navajo institutions to protect sacred places and Navajo culture in general. A more detailed review seems unnecessary since Frisbie (1987, especially pp. 256–320 and 365–400) has already produced one current to the mid–1980s.

"Grass Roots" Opinions and Customary Preservation Methods

Regardless of whether they are aware of the intricacies of Navajo Nation institutional historic and cultural preservation efforts, many Navajos have their own ideas about what such efforts should be.

Before, the beginning, the world was without sound and without movement. It was as if there was a perfectly still body of water. And then a stone was thrown into the middle of this pool and ripples started to move out from the center. At a certain point (now past) the ripples started to turn back around and move back toward this center. Time has turned back around. Soon it will be still again. (Farella 1984:18)

As Farella interprets this statement by someone he consulted,

> Traditionally, after a man died he was left on the ground (in a house that was then abandoned) or he was buried. His body then decomposed and, to oversimplify, his molecules were recycled. His memory, his thoughts, and his descendants are the part that lives on. To put a man into a coffin or to put chemicals into his body to preserve it is viewed with disgust. It interrupts and violates this cycle. . . .
>
> . . . Very often, if not usually, ethnographers set out to preserve some bit of culture that was about to be lost or to die. . . .
>
> A primary theme in [Navajo] stories is the acquisition and loss of knowledge, the point being that all things that come into existence last for only so long and then cease to exist. . . . Thus, our [non-Navajo ethnographers'] attempts at preservation deny the basis of the [Navajo] world view that we are supposedly preserving. (Farella 1984:18–19)

And there is the widespread practice of "returning to the earth" a cherished item, such as a drumstick, cradleboard, or jish, that one can no longer use.

These statements suggest that the cultural preservation efforts of the Navajo Nation government and other institutions described above run against Navajo beliefs. But many Navajos want sacred places and landscapes protected and preserved. They lament that too many younger Navajos aren't interested in Navajo ways. They say that the landscape is an important vehicle for teaching these ways. Although some have burned Navajo medicine bundles (see below), even many Christian Navajos are for preserving Navajo culture, saying, "We all worship the same higher power."

Public discourse among Navajos about the Rough Rock Demonstration School and the Medicine Men's Association, as chronicled by Frisbie (1987:256–320), illustrates these concerns. The Navajo Health Authority Registry of Navajo Religious Practitioners had identified 1029 medicine people in 1981, a third of whom limited their practice to Native American Church [peyote way], herbalism, and divination, alone or in combination, and two-thirds of whom practiced more extensively from Navajo ceremonial repertoires. How many more practitioners weren't identified has not been estimated, but in any case the number of medicine people is small in a population of about 150,000 at the time (Frisbie and Tso 1993). And some medicine people lament that many of these practitioners know only small parts of particular repertoires, that they have learned from tapes and eavesdropping rather than by paying for formal customary instruction.

The Rough Rock School Board's choices of medicine people as instructors were based partly on

> the importance and threat of extinction to the ceremony being taught. . . .
> Their primary beliefs were that Navajo religion and culture must contin-
> ue and that it must always be possible to use traditional mechanisms to
> restore Navajo people to harmony with nature and the universe. (Frisbie
> 1987:261)

Some Navajos criticized the program, but according to Frisbie (1987:265), critics targeted the program's methods more than its purpose.

The Medicine Men's Association came together after Navajo Christian fundamentalists from the Lower Greasewood Chapter in 1976 burned traditional Navajo ceremonial paraphernalia and the Chapter asked the Navajo Nation government for help (Frisbie 1987:207–208, 273).

> Perhaps fears for the future of traditional religion and native healing arts
> had never been so acute; perhaps the decline in numbers of apprentices
> had never been so widely discussed, nor paraphernalia and sacred places
> so openly attacked and defamed. For whatever reasons, in 1976, after the
> Lower Greasewood incident, the time was right to attempt . . . the
> organization of ceremonialists into an association. (Frisbie 1987:274)

Even earlier, in 1973, the Navajo Nation government had held a meeting in Window Rock that fifty medicine people attended. They publicly lamented the decline in Navajo religion and urged the Navajo Nation government to do something to preserve Navajo culture (Frisbie 1987:276). These medicine people advocated more meetings, at least two of which occurred in 1974 and 1976, the earlier one apparently called spontaneously by medicine people themselves (Frisbie 1987:277).

In response to these statements of medicine people, Navajo Health Authority staff started in 1976 to sponsor meetings in various places toward organizing a medicine people's association. The Association incorporated in 1978, but couldn't get the Navajo Nation Council to approve a charter. Council delegates apparently backed away from such support at least partly because many thought their constituents didn't like the idea of a formal organization for medicine people. So Navajo Health Authority staff held public meetings and otherwise worked within the chapters to learn about and address public concerns (Frisbie 1987:277–83).

Both medicine people and other Navajos differed among themselves on cultural preservation issues, including whether the Medicine Men's Association was a good idea. As NHA field staff reported, according to Frisbie,

> "On the road we get opposition sometimes. With the older people, some say, 'If you think it'll do some good, it'll protect and preserve the traditional ways, let's try it.' Others say, 'We never needed an organization before, so why now?' Some of the middle generation people think that the whole thing is an NAC [Native American Church] scheme to destroy Navajo ceremonies. The young people fear that the Association will control them, and that they'll have IRS problems because of it." (Frisbie 1987:286)

Frisbie continues quoting from field reports:

> " 'Those who drink at ceremonies and sing while they are drunk are against the Association and those who drink at Squaw Dances are against it too.' . . . 'Some people want all the songs off the radio; they claim they are hearing songs used in ceremonies and even that public Squaw Dance music should not be on the air. A lot also want rules about doing ceremonies in the right season; they don't like seeing an Enemyway and Ye'iibichei going on at the same time, next to each other so that kids can just wander into one and back out and into the other.' Some people also expressed displeasure 'about the schools teaching anything about traditional religion, the ceremonies, the rules, and all those things; they want that taken out of schools.' " (Frisbie 1987:288)

A medicine man told Frisbie,

> ". . . All of us singers want the ceremonies to be preserved and respected; there is a lot of trouble with those things today. But we don't like their [Medicine Men's Association's] approach." (Frisbie 1987:294)

The Navajo Nation Council at the time of this writing still hadn't chartered the Medicine Men's Association. The Association fell on hard times after the Navajo Health Authority lost its federal funding and no longer existed to support the Association's organizing and other activities. But the Medicine Men's Association continued to function, working with lawyers at DNA, a Navajo legal-aid service, to protect sacred places. In 1983, however, a fire destroyed the DNA building and most of the Association's records, which were housed there. This reportedly so demoralized many members that the Association went into eclipse (Frisbie 1987:290–93). The Association still exists, though. Now known as the Dine Spiritual and Cultural Society, it meets regularly, is active in protesting threatened disturbances to sacred places, and organizes special religious observances like prayers for Navajo soldiers returning from the 1990 Persian Gulf War and pilgrimages to the four sacred boundary mountains (*Navajo Times,* Feb. 7, 1991, and July 18, 1991). The Society's survival even without funding or a charter from the Navajo Nation Council is strong evidence that some medicine people, at least, continue to feel a strong need for such an organization.

Through all these ups and downs, the Medicine Men's Association and other Navajos have acted to protect sacred places, including using federal laws. We discuss these cases in more detail below in connection with areas that we think need extraordinary preservation measures. The cases mentioned show how sophisticated the elders have been in using non-Navajo institutions to protect sacred places.

As far back as 1970, Navajo medicine people joined Hopis, Zunis, and White Mountain Apaches in protesting the expansion of a ski resort that had been on National Forest land on the sacred San Francisco Peaks since 1937. This was the public relations fiasco that evidently led the Forest Service to commission the study by Vannette and Feary (1981). Beginning in 1977, DNA helped them prepare a lawsuit against the Forest Service. The Medicine Men's Association got involved in 1979, with members testifying at Forest Service meetings and in court (*Wilson v. Block;* Frisbie 1987:299–300, 380–84). On another front, in 1977, several medicine men took the federal government to court, claiming that Lake Powell rising under Rainbow Bridge was disrupting their practice of Navajo religion (*Badonie v. Higginson;* Frisbie 1987:379–80). Members of the Medicine Men's Association also made statements at federally sponsored hearings in 1979 on how to apply the American Indian Religious Freedom Act of 1978 (Frisbie 1987:375; U.S. Department of the Interior, Federal Agencies Task Force 1979).

> The Association was also involved in protests against uranium extraction in the Bisti area, further development of the Shiprock Irrigation project, expansion of timbering in the Defiance Plateau and Summit Pine Forests, the management of Huerfano Peak, coal extraction in the San Juan Basin, and other threats to sacred areas. Fearing that significant sites would be destroyed, the Association asked to be consulted during various cultural resource management studies, so that members might help identify sites of sacred or other significance [namely the 1980 and 1982 projects in the Navajo Forest]. . . .
>
> . . . The Association also spoke out frequently against relocation [of Navajos from 1882 Executive Order Reservation lands federally designated as exclusively Hopi in 1977] . . . to suggest that even the native health care system was having difficulty coping with the effects of the Navajo-Hopi land dispute. Among the reasons for ceremonialists' distress were the unmanageable number of requests for ceremonies because of the stress-related illnesses caused by the relocation dispute, and their own inability to perform because of personal distress . . . [T]he Association

was actively involved in efforts to reach a compromise with the Hopis over use of sacred places in [the 1882 Executive Order Reservation]. By December 1983, Association members were also speaking out against mass relocations planned in the eastern part of the reservation in response to federal government and mining, utility, and railroad companies' pressures. (Frisbie 1987:300–301)

Finally, the Medicine Men's Association worked out ways to care for jish that are no longer in the hands of practicing medicine people but have been offered to the Association by family members who don't know how to use them or even by non-Navajo museums and collectors. As Frisbie quotes a Navajo Health Authority staff report on Association policy,

> First, it should go to the [extended] family, . . . someone in that group who knows how to use that. If there is nobody like that, then we think about the community, the local people; is there someone in that area who knows how to use it? If there again is no one then the Association, through its contacts, will notify other communities. . . . The last thing we would consider is the fact that the jish really belongs to the people in the geographic place where the singer lived. The use of that jish has supported that area, spiritually and economically.
>
> Older jish belong in the community where they were originally acquired. . . . Some of those have a history that goes back 200 years; that history is known. (Frisbie 1987:315–16)

And Frisbie testifies to the continuing aliveness of jish, even one that has fallen between the hands of older and younger generations of medicine people.

> [Motion] is characteristic of the lives of jish as they are assembled, used, borrowed, and pawned; transmitted to other Navajos by inheritance, free-of-charge gift, sale, or trade; and disposed of through accidents, deliberate destruction, burial, or return to the earth. Motion also characterizes medicine bundles in the Anglo world from the time a jish is "acquired" by an Anglo throughout its numerous changes of hands. And today, this motion does not necessarily stop when and if the jish reaches a museum. Now, medicine bundles can and do return to the reservation from the Anglo world, and once back in the Navajo Nation, they are pressed into use, through permanent acquisition from the Medicine Men's Association or loan from the NCC [Navajo Community College] jish repository. Thus it is that now Navajo dispositions to Anglos can circle around and result in Anglo dispositions to a Navajo group or institution and then another Navajo-to-Navajo transmission. Thus, in new ways, jish continue to be vital, alive, significant, important, and used. (Frisbie 1987:391)

These actions and discourse about "disposition" of jish relate to sacred places. A jish contains rare elements from all over Navajoland

and beyond. In a way, it is a miniature version of Navajoland that concentrates the power of its rare elements and species. During a ceremonial performance, it focuses that power on the patient and other participants from the surrounding community. The quotations above say that no geographical community should lose the power that the jish brings into it.

The foregoing testimonies corroborate the statements in parts I and II and show that Navajos who care about cultural preservation see Navajo culture as alive but endangered. To be compatible with Navajo philosophy, then, Navajo institutions and the historic preservation bureaucrats who work with them need to focus, not on preserving customs that are effectively "dead" and that "grass-roots" Navajos themselves aren't trying to preserve, but on helping "grass-roots" Navajos keep alive the land-based Navajo customary way of life. The Navajo way needs to evolve naturally, incorporating or producing innovations rather than breaking down under an overload of incompatible innovation from outside. Determining whether an aspect of culture is still in use may not always be easy, especially in light of two other widespread Navajo beliefs:

> There are, moreover, certain subjects which are surrounded with more or less secrecy. To the singer this knowledge is his life or "breath," part of his inner self or soul, which he carefully guards in the firm conviction that, the moment he imparts it to others, his usefulness in life is spent. Pleading and tempting offers are useless, the usual reply being that "when old age is upon me and death is approaching, I will tell." (Haile 1968:31)

and,

> Culture is commonly defined [by scholars] in terms of a shared belief system or of shared knowledge. Here we have a people who share the "belief" that belief is not and should not necessarily be shared, that differences of opinion, differences in ideas, and differences in behavior are a part of human society in general and Navajo culture in particular. (Farella 1984:120)

A corollary to this "discordant voices" model of culture (which, incidentally, is also gaining ground among scholars) is that social consensus is fleeting and provisional at best and is most likely to occur, if at all, when people can freely air their different points of view to decision makers, themselves chosen by consensus, who then incorporate those points of view into their decisions. (This, incidentally, is how local Navajo communities and their leaders were supposed to make decisions in pre-conquest times.)

To reiterate the lessons of part II, bureaucrats and other decision makers can best deal with the questions about what is acceptable to protect and what is best left alone, what measures are suitable, and so forth, by constantly seeking guidance from knowledgeable "grass roots" people about specific undertakings and general policies. If consensus is ever to occur, decision makers must both honor Navajo customary preservation methods within a community as the first line of defense, and open the door to policy making for "grassroots" Navajos concerned with cultural preservation. These people are the least organized and least represented in the modern bureaucratic framework about historic preservation, especially as applied to areas that need special protection. If consensus isn't possible, the next best thing is continuing discourse in a framework open to all concerned parties.

Bolstering Customary Methods

Navajos have naturally evolved their own customary preservation methods. These include preserving the landscape; performing and handing down customs, especially ceremonialism; excluding outsiders, like tourists and developers, from their lands; and telling stories in the contexts of family activities, ceremonial performances, and so forth. These customary methods can be supported in several ways.

Decision makers might help interested communities exclude un-wanted outsiders through site stewardship programs—networks of people each watching particular landmarks as well as archaeological sites and reporting any vandalism or other suspicious activities to law enforcement officers. Chapters also need help in screening scholarly researchers. The Navajo Nation government now requires permits for both archaeological and ethnographic field research and tours. Applicants for ethnographic permits must show that they have contacted the appropriate chapters, but the Navajo Nation government needs to work with the chapters more closely. Tourists could be diverted from areas where residents don't want them to resident-approved places by a chapter and Navajo Nation government program to develop and publicize historic districts that local communities themselves have designated.

The Navajo Nation government could also help communities restrict outsiders by zoning certain natural landmarks and other sensitive areas to be off-limits for pursuits other than Navajo customary ones. Such zoning would also preserve rare plant and animal species and geological deposits required by customary pursuits, and keep their exact locations a secret. Access routes would have to be restricted and watched. Roads in these areas must be kept up for Navajo residents and other Navajos engaged in customary pursuits, but gates and gatekeepers might be possible in some places. The Navajo Nation government tries to help local Navajos work with federal land-managing agencies for similar protection to sacred places on federal lands outside Navajo Nation jurisdiction. Wilderness designations have proved unacceptable in many situations because they forbid the motor vehicles that many old people need. Many Navajos therefore feel that wilderness designations tend to favor recreational hikers over the original users. It is also important to note that well-meaning outsiders who advocate the protection of sacred places often have mixed feelings about the idea that these places should be a community secret. But if communities are willing to share this information with chosen outsiders, the community first needs to have the power to protect the places as it sees fit, and to have precedence over other interested parties, including federal land-managing agencies.

Decision makers also can help communities exclude unwanted outsiders by curbing the excesses of developers. In 1990 in Aneth, Utah, an oil company cleared a well pad of medicinal plants used by a local medicine woman. The company claimed not to have known about the plants until the woman and supporters blocked the bulldozer. This experience led the Navajo Nation government to make explicit that its policy on "emergency discovery situations" (discovery of previously unrecorded cultural resources during construction and development) applies not only to visible cultural materials, but also to stories and customs. According to this policy, developers must avoid further disturbing the places with links to stories and customs that have just come to light until the Navajo Nation government and other historic preservation authorities can learn about the concerns of local people and others. The incident also led the Navajo Nation government to insist that developers be more diligent in identifying local concerns about sacred places on lands proposed for development. The Navajo Nation government had previously accepted cultural resources inventories required by federal and tribal law that consisted only of archaeological surveys. Now, however, the Navajo Nation government requires (and has held workshops for) developers (or the cultural resource consultants they hire) to document concerns of local land users, chapters, and various medicine people and others whom the land users and the chapter recommend (Navajo Nation Historic Preservation Department 1990a).

Many developers have yet to comply with the spirit of this policy. As their diligence improves, however, another problem is emerging: the more sacred places recorded, the greater the need for tight control to keep the locations of these sacred places secret. Such measures might include having developers' consulting ethnographers, the researchers who actually talk with the people, report the information only to the Navajo Nation government. In turn, the Navajo Nation government would keep all records closed to the public and provide the developer, the relevant land-managing agency, and other historic preservation authorities involved only as much information as the developer needs to avoid sensitive areas.

Decision makers can also encourage customary practices, including storytelling. Recording stories and teaching them in schools involve modern settings. These activities, however, may renew participants' interests in Navajo culture and encourage participants to retell the stories at home and in other customary settings where they might otherwise have remained silent. We believe that any talk about Navajo culture, whether in public or private, in customary or modern settings, whether Navajo stories themselves or only talk about the stories and customs, is worthwhile (as long as it's voluntary). Such talk can prompt young Navajos to go home and ask their elders more about it, or prompt older Navajos to take their children and grandchildren aside and tell them more about it. Other efforts described above that limit disturbance to the land also help, because Navajos repeatedly identify the land as a primary vehicle for teaching Navajo ways to the young (Schoepfle and others 1979).

However much one might like to avoid the irony of new social forms to "preserve" Navajo landscapes and the stories and customs that go with them, this chapter shows that these new forms are a fact of life. In the past, the basic institutions for keeping Navajo culture alive were the extended family, local community, and network of medicine people. But colonialism and industrialization since the Depression and World War II have undermined family-based semi-subsistence production as the foundation of the Navajo economy, and replaced it with wage work. The struggle of the Navajo people for autonomy isn't limited to per-petuating (or restoring) the early functioning of the Navajo extended family. It also means Navajo control of modern social institutions like government, schools, businesses, and workers' organizations. There-fore, the struggle to keep Navajo culture alive isn't limited to perpetuat-ing the extended family's role in passing down the stories and protecting the associated landscapes. The modern social institutions are also in-volved in public discourse about keeping Navajo culture and landscapes alive.

9.

Navajo Endangered
Landscapes

Most measures suggested above will protect only particular places. They don't address the problem of keeping whole landscapes alive. In many localities, development is not intensive enough to threaten whole landscapes, and the customary method of preservation through secrecy is best left alone. In some localities, however, land-disturbing development, social fragmentation, or both, endanger whole landscapes and the associated stories and customs—endanger, in fact, the ability of many families to pursue the Navajo way of life on the land. From endangered areas, Navajo people have raised their voices in protest. The discourse not only shows that these areas need extraordinary protection measures for whole land-scapes, but also suggests concrete examples of such measures. This advances our discussion of Navajo concerns about preserving significant areas a step farther. In part II, even though many of the reports covered were prompted by proposed developments in specific areas (construction of a power plant, transmission lines, coal mines, timber cutting), the studies don't report (probably because they weren't requested) many recommendations from people about specific protection measures other than avoiding individual places.

The question in these areas cannot be how close can development come to a sacred place with minimum disturbance, but rather, how (if at all) can development be integrated into the landscape of customary uses with the least disturbance. In many places, local Navajos have organized to put their preservation (often along with other) concerns in front of the Navajo Nation government and outsiders. These groups are ready-made for decision making. Many organized groups, however, don't represent all families with preservation concerns in a particular locality. These other families must also be represented if they want to be. Since many localities of concern are outside the jurisdiction of the Navajo Nation government, these groups and the Navajo Nation government must work with the responsible federal and state agencies.

This chapter is about the sore spots that are under Navajo Nation jurisdiction. Figure 3 shows these areas. This chapter also includes Hopi Partitioned Lands, because the developments that are endangering Navajo life and landscapes there are so tightly bound up with possible developments in other areas that are under Navajo Nation jurisdiction, and because so many Navajos still live there. Chapter 10 covers land outside Navajo Nation jurisdiction, where Navajos for the most part are not living, although Navajo communities may border these areas. It also includes public buildings and central places, because most of these, although on Navajo land, belong to the federal government. Jurisdiction, of course, makes a big difference in the protection framework. Navajo Nation law can protect landscapes on Navajo Nation land but not outside it. The Navajo Nation government is theoretically more accessible to "grass roots" Navajos who demand a role in the planning process, and is structurally better able to accommodate such groups, than federal agencies.

Black Mesa

Coal strip-mine leaseholds of the Peabody Coal Company date back to 1966 and cover a total of about 100 square miles in the northern part of the Navajo Nation. These mines supply coal to plants at Page and (through a slurry line that also mines a tremendous amount of water from deep under the mesa) Bullhead City, Nevada. The plants in turn produce electricity for use outside Navajoland, including pumping water from the Colorado River through the Central Arizona Project canal system to the area around Phoenix and Tucson (Reno 1981:108). Navajos living on these leaseholds have resisted removal and have received news media coverage rivaling that of the so-called Navajo-Hopi land dispute.

Although archaeological surveys (Black Mesa Archaeological Project) began here in 1968 and continued for more than a decade to locate (and later excavate) archaeological sites, there was no comparably intensive effort to locate, let alone protect, Navajo sacred places (other than graves) and landscapes (Russell [1980] conducted the full range of studies that historic preservation authorities required at the time). Yet at least as far back as the Treaty of 1868, documents show that Navajos considered the whole of Black Mesa a Navajo sacred landscape (Barboncito 1868; see also Mamie Salt statement in part I). This is the kind of landform that is also likely to be (and is in fact) dotted with places of great power. Strip mining began here in 1970 and has already made great inroads into this landscape.

THE COAL MINING ON BLACK MESA

[Statement of Black Mesa resident Mary Gilmore published by Forest Lake Dine Rights Movement (1990:2)]

In support of my family's resistance and our attempt to halt mining within the new mining lease area, I would like to elaborate on the sacredness of Black Mesa. Our oral tradition teaches us that these sacred mountains and other places are to remain undisturbed. We exist here as caretakers and we offer prayers and songs as prescribed by our legends. Our ancestors have preserved these sacred sites but some have already been destroyed by the mining and so we are attempting to save those that remain. Mining cannot coexist with traditionalism.

There are many other reasons for our resistance to the strip mining of our homeland, including the adverse health effects for all species, the violation of our human and natural rights, and the desecration of sacred Black Mesa. We want to live in a safe and dependable settlement. We are quickly losing a lot of the resources we once had, especially water. We have shown our resistance and are making our demands known to the public.

Measures to protect human remains and other Navajo cultural resources are, at the time of this writing, being negotiated along with

Peabody's mine permits (Forest Lake Dine Rights Movement 1990). Peabody reportedly consults local residents on places endangered by mining. The quotation above, however, from a member of the Forest Lake Dine Rights Movement, a group of twenty-five Navajo families who still live inside the leaseholds, suggests that this process does not meet the concerns of many.

Maybe nothing can, given the uncompromising tone of the statement, but serious efforts to involve local residents actively in cultural resource protection decisions have yet to be tried. Ideally, an advisory group of present and former leasehold residents with technical help from the Navajo Nation government should work continuously with the company to identify sensitive areas and work out ways to avoid them or minimize damage to them. Perhaps the context most likely to bring concrete and positive ideas from both residents and the company is the "post-mine land-use" planning. Federal law requires mines to develop plans for returning the land to active use after mining and reclamation are over, and furthermore, the planning must involve the people who own and will use the land. The post-reclamation landscape seems like a viable framework within which to integrate the present customary use landscape.

Once a place is strip-mined out of existence, the stories about it are also likely to be lost. Since most Navajo stories are interconnected, the whole narrative structure is weakened. These losses, furthermore, won't be the natural deaths that Farella's teachers had in mind, which result from changes from within a society that replace the outmoded. The losses will result from an abrupt end to local land use that an international corporation has forced on people against their will.

Hopi Partitioned Lands That
Navajos Still Use

Lands occupied by 2,500–4,000 Navajo families that the federal government partitioned to the Hopis in 1977 still support an estimated third or more of those families. Those who have moved still have the right, according to the 1974 law, to use their sacred places on Hopi Partitioned Lands (HPL), just as the Hopis have the right to use their sacred places on the Navajo side of the line (NPL) (*Attakai v. United States* 1990:9).

The Bureau of Indian Affairs, on behalf of the Hopi tribal government, has begun range development projects that local Navajos have protested for various reasons, mainly their multifaceted impact on the

Navajo customary use landscape. The Hopi government has also proposed more coal mining, a coal slurry line, and a power plant in the parts of HPL where most Navajo resisters live, Big Mountain and Star Mountain near Teesto (Forest Lake Dine Rights Association 1990). While these proposals may be only a legal ploy to bolster Hopi water claims, the BIA has also pushed range fencing across the slopes of both Big Mountain and Star Mountain, provoking protests from Navajo families about intrusions onto sacred landscapes (*Attakai v. United States* 1990:1–9).

Neither the BIA nor federal courts take these protests at face value, viewing them as cynical ploys by people who "only" want to keep their (customary) rangelands. They question the people's claim that these developments disrupt their religious practices, since they say that the developments don't prevent the people's access to places for "religious" purposes. They fail to see that "religious" observances on the land are part of Navajo range use and all other land-based productive activities, and that users want to decide for themselves how to zone the land for various customary uses (see, for example, Wicoff 1991b). The BIA and courts also fail to acknowledge that American Indian religious freedom requires not only preserving access to sacred places, but also preserving their natural condition and that of the surrounding landscape, a point recognized by the Andrus Commission report on 1979 hearings about how to use the 1978 American Indian Religious Freedom Act but largely ignored since then (U.S. Department of the Interior, Federal Agencies Task Force 1979:51–55; Frisbie 1987:388–89).

The more Navajos who are relocated from HPL, especially those who move too far away to use their access rights, the more stories about the land will be lost, and the greater will be the danger that developments will disturb or destroy Navajo sacred places. These lands are outside the jurisdiction of the Navajo Nation government. As we learned from attending meetings during the Star Mountain fencing controversy (Wicoff 1991b), the Bureau of Indian Affairs "manages" cultural resources, but contends that it has little or no obligation under the National Historic Preservation Act to "take into account" how its projects will affect Navajo (or Hopi) sacred places. The BIA also refuses to acknowledge the geographical extent of such places.

Some sort of agreement between the Navajo and Hopi governments is necessary to insure protection and continued use of the customary landscapes of each tribe on the lands of the other. Meanwhile, the Navajo Nation government has told the BIA that, as federal land manager, before each proposed development on HPL, it must consult Navajo (not to mention Hopi) users of sacred places and landscapes about how to protect them from the developments at hand. In various parts of HPL, Navajo residents have organized (Dine Bikeyah Committee of Teesto, Big Mountain Dine Nation) to deal with the Navajo Nation government and other groups on relocation issues, although not all the remaining local residents necessarily belong to these groups. These organizations, and also the families that they don't represent, must be actively involved in efforts to protect sacred places and preserve access to them. Navajos living on and near HPL, including the Teesto Chapter (in a resolution) have advocated such efforts (Wicoff 1991a).

Lands to Be Developed under the Navajo Rehabilitation Trust Fund

The Navajo Rehabilitation Trust Fund is to pay for roads, utilities, services, and jobs in areas where most Navajos from HPL have relocated: Navajo Partitioned Lands (NPL) and other lands on the Navajo Reservation in Arizona, the Arizona boundary of which was confirmed by act of Congress in 1934 (U.S. Congress 1934).

The Navajo-Hopi Land Settlement Act and its 1980 amendments also allowed the Navajo Nation to acquire "new" lands to compensate for the lands lost to the Hopis (although the authorized acreage is less than half the total lost). Among those lands was the Paragon Ranch and half its coal rights (the other half went to the State of New Mexico according to terms of the San Juan Basin Wilderness Protection Act of 1984, which broke a stalemate over land transfer that followed Secretary of Interior James Watt's attempt virtually to give the coal away to several large corporate lease applicants) (Radford 1986:148–52, 221; Whitson 1985:394). The Paragon Ranch is south of Dinetah in the eastern Navajo country, the "national sacrifice area" for Carter and Reagan-era energy policy, where Navajo individual allottees and tribally owned (fee land) ranches are checkerboarded with BLM land and other non-Indian lands. Navajos may have used the lands in the Paragon for at least 200 years until the 1920s, when an Anglo rancher took possession of the land and kicked them out (York 1979:267–76; Kelley 1986a:25). When the Navajo Nation got the ranch in 1984, the descendants of the evictees hoped to regain the use of the land. But that evidently cannot be. For the Navajo Nation must repay the loan to the Navajo Rehabilitation Trust Fund by mining coal from the Paragon or using it to make money in some other way.

All these areas, of course, contain Navajo sacred landscapes, both recorded and unrecorded. In fact, most of the studies connected with coal development in the eastern Navajo country described in part II cover parts of the Paragon Ranch or surrounding tracts. These areas were all supposed to supply coal to a power plant that Public Service Company of New Mexico wanted to build on the Paragon Ranch before the Navajo Nation selected the land under terms of the Navajo-Hopi Land Settlement Act. The crane petroglyph site (see story, chapter 5) is on the Paragon, and the route of Changing Woman from Huerfano Mountain to the west may pass through it.

When the Navajo Nation government and various federal agencies plan developments on NPL and the 1934 Act Reservation, they must also work with residents in each affected chapter area (preferably organized into historic preservation committees) to fit proposed roads, utility lines, housing areas, and so forth into sacred landscapes with the least disturbance. More intensive measures may be necessary to cope with strip mining in the Paragon. Since many Navajos seem to be uncompromisingly opposed to strip mining, forming advisory committees may be extremely difficult unless the Navajo Nation can find a moneymaking alternative to strip mining.

In fact, the Navajo Nation is developing other plans, since right now there is little pressure from outside on the Navajo Nation government to generate power here, a respite that will probably last only as long as PNM has excess electrical generating capacity (Ward 1992). The Navajo Nation has recently formed a planning group to look at other possible uses, including the extraction of previously unrecoverable natural gas from coal seams, a practice which is booming in the surrounding region; an energy research institute; extraction of baked shale; grazing; a tourist complex (hotel, RV park, craft shop, guided tours of surrounding famous Chacoan Anasazi archaeological and Bisti paleontological sites); an educational complex (visitor center, roadside exhibits, primitive campground, research camp for archaeology and geology); or a movie location (Poster 1992). The surrounding chapters need to be represented in the planning group by people with ideas on how to structure the landscape of each alternative to allow local people to reintegrate the landscape into their customary activities.

Chambers-Sanders Trust Lands

The Navajo-Hopi Land Settlement Act and its 1980 amendments also brought the Navajo Nation this 570-square-mile area in eastern Arizona just south of the 1934 Act Reservation. Navajos were living here by the 1750s (Stokes and Smiley 1966), perhaps having fled from

Old Navajoland around Huerfano Mountain (see chapter 10, "Old Navajoland"). They continued to do so until the 1934 Arizona Navajo Boundary Act. As part of the federal effort to consolidate land into large management units that accompanied the stock reduction program and Taylor Grazing Act, this law also gave railroad land inside the boundary to the Navajo Nation in exchange for scattered small tracts allotted to individual Navajos outside the boundary in this area. The federal government then evicted the Navajo residents from their former allotments. The railroad soon sold the lands thus acquired to several ranchers, mostly non-Indian (Kelley 1987; Stokes and Smiley 1966; Navajo Nation n.d.a) Beginning in 1985, the ranchers sold the land to the Navajo Nation, although they have kept the mineral rights.

Descendants of the Navajos evicted in the 1930s, like descendants of the Paragon Ranch evictees, hoped the Navajo Nation's acquisition would right old wrongs and give them back their land, but that was not to be. The land was intended for Navajos evicted from HPL, and so far about two hundred families have been resettled there (Kelley 1987; Reid 1991a).

Because the original Navajo families have been cut off from this land for almost 60 years (at least for subsistence and residence), knowledge about sacred landscapes is in danger of being lost prematurely. Furthermore, rapid development of residential and grazing lands for families relocated from HPL threatens to disturb such places. The Office of Navajo-Hopi Indian Relocation (ONHIR) (formerly the Navajo-Hopi Indian Relocation Commission) is responsible for developing these lands. Since it is a federal agency, one would expect it to follow the National Historic Preservation Act, if not AIRFA, and to take into account the effect of its actions on cultural resources. The agency did almost nothing to identify Navajo sacred places (or those of Zunis or Hopis, which are also reportedly in the area), let alone whole customary landscapes. Because the development planned is intensive, an effort to identify sacred landscapes and plan around them should have covered the entire Chambers-Sanders Trust Lands before proceeding. Yet development is already well under way.

Belatedly, ONHIR has agreed to fund the Navajo Nation government to develop such a plan. One hopes that this plan will have guidance from former residents and their descendants, as well as other Indian communities that have used the area, to plan around intertribal sacred landscapes. Guidance should also come from relocatees from Hopi Partitioned Lands, since they may have started learning local stories and are already using the landscape for customary purposes. Many may already have known something about the landscape before they moved there, like an herbalist resident of HPL who told us she had checked out the area to see what medicinal plants might grow there. Relocatees have recently formed their own chapter, which ideally could form a customary land-use committee to work with planners.

The Navajo Forest

Efforts to identify sacred places in the Navajo Forest during the 1980s preceded heavy logging to supply rampant construction in Phoenix during the boom in urban real estate speculation, itself the result of Reagan-era deregulation of financial institutions. Environmental protection measures have been inadequate, according to residents, forest managers, and even workers at the sawmill that the Navajo Nation government owns. The demand for much of this lumber has dropped since the Savings and Loan crash of 1990. But the Navajo Nation is under much financial pressure to keep cutting and selling timber to the Navajo Nation sawmill partly because it needs the stumpage payments (now in arrears), partly because several hundred Navajo mill workers would perhaps lose their jobs, and partly because of poor management, according to a statement published by sawmill workers (*Navajo Times*, May 3, 1990, May 10, 1990, and Dec. 27, 1990).

The Navajo Nation Forest has a high concentration of mountain peaks and a wide range of plants, animals, and minerals used in ceremonies, a long history of Navajo residence, and many recorded sacred places, as even the limited work mentioned in part II shows, and our own ongoing review of published ceremonial stories confirms (see chapter 3, note 1). It therefore is likely to have a very high density of unrecorded sacred places and probably constitutes a single large sacred landscape as well.

Timber cutting and customary uses are not now well integrated, according to professional foresters (Einbender and Wood 1991; Einbender 1990). In 1989 and 1990, forestry student LeGrand Einbender and Navajo Nation government (Forestry Department) staff interviewed members of several dozen families who live in the Navajo Forest. They found that "Forest residents depend on these [customary] uses for both physical and spiritual subsistence"—grazing, wood for architecture, fuel wood, sacred places, foods, plants for ceremonies and medicines, materials for ceremonial items, and raw materials for handicrafts. About half the people interviewed said that their families have sacred places in the forest, and most collect plants for ceremonies, medicine, or both. Although Einbender and Wood report that most of the people they interviewed didn't think that logging had "greatly impacted" most customary uses, it was interfering with grazing. They also note that logging contributes to decreasing diversity of the ecosystem, which in the long run will "adversely affect these [customary] uses." Furthermore, almost all the people whom Einbender interviewed in 1990 expressed concerns that timber operations need to respect sacred places and leave them alone.

Einbender and Wood suggest that logging and customary uses of the Forest can coexist. "The traditional land ethic does not appear to prohibit logging operations, the earth is to provide for man." But they criticize the Navajo Nation government's present forest management plan because it has overemphasized timber production and "addressed traditional uses only superficially. The challenge for NFD [Navajo Forestry Department] is to consider the natural resource and cultural needs of the forest users." They recommend that Navajo Nation foresters "educate and work with land users" and that they adopt a more diversified land-use plan, which implies less logging.

Many forest residents show a greater sense of urgency about dangers to the traditional landscape than Einbender and Wood report. Organized community opposition stopped one plan to cut timber on a pair of well-known sacred buttes on Changing Woman's route to the west. This incident prompted the Navajo Nation, when it assumed responsibility for the archaeological surveys that the National Historic Preservation Act requires before each timber sale, to revive the practice (originally requested by the Medicine Men's Association) of interviewing residents and users of the tract to identify the sacred places that timber cutting or thinning crews should avoid. This effort, however, focuses on places more than landscapes.

Einbender and Wood see logging and customary uses as compatible—"This contentious situation is unfortunate since logging essentially complements grazing (reduced tree density should increase forage yield)"—and forest residents may, also, in principle. But some residents think that logging has been so excessive that it must stop for the foreseeable future so that the customary landscape can regenerate. Foresters counter that overgrazing by forest residents' stock impedes reforestation, a problem that Reno (1981:96–97) recognized a decade earlier, before the present round of heavy cutting. He suggested that allocating more forestry revenues to local communities would provide an incentive for residents to control grazing. Organized residents of several chapters in the Navajo Forest also insist that the Navajo Nation government do a better job of managing the forest to accommodate customary uses. The Navajo Nation government is now planning for the next ten years of forest management and has an "interdisciplinary" planning team, but community representation has been insufficient. According to a Resolution of the Tsaile-Wheatfields Chapter (March 18, 1990, passed by a vote of 49 to 0), among other deficiencies in forest management, there are

> No significant efforts by the department of Tribal Division of Resources, the Navajo Tribal Resources Committee and/or the Navajo Tribal Council to develop the governing policies and procedures applicable to cultural or traditional ties to places of special significance, no known initiative to identify and designate such areas and non-existence of protection and preservation policies in the Natural Resources Policies. . . .
> . . . It is time the local chapters be given some voice in the forestry programs; and . . . the allowable annual cut is extremely high and hereby demands a reduction rate; and . . . The . . . Chapter hereby respectfully requests that these concerns and/or needed programs be incorporated in the development of the next 10-year Forest Management Plan. (Tsaile-Wheatfields Chapter 1990)

While this resolution errs in stating that the Navajo Nation government's forestry program has taken "no known initiative to identify sacred places," the chapter members who voted on the resolution probably wouldn't have made this mistake if the actual efforts had reached enough people, including through presentations at chapter meetings. Probably the best way to protect not only isolated sacred places but the customary forest landscape and its continued use is to be sure that the 10-year planning group includes representatives of each chapter that lies within the forest, and that among these representatives are people concerned with cultural preservation.

TIMBER CUTTING IN THE NAVAJO FOREST

[The following letter to the Editor of the Navajo-Hopi Observer *appeared on August 5, 1992 (Begay and Suen-Redhouse 1992). The authors are members of Dine CARE, the most outspoken critics of the Navajo Nation government's management of the Navajo Nation Forest, particularly in relation to the customary-use landscape. Technical and financial details of forest management have been omitted here to make the authors' points about the sacred landscape stand out more clearly.]*

In 1880, the Bureau of Indian Affairs (BIA) Forestry Department began the logging business on Navajoland when they started timbering the ponderosa pine. Then in 1958, Navajo Forest Products Industries (NFPI) was established, a for-profit business. NFPI expanded their establishment by constructing an enormous plant at Navajo, New Mexico, in 1963, which allowed NFPI to begin operating 24 hours per day. To make any profit, the plant must at least have 40 million board feet of timber annually. Apparently, the limited commercial forest base was not realized. Nor were the 150 years it takes pine trees to mature. Again, NFPI borrowed money to scale down their equipment to cut the smaller trees. As a result, the Navajo forest is a shrinking forest.

The Navajo Nation Forestry Department has a ten-year forest management plan, which covers the time span between January 19[8]2 and December 1992. This plan calls for an annual allowable cut of 40 million board feet of timber. It also states that the pine trees would have a one-hundred-twenty-year cycle— allowing for them to be cut at one hundred twenty years old, and allow twenty years to elapse before re-entering into a compartment for further timbering.

There are 62 compartments with each compartment covering approximately 8,046 acres. Of the 62 compartments, 26 compartments were planned to be logged within the cycle of this ten-year plan. To bring in compartments that are not originally slated for cutting is also clearly stated as a violation. Areas to be avoided while timbering in these designated areas are riparian zones, areas of 40 percent or greater slopes and archaeological sites, sacred sites qualify under this clause.

However, NFPI has blatantly violated many of the regulations. In November of 1991, we realized that the ten-year forestry plan was literally completed, when it became apparent that the 26 compartments withdrawn to be logged were all cut. We also noticed NFPI's obtrusive logging practices. . . .

All this outright disregard for the environment is due to NFPI's many financial losses that [have] been jeopardizing its primary source of raw material. As of November of 1991, we learned that NFPI was in debt $21.8 million plus interest. NFPI owed $2.5 million to the Navajo Nation [government] for stumpage fees, $.8 million to the Navajo Nation for retirement benefits, $10.5 million to the Economic Development Administration (EDA) for the particle board plant and $8 million to Citibank for mill improvements.

Today, NFPI claims that they are only $10 million in debt. . . .

. . . Navajo Nation President Peterson Zah and the majority

of the Navajo Nation's Resources Committee [a standing committee of the Navajo Nation Council] were instrumental in relieving NFPI of its overdue financial obligations.

We started opposing the logging operations when it became evident that NFPI was bringing in compartments not planned to be timbered. . . . [Two compartments] are watersheds for Wheatfields Lake and Canyon de Chelly. Cutting in these areas would have significant impact on their water source [including increasing erosion in Canyon de Chelly and consequent damage to the cultural landscape there]. [Another] is . . . one of the few scenic lakeside areas, which has the potential to be a profitable recreation site. Compartment 34 . . . has quite a number of yellow pine, numerous sacred prayer offering sites and medicinal herbs. It is also the last green canopied area in the Chuska Mountains.

When we began approaching the public and the politicians in Window Rock with our concerns, there more or less was a turn of the shoulder—it seemed as though it was because our charges lacked "professional credibility." So, an assessment was done by a professional forester from Forest Trust. We were reaffirmed in our observations of NFPI's overcutting and offensive environmental indifference. NFPI's logging was leaving virtually no cover for wildlife. . . . The cutting was leaving only two to three seed trees per acre. . . . [From here, the story is almost like a modern version of the Twins' visit to their father, and the trials he put them through, if one substitutes "the Sun" for the Navajo Nation government and "the Twins" for the local residents.]

With [their] assessment, [the Twins] approached [the Sun] when the . . . timber sale [not included in the current ten-year plan] was proposed before them. . . .

When presented with [the Twins'] concerns, [the Sun] used [their] request for an Environmental Impact Statement (EIS) as propaganda—distorting it as a means which would result in livestock reduction for our elders. In December 1991 [the Sun] made a decision to allow the continuation of timbering in the Chuskas just to keep 400 people employed [at the mill and logging sites.] The [Sun] aligned with NFPI Board and Management to approve the [timber sale]. The final decision for approval rested with the BIA, who gave their approval with a decision of Finding of No Significant Impact (FONSI). The day after the BIA approval, NFPI began cutting. . . .

At this point, [the Twins] appealed the BIA's decision to approve the timber sale based on several reasons. . . . Cultural and spiritual concerns were also part of the reasons for appealing. When the appeal went into effect by the cease and desist order by BIA to stop the logging, [the Sun] enlisted the help of [Assistant Secretary of the Interior for Indian Affairs] Eddie Brown and his superiors . . . who then lifted the appeal. The only reason was to allow the 400 employees to continue working.

[The Twins'] next recourse was to file a lawsuit to halt logging. At that point, [the Sun] contacted [the Twins'] attorneys to freeze the lawsuit, so a compromise could be worked out. However, when a meeting was set for a compromise to be reached, there was no definite decision made by [the Sun].

Then, a meeting to negotiate was planned. . . . At this meeting [the Sun and NFPI personnel] tried to intimidate [the Twins] into giving in on the negotiations.

There were nine points to negotiate, three of which were non-negotiable. The first is to remove two non-Navajos from the Navajo Forestry Department and NFPI. The second is an EIS to be completed within a year. The third is to preserve Compartment 34 in its entirety as a cultural and religious reserve.

Currently, the lawsuit is still pending and no compromise has been reached. . . .

The Universe, Mother Earth, mountains, trees, herbs and wildlife are the core of Dine beliefs. President Zah said so when he said, "Respect should be given to a religion that does not involve going to church, one day a week, but which is based on the animals, the world and the universe, and whose church is the mountains, clouds and sky" at the American Indian Religious Freedom Summit in Albuquerque, New Mexico, on Nov. 22, 1991.

Yet, the bottom line is, our Navajo leaders have refused to conserve and preserve what is left of our few natural resources in the name of economic development.

[Since this letter appeared, the Navajo Nation government has started work on an environmental impact statement for the next ten-year plan, including a series of public meetings around Navajoland. Dine CARE remains critical of these efforts.]

Aneth Oil Field

The Aneth Oil Field is in the far northern part of the Navajo Nation in Utah. The first wells here date from the 1930s, but the field really began producing in 1957. The royalties historically have provided important revenue to the Navajo Nation government (Young 1978:152). Production, of course, has fluctuated with world and regional market conditions. Market upsurges have caused development intense enough to provoke local residents to protest that their community bears the costs without getting its fair share of the benefits. One of the most recent such incidents was a protest in part about the well pad that destroyed the medicinal plant bed.

> In a telephone interview late Sunday night, Yanua Morgan, speaking on behalf of her [husband's] 81-year-old [grandmother] Bessie Adakai Morgan, said the elder wants the oil company out of her grazing area located 13 miles northeast of Aneth Chapter. She never released her grazing permit so that the company can prepare for a drill site, she said.
>
> "She asked us to tell the company to stop the clearing because she collects herbs for her medicine from the spot, and she also uses the soil from there for sandpainting for various ceremonies," the younger Morgan said. (Reid 1990)

Development in this field is surging again, with several different operators drilling and installing new gathering systems cheek by jowl. Now each company does its own cultural resource inventories, with the result that impact assessment is strictly limited to each company's right-of-way and neither indirect impacts nor the cumulative effect of all companies are being addressed. Such intensive development, however, requires a single overall plan to try to fit the oil facilities around cultural landscapes. The inevitable damage to these landscapes, no matter how good the plan, requires that the planning group include a cross-section of local people, including the elderly, chapter officials, and families occupying the acreage to be developed. In a community where jobs and other oil-related income seem to have split many families, such a cooperative effort may be impossible (doubtless to the relief of the oil companies). Trying to do the right thing might nevertheless produce a worthwhile compromise.

Canyon de Chelly National Monument

We have described above what makes Canyon de Chelly National Monument a candidate for extraordinary protection measures—the enormous influx of tourists. (Monument Valley may also be a candidate, for similar reasons, although the park there is managed exclusively by the Navajo Nation rather than jointly by the Navajo Nation and National Park Service, as is Canyon de Chelly, and we are unaware of complaints by residents.) One resident reported that, a few years ago, fifty-five jeeps in one hour entered the canyon. The noise, invasions of privacy, traffic congestion, erosion of the canyon floor that serves as an increasingly treacherous roadway, all discourage many residents from prolonged stays in the canyon. So have Park Service requirements that residents have land-use permits. Also, many younger family members don't live in the canyon because it is isolated from the larger towns inside and outside the reservation, where even the impoverished can buy into modern consumer culture. The canyon may present an extreme example of how development (even a type considered potentially "low-impact") is disrupting Navajo customary uses of the land. For the canyon, according to many Navajos, forms one sacred landscape with a high density of places of special power, among which Navajos live, farm, and keep livestock. This quality, in fact, is what attracts so many tourists.

Like all the other areas described in this chapter and the next, the canyon needs a plan to try to integrate tourism into the customary use landscape with as little disruption as possible. At the same time, more of the money from tourists should go to canyon residents, not only those who work as independent guides and jewelry sellers, but also to those who need money for land maintenance and services that will help them sustain life in the canyon. The planning body must include both the local Navajo Guides Association and residents themselves, vested with decision-making authority.

This case is unusual in that the Monument Superintendent and his staff have tried to consult local residents in their planning. Their difficulties are probably prophetic for all the other areas discussed: divisions among residents manipulated (or even, to some extent created) by the businesses that profit most from uncontrolled development. The problem is often compounded when local and Navajo Nation government bodies, over which residents of the affected area have little influence, endorse these developments. Thus, a Monument staff proposal for zoning in the canyon to restrict tourist access to some of the most densely populated parts has apparently received mixed reactions from residents. This experience suggests that residents and other customary users need to be formally integrated into the planning process, not just through open public meetings, but through a formally constituted planning body, with representation carefully structured to balance potential conflicting factions.

10.

Endangered Landscapes outside Navajo Jurisdiction

Much of the customary Navajo homeland is beyond the jurisdiction of the Navajo Nation government. Figure 4 shows the locations of areas where Navajo customary landscapes are in greatest danger today. Tomorrow's endangered landscapes could be anywhere in this area.

Dinetah

This far northeastern part of Navajoland was the cradle of what we think of as Navajo culture. It is where the Navajos' Athabaskan ancestors apparently arrived when they moved into the Southwest, possibly during the 1400s or earlier. It is also the setting of most of the Navajo creation stories sketched in chapter 1.

OLD NAVAJOLAND

[Navajo political activist and historian John Redhouse (1985b:2–8) has sketched this landscape and its multifaceted importance in Navajo culture, reproduced with permission from John Redhouse. Bracketed material is our interpolation. Deletions are to limit length by not repeating stories given above. Readers are urged to consult the entire work.]

And so the People with five fingers lived at the junction of the west fork and east fork of the San Juan River. They hunted, gathered, and fished in the shadow of Wolf Creek Pass deep in the San Juan Mountains. Soon they moved to Chimney Rock and down the Piedra River to its confluence with the San Juan River. Here they wrote drawings of their migration on the rocks and cliffs so that future generations of Dine will always remember their tribal roots and destiny. . . .

From their emergence [from the lower worlds] at Hajinei to the cool water of To Aheedlii [junction of Los Pinos and San Juan rivers, now flooded by a water storage project], their migration trail had finally led them to the dawning of Dinetah— their promised Land in the Fourth World.

Mindful of their spiritual responsibility, the Children of Kayah, the To'aheedliinii clan, stayed at To' Aheedlii while the rest of The People moved into the rugged canyonlands and windswept mesas of the Dinetah Plateau in what is now northwestern New Mexico. . . .

First Man and First Woman lived in a hogan atop Dzil Na'oodilii (Huerfano Mesa). Early one morning First Man looked to the east and saw a dark cloud descend over Ch'ool'i'i (Governador Knob). Upon investigation of this phenomenon, he heard a baby crying [Changing Woman, who later gave birth to the Hero Twins, who] were sent to kill the monsters and make the world safe for present and future generations of Dine [Navajos]. . . . After slaying all the beasts, they went to To' Aheedlii, where they are enshrined today [petroglyphs inundated by Navajo Lake]. . . .

But by 1630, the armed and mounted Spanish cavalry had begun to launch slave raids into the heartland of Dinetah. That same year, Fray Alonso de Benavides noted in his Memorial that the Dine' were "very skilled farmers, for the word Navajo means 'large cultivated fields.'" After that, the people with five fingers became known as "Navajo-Apaches" or simply "Navajos." . . .

[After the Pueblo Indian Revolt of 1680 and Spanish Reconquest of the 1690s,] [w]hen the Spanish were not raiding them, the Navajos and Refugee Pueblos [Indians fleeing Spanish reconquest along the Rio Grande] lived peacefully in Dinetah. Here they farmed and built an advanced bicultural civilization in the Upper San Juan River valley and its tributary streams. A unique defense system was also established, with fortified pueblitos and hogans, high walls, and watchtowers for early warning and long distance communication. In addition, there were other advances made in architecture, pottery-making, rock art, and religious organization.

[Raids from the Utes and Comanches, partly stimulated by the Spanish slave trade, eventually drove the Navajos from Dinetah. Sedentary farming made them too vulnerable, and they came to depend more on herding sheep and goats captured from the Spanish, so that they were not such easy targets for raiders.] From 1775 to 1863, Dinetah remained largely unoccupied. Then fleeing from the advance of Colonel Kit Carson's Roundup in 1864, some Navajos retreated into the extensive canyonlands of their former homeland and hid until a peace treaty was signed between the United States government and the captive Navajo tribe of Indians at Fort Sumner, New Mexico four years later. The unequal Treaty of 1868 "gave" the Navajos a small reservation to the west and, within a few years, old Dinetah was opened up to the public domain. . . . [T]his energy-rich region is now under the colonial administration of the U.S. Bureau of Land Management and National Forest Service. . . .

. . . [I]n 1956, after overruling Navajo medicinemen's objections, the Federal Communications Commission licensed the construction of "an orgy" of microwave television towers and translator stations on Dzil Na'odilii. An access road was bulldozed up to the top and later a racetrack built near the center.

These are the developments mentioned in the preceding chapter that the Medicine Men's Association opposed. In the early 1960s, a windfall for Albuquerque real estate speculators came from the diversion of water from the San Juan into the Rio Grande drainage (incidentally supplying water to the Navajo Indian Irrigation Project, so that the Navajo Nation would consent to the limits on its unlitigated water rights as the deal required) (Kelley and Whiteley 1989:143; Reno 1981:46, 60). A component of this project, Navajo Dam, flooded an important part of Dinetah landscape, the river banks, including the

Twin War God shrine recorded by Van Valkenburgh for the Navajo Land Claim before the Indian Claims Commission. Dinetah has also, as Redhouse points out, sustained almost forty years of oil-and-gas development. Another round has already started with a new technology to pump natural gas (methane) from coal seams and a new (1991) pipeline that links Dinetah to east-west natural gas transmission lines across the southern edge of Navajoland. The pipeline companies are enlarging these, as well, evidently in a neck-and-neck race for the West Coast market. Vandalism of ancestral Navajo sites in Dinetah is therefore a growing emergency.

In an effort to salvage as many stories about the landscape as possible, Harry Walters, Director of the Ned Hatathle Museum at Navajo Community College, and pictograph specialists Harry and Sallie Hadlock, have brought medicine people to Dinetah to look at the pictographs and other Navajo archaeological sites—the pueblitos, fortifications, towers (Olin and Hadlock 1980). Further threatening this early Navajo heritage is the BLM's plan to "develop the recreational opportunities" of Dinetah for tourists. A mask recently auctioned at Sotheby's (the mask's purchaser, Elizabeth Sackler, deserves praise for offering to return it for Navajo use [Wallach 1991a, 1991b, 1991c]) may be an early Navajo ceremonial item looted from here.

Discussions about the mask (as reported by Wallach [1991a, b, c] and during various meetings that we attended) illustrate a range of Navajo interests in the cultural resources of Dinetah in general. Medicine people and other Navajos who saw the mask agree that it differs from masks now used in Navajo ceremonies. Some recalled as children seeing a similar mask in a particular nine-night ceremony supposedly no longer performed. Walters and anthropologist Jim Faris (personal communication, Aug. 28, 1991) say that the mask also resembles other masks, now in museum collections, that came from archaeological sites in Dinetah (Olin and Hadlock 1980:30), as well as masked figures in certain petroglyphs in Dinetah. The iconography in the Dinetah petroglyphs closely resembles that of sandpaintings used in Navajo ceremonies today or in those recorded in connection with Navajo ceremonies of the late nineteenth and early twentieth centuries. But Navajo custom has long prohibited making images on rocks for religious purposes. The source of these prohibitions is Blessingway (Wyman 1970:58–59).

Both the petroglyphs and the mask, then (not to mention the pueblitos) seem like the kind of things that, according to the people Farella consulted, have had their day but are now dead and best left alone. Indeed, this idea may have prompted some Navajos to say that the mask couldn't be used in ceremonies. But Walters felt that he wouldn't be violating his own understanding of Navajo custom to use the mask—and other Navajo cultural remains in Dinetah—to teach Navajo students about the evolution of Navajo culture. These things would still be part of Navajo life, not as they originally functioned, but to teach the old Navajo lesson that all things change.

The first thing decision makers should be doing is curbing vandalism. Anti-vandalism measures could include some sort of cooperative agreement between the Navajo Nation, the State of New Mexico, and BLM to provide heavy patrolling of the area. They could perhaps also involve the Dine Spiritual and Cultural Society, other interested practitioners, and the nearest Navajo chapters (Huerfano and Nageezi) in a site stewardship program. A cooperative agreement among the same parties should guide any archaeological and other field research.

Recording stories about the area before they are lost is also important. Medicine people and others in the nearby chapters (and presumably elsewhere) still seem to know a lot about the landscape. Many stories undoubtedly have already gone but may be worthwhile to reconstruct indirectly through combined study of archaeological remains, Navajo and Puebloan stories, and records. Some Navajos may not approve of such reconstructions, but others will probably consider them worthwhile. The insights and guidance of Navajos on all sides of these questions are essential.

To take these actions and, more important, incorporate them into a plan for protecting the whole Navajo landscape of Dinetah, the BLM should work with an advisory group of nearby Navajo residents, medicine people, the directors of the Ned Hatathle and Navajo Tribal Museums, and the Navajo Nation government. The plan should also encourage Navajo visits to Dinetah and especially use by medicine people.

Other Federal Lands outside
Navajo Nation Jurisdiction

The Navajo Nation is surrounded by land under the jurisdiction of the U.S. Forest Service, Bureau of Land Management, and National Park Service. These lands, like Dinetah, are under direct federal control (in contrast to land under the jurisdiction of the Navajo Nation government) and lie within the Navajo pre-conquest use area (see Figure 4). This land includes the Eastern Navajo or "checkerboard" area, where energy development proposals from the late 1970s-early 1980s have died down for the moment but will no doubt come back to life one way or another. Among the most powerful of the Navajo landscapes are those around the mountains of the four cardinal directions, which represent the outer limits of the Navajo homeland. All four are in outlying federal jurisdictions, mostly Forest Service.

The most heavily developed of these mountain landscapes consists of the San Francisco Peaks and surrounding smaller mountains, where a Forest Service lease for expanding the Snow Bowl ski resort drew protests as early as 1970 from Navajos, Hopis, Zunis, and Western Apaches, who hold the mountain sacred.

In 1977, the tribes took the Forest Service to federal court, claiming, among other things, that the San Francisco Peaks are eligible for the National Register of Historic Places because of their association with age-old religious activities, and that the development, by interfering with those activities, would compromise the qualities that make the Peaks eligible for the Register. The Forest Service and the Arizona State Historic Preservation Officer both contended that the Peaks are not eligible for the Register, although they did not consult the ultimate authority on eligibility, the Keeper of the National Register in the National Park Service in Washington, D. C. The final federal court ruling relating to the National Register declared the question of eligibility settled by the agreement of the Forest Service and State Historic Preservation Officer, thus allowing the expansion of the Snow Bowl. In 1983 and 1984, the Supreme Court refused to hear any aspects of this case (*Wilson v. Block;* Frisbie 1987:299–300, 380–84; Bell 1985:65).

After this defeat, largely to make a bulwark against further development, the Navajo Nation in 1984 acquired a Forest Service grazing lease for nearly all the land around the Peaks themselves, which are in a wilderness area. This leasehold, however, hasn't prevented such Forest Service proposals as more recreational facilities to accommodate the growing tourist business in the neighboring city of Flagstaff, more transcontinental natural gas pipeline construction (which will carry gas from Dinetah), and a telecommunications fiber-optic buried cable.

With Navajo Nation government help, developers on two separate occasions consulted Navajo medicine people about how the fiber-optic cable and the gas line respectively would affect the sacred qualities of the San Francisco Peaks. In both cases, medicine men asked to conduct Blessingway prayers at or near the construction site on the mountain and make offerings before construction. This practice is like making an offering to the inner forms of the mountain, plants, or whatever one wants to collect before collecting them—to "give something back" to the mountain when taking something away. One, if not both, medicine men evidently thought that, as a custodian of the landscape, he must at least pay respect to the mountain for damage he considered inevitable; one at least may have thought that the project would benefit the Navajo people (Downer and others 1993 [in press]).

On another occasion, after a public meeting in which Navajos, Zunis, and an Apache ceremonial practitioner had most strenuously opposed any more development on the San Francisco Peaks, the Forest Service (again assisted by the Navajo Nation government) worked with a Navajo medicine man who had spoken at the meeting to correct an overall plan for rerouting trails, modifying springs, and putting up fences so that these improvements could both serve the functions intended by the Forest Service and keep tourists away from places on the mountain that medicine people visit and use. The relevant Navajo Nation programs, unfortunately, often lack the wherewithal to follow up such consultations and keep after federal agencies to carry out Navajo recommendations.

Developments on both National Park Service and Bureau of Land Management land east and southeast of the Navajo Nation have also drawn protests from members of the Ramah Navajo Chapter, a small reservation southeast of the main Navajo Reservation. The NPS and BLM administer a National Monument/National Conservation Area, El Malpais, created by act of Congress in 1987, in a large lava flow that is also a self-contained sacred landscape for Navajos and for the Pueblos of Zuni, Laguna, and Acoma. The Ramah Navajo Chapter has opposed the BLM and NPS plans to expand the area's "recreational opportunities" to attract the tourists that businesses in nearby Grants, New Mexico, covet, after losing uranium mining around 1980. The Ramah Navajo people dispute the NPS's claims that the chapter has been involved in any meaningful planning of the monument (USDI Bureau of Land Management, Albuquerque District Office 1990 [April], 1991 [January]; USDI National Park Service 1990a [January], 1990b [October]).

Adding to the sting is the fact that the Navajo Nation government owned the land for a short time in the early 1990s, having bought it from a railroad land company to trade to the federal government for scattered tracts of BLM-administered land in the "national sacrifice area" to the north, occupied by Navajos who were in danger of eviction for coal mining. (They are still in danger, since the Navajo Nation didn't receive the mineral rights to these tracts and didn't get even the surface ownership of land many families occupy that coal companies had optioned between 1971 and 1973 as Preference Right Lease Applications during the 1971–1979 Congressionally imposed moratorium on coal leasing; these PRLAs in any case are exempt from surface user consent required by the Surface Mining Control and Reclamation Act of 1977 [Radford 1986:16, 43, 84–87; Kelley 1986a].)

EL MALPAIS

[The Ramah Navajo Chapter stated its concerns in a Resolution of January 13, 1989 (passed by a vote of 29 to 0), which is also of interest because it describes the components of a Navajo customary-use landscape (Ramah Navajo Chapter 1989).]

a. Because the Ramah Navajo Community was not informed about the El Malpais until nearly seven (7) months after the [authorizing] bill's passage by Congress, the community must be given adequate and reasonable time (i.e., September 1989) to examine the full impact of the El Malpais on the Ramah Navajo people and then to develop a response to issues regarding the Malpais.

b. The Ramah Navajo Community must be represented throughout the NPS-BLM planning process to develop a draft management plan for the Malpais. To facilitate the Ramah Navajo Community's participation, the BLM-NPS should provide funds for a liaison, appointed by the Ramah Navajo Chapter, to work with the community, to attend all meetings on the Malpais, and to be a contact person between the Ramah Navajo Community and the BLM-NPS.

c. The entire Malpais is very sacred to the Ramah Navajos. There must be no development near sacred sites to ensure privacy for Ramah Navajos carrying out traditional practices. These sites must be protected and left as they are.

d. Ramah Navajos must be allowed unlimited and unrestricted access to the El Malpais to gather plants, native foods, medicines and salt required for traditional purposes, to make sacred offerings, and to carry out other traditional cultural practices and uses.

e. Any evidence of Navajo habitation (log homes, forked stick hogans, horse and deer corrals, rock piles, fireplaces, burial sites, bones, etc.) must be left undisturbed and are not to be used in displays or referred to in NPS-BLM publications and other interpretative materials developed on the Malpais.

f. Offerings that are found on mountains and cinder cones in the Malpais must be left undisturbed, just as they are found. Feathers are not to be collected, but left where they are originally sighted. No offerings or feathers are to be used in any interpretative/museum displays or publications.

g. A consultative process regarding sacred areas and objects of special significance to the Ramah Navajos must be established by the Ramah Navajo Community and the NPS-BLM.

h. The Ramah Navajo Community must be involved in the planning and development of any interpretative and support materials about the Ramah area. The NPS-BLM should assist the community to locate funds to work on a community history, which would provide accurate information about the Ramah Navajos for interpretative displays and materials. The history project would be carried out by the Ramah Navajo Community to ensure the proper handling of sensitive information that is not for public dissemination.

i. The preparation of all interpretative materials about the Malpais should be done by native people, especially those from the Indian communities for whom the Malpais is a sacred area, and reviewed by these communities before dissemination. A review process to assess interpretative materials should be set up by the Ramah Navajo Community and the neighboring tribes impacted by the Malpais.

j. Species native to the Malpais, such as the bighorn sheep, should be reestablished if the natural environments to support such species presently exist or can be strengthened.

k. The Ramah Navajo Community should play an active role in the process of designing visitors' facilities in the Malpais, so that the buildings constructed will reflect the native people who have long inhabited the area and continue to do so today.

l. Because of the Ramah Navajo Community's expanding population and the need to reestablish its land base, landowners who will be exchanging, transferring, or selling their lands in the Malpais should not be allowed to buy or exchange land within the Ramah Navajo Community area.

m. The continual habitation of West Central New Mexico by Indian people is a primary reason for designating the Malpais as a natural and cultural resource. It is only fair that native people, facing 80% unemployment, should benefit directly from any development of the Malpais . . .

To deal with the new appropriators, the Ramah Navajo Chapter organized the Ramah Navajo History Committee, a group of elders who work with chapter officials to, among other things, advocate specific cultural preservation measures with the Navajo Nation government and outside authorities like the National Park Service, Bureau of Land Management, and corporate developers. We believe just about all chapters could benefit from organizing similar committees, some of which might work out of the senior citizens' programs that most chapters operate.

The Ramah Navajo Chapter is also protesting a coal mine (Fence Lake Project) proposed by Salt River Project (SRP), a major utility company based in Phoenix. SRP owns a power plant in the northwestern Navajo Reservation that uses Peabody coal from Black Mesa, as well as two other power plants south of the Navajo Nation that would use the coal from the proposed mine (these plants now use coal from another mine on Navajo lands, the McKinley Mine near the Navajo Nation capital of Window Rock, Arizona). The Fence Lake Mine is proposed on BLM land that is part of the customary, pre-conquest use areas of the Ramah Navajos and the Pueblos of Zuni and Acoma, and possibly some of the Hopis (Kelley 1988; USDI Bureau of Land Management, Las Cruces District Office 1990 [September]).

These federal agencies recognize that they must take into account how their various undertakings might affect places significant to Indians if they are to comply with the National Historic Preservation Act. Moreover, following the American Indian Religious Freedom Act of 1978, federal agencies were to develop policies to carry out the law's intent, to insure that American Indians can fully exercise their constitutional right to practice their customary religions. The need for such policies is evident from hearings in 1979 that the Federal Agencies Task Force held before making recommendations on how federal agencies could meet their new responsibilities under AIRFA. At these hearings, Navajos complained about: lack of access to animals for ceremonial use on federal lands; mineral resource development threats to sites; Forest Service personnel's rudeness to medicine men; lack of access to sacred sites; too many interrogations about herb gathering, and the lack of one permit to give a medicine person permanent access; ski development and non-Indian drinking and carousing at the San Francisco Peaks; non-indigenous plants used to reseed strip-mined areas driving out medicinal herbs; lack of access to Mount Taylor, Blanca Peak, and Hesperus Peak; (the need for?) a list of native flora at Black Mesa; the lack of consideration of AIRFA in the BLM environmental impact statement on strip mining in the Star Lake-Bisti areas; the lack of access to feathers; whites illegally in possession of eagle feathers; museums seizing artifacts; lack of access to museum personnel to petition for return of objects; missionary interference with traditional practices;

conflicts between traditional and non-traditional forms of government; the lack of bilingualism in southwestern federal agencies, which limits service to Indians; and the Task Force's failure to schedule hearings on the Navajo Reservation (U.S. Department of the Interior, Federal Agencies Task Force 1979: Appendix C).

The Task Force's recommendations most directly relevant to land included accommodation of native religious practices to the fullest possible extent under federal land and resource management statutes; appointment of American Indians to existing advisory boards on federal land and resource planning, management, and practices; and reserving and protecting federal areas of special religious significance to Indians (U.S. Department of Interior, Federal Agencies Task Force 1979:51–64).

But many federal agencies have yet to develop policies to carry out AIRFA, and those that have, like the National Park Service and the Bureau of Land Management, took a decade or more to come out with policies more modest than those that the Task Force report recommends. In 1980, the Medicine Men's Association said about AIRFA,

> It's like those agencies consult [us] because they have to. So they do a little of that, but they don't really care about our opinions, our concerns about protecting our sacred things; they just go right ahead with their plans while we are talking. Even the courts don't respect that Religious Freedom Act. Just look at the Peaks fight. . . . That Religious Freedom Act is just on paper. It has no teeth in it. (Frisbie 1987:378)

Frisbie (1987:397–98) suggests that in some ways Indians have been worse off with AIRFA than without it, even before a 1988 Supreme Court decision gutted it. To back up claims against federal agencies under AIRFA, Indians have had to reveal religious beliefs and practices that should be kept secret, yet AIRFA guaranteed no protections in exchange for these sacrifices. As mentioned in connection with Hopi Partitioned Lands, federal agencies also have tended to define Indian religious rights very narrowly as access to sacred places. The vagueness of the law allows them, furthermore, to place Indians in a double bind by saying that as long as they can use a place, there is no problem with access and therefore no basis for a claim, no matter how much development disrupts the condition of the place, and that if they aren't using a place (because access is difficult), then that may invalidate their claim that the place is important in their religion.

Federal courts also have been notoriously unsympathetic to Indian claims to stop developers on federal lands from desecrating sacred places. The crowning blow has been the 1988 Supreme Court decision about a Forest Service road in northern California, the Gasquet-Orleans

Road, which guts the already toothless AIRFA (*Lyng v. Northwest Indian Cemetery Protective Association* 1988). In this decision,

> The Forest Service proposed to build a six-mile paved logging road that would have opened the high country to commercial logging, destroying the isolation of the ceremonial sites of three tribes and introducing new processes of environmental degradation. . . . The Supreme Court, nevertheless, insisted on deciding the religious issues and ruled that even the Free Exercise clause did not prevent the government from using its property any way it saw fit. (Deloria 1991:2)

—as long as its property-managing acts didn't have the purpose of infringing on the religion and didn't force people to act against their religious beliefs (American Association for Indian Affairs 1990). In this case, because places are essential to Indian religious practice, the Constitutionally guaranteed freedom of religion came squarely against property rights, and, not surprisingly, property rights won. The Court was concerned that the religious practitioners' need for privacy and unspoiled surroundings "could easily require de facto beneficial ownership of some rather spacious tracts of private property" (*Lyng v. Northwest Cemetery Protective Association* 1988). Another example is the case of the San Francisco Peaks.

The medicine men's suit against the National Park Service about Rainbow Bridge National Monument is another example of judicial insensitivity (*Badonie v. Higginson* 1981). The medicine men claimed that the rising of Lake Powell under the arch, and the tourists who ride in on the water, disrupt certain religious acts around Rainbow Bridge on Park Service land, thereby infringing on their First Amendment religious rights. The medicine men originally filed suit a year before AIRFA but appealed their case after AIRFA. In 1981, the Supreme Court ruled against the medicine men. The court acknowledged that the religious rights of the medicine men had been violated, but that to correct the violation would require the drastic action of lowering the lake by half, thus jeopardizing the federal government's other compelling responsibilities of controlling water and producing power from Glen Canyon Dam (*Badonie v. Higginson* 1981). This decision shows how the federal government can use even an acknowledged violation of Indian religious rights to justify trampling on them further, by defining the action needed to restore those rights as being so drastic that it would interfere with other compelling government responsibilities. And since the 1988 Gasquet-Orleans road decision, the government hasn't even had to show that its other responsibilities are compelling.

The new Native American Graves Protection and Repatriation Act

(1990) (P.L. 101–601) is another federal law that vests ownership and control of human remains and various other cultural items in federally recognized tribes that meet certain qualifications (U.S. Congress 1990). This law is new, but stories are beginning to form around it (Kelley, Downer, and Roberts 1993).

Despite these laws, policies, and commitments, the federal agencies usually offer the Indians too little, too late, in the planning process. They usually say, "Here is our proposed developed landscape, but we can tinker with it a little here and there if you tell us where your sacred places are (but remember, they've got to be small)." Better protection would result if the agencies would say, "We know that large areas of this landscape have customary uses. We want to develop a project that has a specified set of components. Where can we put these various components with the least disruption to the customary-use landscape?"

If federal agencies are going to do more than token consultations with Indian communities, they must integrate representatives of those communities into their planning process rather than expecting the communities to wait patiently until the agency chooses to consult them, and then only about matters of the agency's own choosing. Such thorough integration is necessary if there is any hope of fitting agency plans into Indian customary-use landscapes to minimize the disturbance to those landscapes.

One promising vehicle may be the intertribal advisory group. The San Juan and Rio Grande National Forests in southwestern Colorado (Rocky Mountain Region) have organized such a group, although it hasn't become embedded in the planning structure (and as time goes by, one wonders why). Such groups would generally function at the level of the large administrative unit, such as whole National Forests or BLM districts (or might interlock to cover several large administrative areas of various federal agencies in a region, depending on the extent of the aboriginal use areas of the tribes represented). Smaller units like the San Francisco Peaks Ranger District and El Malpais, however, which have both dense sacred landscapes and a lot of pressure for intensive development, need their own boards.

Sacred Places on Private Land

Among the most recalcitrant problems of protecting sacred places are those on privately owned lands, which are often (but not always) beyond the reach of federal, state, and tribal laws. Two examples show that existing laws are neither entirely useless nor completely effective in backing intertribal and local Navajo initiatives to protect endangered sacred places on these lands.

Woodruff Butte is an isolated volcanic cone south of the Navajo Nation boundary. It is an important source of ceremonial plants for Navajos, Hopis, and Zunis, as well as figuring in Puebloan stories and in the origin stories of the Navajo Frenzyway, Waterway, and other ceremonial repertoires (see chapter 7). But as of this writing it remained in the hands of the descendant of an early Mormon settler of the adjoining village of Woodruff. In 1990, the owner leased the land to a gravel company for resurfacing a nearby federal highway. Residents of Woodruff sounded the alarm to the Hopis. They themselves said they were incensed at the defacement of a symbol of their own community origin, ignoring the irony that the settlement established the property rights that allowed the defacement they opposed. Both Woodruff residents and a lawyer for certain Hopi villages called the Navajo Nation government, and the alarm was also sounded at Zuni. The nearest Navajo community, Indian Wells Chapter, stated the following concerns in a resolution of August 19, 1990 (passed 34 to 0):

> 3. Woodruff Butte (Toh-ji-hwe-zho) is the originating place for highly sacred Navajo ceremonies, where only medicinem[e]n can go alone or with afflicted patients and is considered a prohibit[ed] sacred religious site to all other Navajo; and
> 4. Woodruff Butte (Toh-ji-hwe-zho) is where sacred herbs grow, medicine men provide offerings and prayers before the sacred herbs are collected for ceremonies to heal patients; and
> 5. Indian Wells community members are deeply concern[ed] and demand an end to the destruction of Woodruff Butte (Toh-ji-hwe-zho) a highly sacred religious site. (Indian Wells Chapter 1990)

Because the gravel was intended for a federally funded highway project, the responsible agency was required under the National Historic Preservation Act to see whether the proposed gravel mine would damage any cultural resources listed on or eligible for the National Register. Therefore an archaeologist surveyed the area, locating archaeological sites but neglecting to ask nearby Indian communities about the Butte's significance or to consult previous studies of Indian customs about the Butte's significance. When a State Historic Preservation Office staff member reviewed the report, he asked the Navajo, Hopi, and Zuni governments.

The protests of the three tribes led the archaeologist to amend his report and the State Historic Preservation Office to recommend that the highway project find another gravel source, which it did. The gravel supplier, however, found other clients not subject to federal law. The landowner later offered to sell the land to one or a group of the tribes, and began talks with the Hopi government, but with no result as of this writing. (Mitchell and King 1990; Morse 1990a, 1990b, 1991; Hardeen 1990, 1991; Zuni Tribal Council 1990; Navajo Nation Nation Historic Preservation Department 1990b). Meanwhile, mining continues to deface the butte. Tribal purchase in any event would set a bad precedent by encouraging near-bankrupt landowners to threaten sacred places to extort excessive payments from concerned Indian communities.

In 1991, a company proposed to put an asbestos dump on private land in the eastern Navajo country about four miles east of Huerfano Mountain, the home of Changing Woman on the southern edge of Dinetah. The dump site is near enough to the mountain to make a potent symbol of non-Indians polluting the core of the Navajo homeland and desecrating the core of Navajo beliefs. It is inside what one resident described as a sacred preserve around the mountain, the edge of which is marked by certain landmarks several miles in every direction and within which, "in the old days," Navajos weren't supposed to live. The site is also surrounded by the Nageezi Navajo Chapter area.

ASBESTOS WASTE DUMP COMING TO MY BACKYARD

[Nageezi Chapter resident Johnny Russell describes the customary-use landscape and the project's threat to it in this letter sent to the editors of local newspapers (Russell 1991).]

An Asbestos Waste Dump is coming to T'iistah Diiteeli (Spread out Cottonwoods) in the Blanco Canyon portion of Nageezi Chapter Community. Huerfano Mountain is less than 5 miles due west of the proposed landfill site which is 160 acres.

Huerfano Mountain is also known as Dzilth-Na-O-Dith-Hle, a sacred place for all Navajo people. Dzilth-Na-O-Dith-Hle is located 26 miles south of Bloomfield, New Mexico, and just east of New Mexico Highway 44.

We the people who live in Blanco Canyon area heard of the Asbestos waste landfill dump around the first part of March 1991. The company that is planning the landfill is ICU, which stands for Insulation Contracting Unlimited.

We passed a resolution at the Nageezi Chapter opposing the proposed asbestos waste landfill. The people at Carson Chapter passed a resolution too.

We have great-great grandparents who are buried in the area and other relatives too. Members of a Mexican family who ran a trading post at the site of the proposed landfill in the late 1880s are buried inside the 160-acre parcel. The foundations of the trading post building and other buildings still exist. The Mexican store owner's name was "Lomalo" (Romalo) Martinez. He was known to Navajos as 'Atsoo'ii, a Navajo word that stands for "tongue."

The area where the landfill is supposed to be located is covered with thirteen different natural herbs which are still used in Navajo ceremonies such as the Squaw Dance. The natural herbs help the sick recover and chase away evil spirits.

The area is also covered with remains of Navajo sheep camps, wind breaks, woodchip piles, and hogans. The hogans were blessed by medicine men before being completed. Just to the west of the proposed dump there is a standing sweat house.

Anasazi items including arrowheads, pottery and grinding stones are within the parcel.

The 160 acres is full of beautiful trees, natural herbs, cactus, and other plants including sagebrushes, as well as wildlife and petrified wood. The area is a rolling valley going down to the Blanco Wash. We have natural springs in the Blanco where we water our livestock. When it rains, it makes a run-off from the rolling valley to the Blanco Wash. Once in the Blanco, the run-off goes down the canyon where relatives have homes and graze livestock.

After the water runs through the Blanco Wash it joins with water in the Largo Wash. It soon goes down into the San Juan River and on west to Lake Powell.

We had a [Navajo Nation Council] Natural Resource Committee meeting at Dzilth-Na-O-Dith-Hle Boarding School. We met with the people from Window Rock and other local area residents. After the meeting we took a tour of the proposed landfill site with the Resource Committee. The Resource Committee thought that the site was supposed to be a flat place, but after seeing it their response was "what a beautiful place going to waste."

It was raining that day when we did the tour. The water was running off the valley into the Blanco Wash. After we left the area there was a beautiful rainbow sitting over the landfill site.

I'm writing this article because I sure do love my land and

country which my ancestors originally came from. It is sacred to me and all my families who come from T'iistah Diiteeli and elsewhere along Blanco Canyon. I am sure that other people who appreciate their land would fight for it. I respect that Grandma from Aneth, Utah, who fought to save her land and the natural herbs that grow in her area.

We the Navajos (Dine) can save our heritage if we fight for our land and not let the white people take over what we have. I would like for the Asbestos Waste Dump to go elsewhere, but not anyplace on our Navajo Reservation or on any other Indian reservation.

The Nageezi Chapter, the Navajo Nation government, the Dine Spiritual and Cultural Society, and Dine CARE (of Navajo Forest fame; see chapter 9) mobilized opposition to the project. Hazardous waste dumps require a state permit, and this permit application included an archaeological survey report for the tract to comply with state and federal laws (including the National Historic Preservation Act) that protect cultural resources. The survey was evidently deficient, however, for it didn't mention the Navajo sites or graves that local residents repeatedly wrote about and pointed out. The state delayed issuing the permit until after a public hearing to address the issues whether ICU had taken adequate measures to identify and protect cultural resources and to protect public well-being. ICU commissioned a second archaeological survey, which did record the Navajo and "Mexican" archaeological sites and graves but didn't record any sacred places (the archaeologists didn't interview local people).

The public hearing in spring of 1992, near the mountain itself, produced such an outpouring of indignant testimony from local Navajos and many others that, before the Navajo Nation's lawyers had a chance to parade all their expert witnesses, ICU asked for a break while they tried to find another site. As of this writing, the Navajo Nation and ICU are trying to work out an arrangement that would give the Navajo Nation title to the ICU site (Shebala 1991; Reid 1991b; Nageezi Chapter 1991 [April 21]; Taliman 1992; Linthicum 1992).

Public Buildings and Central Places

Throughout this work we have emphasized sacred places and customary-use landscapes, mainly because our own work and the work of others tells us that they are of greatest concern to Navajos. Another reason is that the questions how and even whether historic preservation laws and regulations should apply to sacred places are still debated, whereas those laws and regulations seem to apply routinely to "historic" public buildings. Yet Tuba City Cultural Projects, Inc., would probably dispute the last statement, as would other Navajo communities that have struggled, usually without success, to preserve and reuse these buildings. We therefore list central places with public buildings—administrative centers, schools, trading posts, chapter houses—as a category of place that needs extraordinary preservation measures, both because of demonstrated local Navajo desires for such preservation, and because the existing preservation framework has not worked well.

The main government and military compounds in the Navajo country are Fort Wingate, Crownpoint, and Shiprock, New Mexico, and Fort Defiance, Tuba City, Leupp, Chinle, and Window Rock, Arizona. The earliest compounds, Forts Defiance and Wingate, were originally military compounds established in 1851 and 1860, respectively, for deploying the troops that conquered the Navajos in 1864. The others were originally federal administrative outposts, many with schools and hospitals, established in the late nineteenth and early twentieth centuries, later becoming also centers for Navajo Nation government administration. Window Rock, the capital of the Navajo Nation government and the highest-level regional center of federal administration, was built in 1936. During the same period, the federal government and missions built boarding schools and, beginning in the 1930s, day schools, in various other, more isolated, places. These centers attracted trading posts, which proliferated also in many isolated parts of the Navajo Nation, most built and run by non-Indians after 1880 (although a few early traders were Navajos, and the remains of these trading posts are especially significant) (Van Valkenburgh 1941; Kelley 1985b).

Many early buildings of these types survive, but they tend to be poorly maintained. Their owners, whether federal government, Navajo Nation government, or private, usually prefer to demolish and replace them than to restore them. To make matters worse, even where the federal or Navajo Nation government abandons a building, local communities that want to restore and reuse it have found themselves thwarted by the complexities of transferring ownership before teenage gangs, partyers of all ages, and others who don't "subscribe to a preservation ethic" vandalize it beyond redemption.

This happened in Tuba City, an "oasis" in western Navajoland settled in 1875 by Mormons, who sold their property for the federal government to use as a compound when the government annexed the surrounding region to the Navajo Reservation in 1903. At various times before and after the Mormons, the locality was an oasis for Navajos, Hopis, Paiutes, and Havasupais from the Grand Canyon region (Van Valkenburgh 1941:109–10; Threinen 1981).

In 1987, a group of Navajo and non-Navajo residents formed Tuba City Cultural Projects, Inc., a private, non-profit organization whose goal was to acquire one of several abandoned government buildings to restore and use as a community museum and cultural center. A prime candidate was a former trading post, later school laundry, built in 1900. In 1991, after years of stalled negotiations with the BIA over title transfer, fire gutted the building and destroyed the roof. Stalled negotiations may result in a similar fate for three other possible choices, dormitories built in 1919, if not in their demolition by the BIA. Coconino County Supervisor Louise Yellowman, a member of Tuba City Cultural Projects, said,

> It hurt my heart to hear they want to demolish those buildings. . . . Nobody makes buildings like that anymore. Now, we live in trailers and it's just not the same. (Quoted by Bindell 1991)

The laundry building may still be restored (although the cost will be much higher), and Tuba City Cultural Projects is still, as of this writing, working with the BIA and the Navajo Nation to get the building. This example shows a clear need for, at a minimum, some sort of general agreement between the BIA and the Navajo Nation government on behalf of local community organizations to encourage and streamline the process of title transfer to local organizations that can meet reasonable standards for their ability to restore and maintain these buildings. Preserving and restoring historic buildings can have the added possible benefit of drawing tourists to them and away from sacred places where local people don't want them.

Future Developments

New expressions of concern about customary landscapes continue to emerge from the Navajo "grass roots." Organizations of Navajos like Tuba City Cultural Projects, the Ramah Navajo History Committee, the Dine Spiritual and Cultural Society, and Dine CARE are new. As such "grassroots" advocates of landscape preservation become more organized, their opponents will try to isolate them from a potentially sympathetic public by painting them as "special interests" insensitive to the needs of ordinary workers, as developers have characterized advocates of environmental protection elsewhere. Local workers and local advocates of landscape preservation in Navajoland, as elsewhere, have common goals (not to mention that most preservationists are employees, too)—for local people to have as much say in development planning as possible, to minimize exploitation of both local land and local workers, and to maintain the local "quality of life" in which people incorporate modern ways into Navajo customary life.

AN OPEN LETTER

[In an open letter of October 15, 1991, to the Navajo Nation President, members of Dine CARE (then calling themselves Dine BiWilderness Society) stated:]

With great concern we forward this letter to voice an ecological consciousness in hopes to impress an awareness in your heart.

Before, we Dine (the People) set forth our spiritual being on the surface of Nihima Nahasdzaan (Mother Earth), the Diyin Dine'e (Holy People) enacted laws for us to ensure a harmonious coexistence with nature through a strong understanding of beliefs. The gods set prophecies through time to which we respond with respect. Precedent to our time, nihastoiyee (our forefathers) conducted ceremonies to request guidance and protection of the Diyin Dine'e. Through that profound relationship based on kinship and reciprocity established with the Diyin Dine'e, we show reverence and appreciation by process of Naa'iiniih doo nitl'iz neha'niil (offering of pollen or white/yellow corn in the morning and offering precious stones).

Thus, we were empowered by the Diyin Dine'e through nihiyiin, nihisodizin doo nihe'oodla' (our spiritual songs, prayers and beliefs) to implement our role as the caretakers of Nihima Nahasdzaan and Ya dilhil Nihitaa' (Father Sky). One of the most important beliefs with the Dine is, there is a cyclical interdependence deeply rooted in knowledge intricately webbed in taboos, symbolisms, songs, prayers and ceremonies between the Dine and all the other nihokaa' naaldeehii and nanise'ii (living creatures and plants). Once, we often heard nihicheii doo nihimasani (grandfather and grandmother) advising us, "Shoo, shiyazhi, eii doo akot'ee da. Kojigo ei ya'at'eeh." (My child, that is not wise. This is the way.)

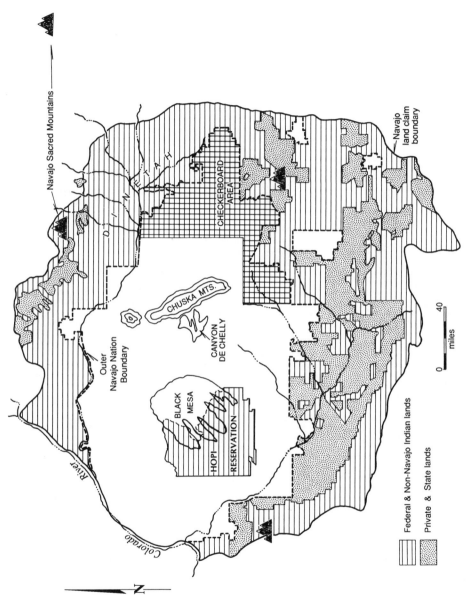

Figure 4. Lands in Navajo aboriginal use area outside Navajo Nation jurisdiction.

PART FOUR

HIDDEN

AND

MANIFEST

LANDSCAPES

IN

STORIES

11.

Analytical Framework

The first three sections of this book show that places important to Navajos are parts of larger landscapes. Navajos use these landscapes for a whole range of customary purposes. They tell stories about the landscapes that teach, guide, and justify various activities in various parts of the landscape. These stories are about all kinds of things—the origins of the present world, the Navajo and other peoples, Navajo customs; family chronicles; encounters, both hostile and friendly, between Navajos and other Indians and non-Indian colonizers; interaction, both long ago and recent, between particular Navajos and the immortals who inhabit the land, and so forth. They define, "construct" the landscape by telling, explicitly or implicitly, about different places on the landscape and how each relates to the whole. The stories map the place and the landscape onto a dense structure of powerful cultural symbols, images, and beliefs that give meaning to that landscape and place. When one asks people to identify culturally significant places, many respond with the statement that "the whole land is sacred" and then tell, or at least refer to, some of the stories that define the landscape.

People interviewed also say that disturbance of these landscapes will speed the loss of Navajo stories and culture, which many feel is imminent under the weight of "economic development." The stories and the land are not only powerful symbols, but also constituents, of Navajo ethnicity.

In part IV, we look more closely at how these stories define the landscape and map it onto systems of symbols and beliefs. The stories do a lot of this defining and mapping only implicitly. In this chapter, therefore, we discuss our framework for bringing out possible hidden meanings. In chapter 12 we analyze two very short stories about places to show concretely how such stories can define whole landscapes around each place and invest the landscape with meaning.

These stories, and most others reproduced throughout this book (especially those in parts I and II) are constructed, obviously, by their tellers. But they are also built from elements that generations have passed down. Therefore, they might contain some information that the teller may not be aware of. Included in this information may be that immortal figures, episodes, and symbolism in a Navajo story may also occur in the stories of neighboring Zunis, Hopis, other Puebloans, Apaches, and so forth. Chapter 13 uses one of the short stories from chapter 12 to make this point. Many storytellers are aware of these common story elements and beliefs. How can these stories contain so much "non-Navajo" material and still contribute to Navajo ethnic identity, and their loss indicate the loss of that identity? Chapters 13 and 14 address this question. The answer we propose involves the emergence of the Navajos as a distinct ethnic group forged in the crucible of Spanish rule from pieces of many disparate communities, mainly Puebloan and Athabaskan. The story we construct suggests the possibility of a nativistic movement to forge the various stories and customs of these refugees from Spanish rule into a coherent belief system to help unite these resisters, fighters for the land, at a time when organization and unity were essential for survival. A similar movement is the one that Gill sees today, in Indians of various tribes forging an intertribal belief system centered on "Mother Earth" to unite them and set them apart from the "European Americans" (or, from our viewpoint, the land-, resource-, and market-hungry corporations and their governmental allies) against whom they are still struggling to control what little land (and its cultural associations—the cultural guides to its customary use) they have left. Our story involves the Anasazis, ancestors of many (perhaps most) of the groups who joined to become Navajos, and the puzzle of why many Navajos see little continuity between the Anasazis and themselves.

To be told properly, this story needs an entire book. But we want at least to sketch it here because it answers the lament that has grown louder as this book has progressed: how Navajo ways can be kept alive in the face of ever-growing economic development. Our story supports the insight of "grassroots" people that they themselves (not just their government) must keep control of the land if their stories, customs, and ways of life are to stay alive. When people succeed in holding the land, as the diverse ragtag bands that coalesced to form the formidable Navajo tribe of the seventeenth, eighteenth, and nineteenth centuries did, they can incorporate new things from their would-be rulers without being swamped. The culture changes are part of life. But change doesn't have to come by throwing out old ways like disposable diapers. It can come by renewing and recycling old ways and integrating the new among them.

Stories from the Past Have Hidden Meanings

Information in stories that generations have passed down by word of mouth is often given poetically through symbolism, and figures of speech like metaphor and metonymy. If people are to remember and pass down by word of mouth the accumulated knowledge of generations, they must compress it. Figurative language does that. So do the common practices of mapping stories onto the landscape, tying them to music, fitting them into standard plots of action, and associating story elements with ceremonial and other items that are assumed to influence the perceptible world through the same mechanisms that cause metaphor and metonymy to evoke ideas or images in one's mind—the interchangeability of things that resemble each other, the influence that two things once physically connected can exert on each other when physically separated (Basso 1990 [1983]; Connerton 1989; Foley 1988; Schoepfle and others 1979).

Two aspects of generations-old stories about the past, especially "origin myths," that many scholars consider distinctive, are the character of time and its association with religion. Many scholars characterize time in such stories as, to use Eliade's (1965:ix) terms, "mythical," which they contrast with "historical" time. Indeed, Eliade implicitly associates "mythical" time with religion by characterizing "historical" time as "profane." He then places the traditions of "archaic" or "primitive" societies on the "mythical" time—religious content side—thereby contrasting them with so-called modern societies.

These dichotomies seem false to us because of the way we see the nature of stories about the past. For us, like Gill, such stories try to make sense of information about, or evidence of, the human past. The evidence comes in many forms—archaeological deposits, other past human changes of the landscape, architecture, myths, stories, even riddles and rhymes, music, rituals (all the way from large-scale public religious or commemorative ceremonies down to seemingly trivial, stereotyped practices like table manners), documents, "history books," and so forth. Some of this evidence itself consists of stories like cosmogonies, documents, or history books, for example. Other evidence ordinarily doesn't, such as archaeological deposits.

In all societies, people interpret evidence about the past within their own contemporary frames of reference. These interpretations express, either openly or covertly, "the conflicts which dominate our lives and symbols of their resolution" (Holmes 1989:30). A particular type of story about the past—say, "myths," national history textbooks—that is made or handed down by a particular part of a society—elders, "the state"—is bound to reflect, among much else, the concerns of its creator-custodians. These stories are likely, for instance, to validate the status of the creator-custodians by grounding that status in some kind of beginning—the origin of the world, the founding charter of the state. Stories about the past may also contain accumulated knowledge of former generations that is a true help to individual and group survival. Stories about the past grow in these and many other ways from the material and social conditions of the lives of the people who make and use those histories (Campbell 1969 [1959]:36–131; Connerton 1989; Detienne 1986 [1981]:22–42, 127; Ewen 1988; Gal 1989; Hanks 1989:118–19; Althusser 1969, 1971).

In "archaic" or "primitive" traditions, Eliade (1965), like many other scholars, observes "archetypes"—stereotyped narratives, or narrative structures or outlines, into which people mold evidence of the past (see also Connerton 1989:44; Doe 1988:204–207; Foley 1988:47). Many traditions even explicitly state that at the beginning of things, the creators had models of all things, and life must replicate these models to go on. In some societies, people use tiny replicas of game animals, for instance, along with procedures that the creators originally dictated, to renew game (see also Chapter 5, "The Origin of Horses"). In others, people engage in often highly ritualized political acts to bring a deviant national government back to the form that they think the nation's constitution dictates. To us, all the models here are "archetypes." We believe that all stories about the past interpret evidence of the past using some kind of preconceived patterns that reflect the interests and needs of the creators-custodians of those stories. Those patterns may be anything from Eliade's "archetypes" to an anthropologist's "model" of culture change.

We don't deny that there are real differences among different kinds of stories about the past—for example, between "myths," like the Navajo creation stories sketched in chapter 1, and scholarly chronicles like the story of Navajo encounters with colonialism later in the same chapter. But we think that the apparent qualitative difference in the character of time and the association with religion are really in large part differences in the degree of compression, mentioned above, which stories passed down orally need much more than do written stories. It should be clear from the preceding paragraph that we don't see stories passed down orally as simply telescoped versions of written chronicles of observed events, let alone as "just-so" stories or naive explanations of natural phenomena. We see stories passed down orally as highly compressed interpretations of evidence of people's past in a way relevant to their present lives.

In learning these stories, people learn the ideas associated with figures of speech, names, and terms, by hearing those figures, names, and terms used recurrently by certain people in specific times, places, events, and social situations along with certain other verbal symbols, objects, acts, and concepts. These associations may be so deeply ingrained in most people that they can't explain them, any more than most people can explain the grammatical rules of their native language. By learning what people associate with a particular name, term, or phrase, an outsider can guess at its possible range of deeper meanings to the people themselves, recognizing that no two members of the society will have exactly the same range of associations with a particular name, term, or phrase, because no two people have identical learning experiences (Doe 1988:188–96). The more of the relevant experiences people share, however, the more their interpretations will have in common.

Placing the Place in the Past and in the Landscape

Many decision makers, such as bureaucrats who are responsible for deciding whether a place is "significant" enough to be "worthy of preservation," don't accept the idea that such stories make up a proper framework for establishing the significance of these places. Yet even if one does accept that framework, what people say about the place may not relate it to stories about the past explicitly, but only implicitly. Nevertheless, one can learn something about how someone places the significant place in a landscape and in the past by the overall structure of the person's statement about the place and by identifying the figurative or symbolic elements of the statement—the parts of the statement most heavily freighted with connotations—and the ideas associated with those elements. One must learn from other stories and statements what ideas are associated with particular elements.[1]

The next two chapters offer examples of the analytical convolutions ("semiotic" and "hermeneutic" analyses) sometimes needed to connect what people say about a place to stories about the past. Semiotics and hermeneutics may seem very esoteric tools for an applied anthropologist, but the methods can be straightforward. Our analytical methods consist mainly of taking a statement and looking at the elements that seem to have the most unstated cultural associations. These may be virtually all the noun phrases in a very compressed statement, or only the elements embellished in some way, such as by rhetorical or poetic devices. We look at how those elements may be interrelated through association with a particular symbol (color, direction, and place are common in Navajo stories), at how the internal structure of the statement interrelates those elements, and at the situation in which the statement was given (Hanks 1989:101–17).

A cautionary note: because stories about the past in oral form reflect contemporary concerns, they are likely to differ in each telling (Foley 1988). Therefore the notion of one authoritative version is decidedly unsophisticated. Decision makers must abandon the quest for the chimerical authoritative version on which to base judgments about the "significance" of a place.

12.

Hidden and Manifest Landscapes in Two Stories

Both stories in this chapter were given to us in similar settings—small gatherings at the homes of Navajos still living on Hopi Partitioned Lands where people could tell us about Navajo sacred places on HPL for the study mentioned in part II. Each teller intended to communicate the importance of a particular place. Both imply more than they state about how the place fits into a larger landscape and what the other parts of that landscape are. We will discuss each of these two short, very compressed stories to bring out its most obvious implications. Since each teller gave his story as part of a more general statement, we also summarize those statements.

A close analysis of the larger statements isn't necessary to make our point about how stories place a significant place in a particular landscape through implication and figurative language. But certain differences between the two statements are worth noting here. The first statement validates the story about the place with the kind of remarks that Gill notes in Indians' statements to "European-Americans" to validate Indian land rights (see chapter 6). The second, in contrast, validates the story about the place with a simple, factual chronicle of the teller's family's residence on the land, their sufferings in defense of their land rights, and his knowledge as a medicine man. Both statements seem consciously pitched at the non-Indian audience for whom everyone knew we were writing our study. The statements seem intended to communicate directly, once translated into English, with relatively little cultural interpretation. But the first speaker tries to do this by incorporating the widespread pan-Indian form of discourse that Gill describes, and interpolates symbols and other allusions to Navajo beliefs to make the statement relevant to the virtually all-Navajo audience at hand. The second speaker avoids these complexities.

JESSE BIAKEDDY: BIG MOUNTAIN

[Mr. Biakeddy's statement is from May 1991. Translation by Harris Francis, reproduced with Mr. Biakeddy's consent. We have added explanatory information enclosed by brackets. Mr. Biakeddy asked us to add that he is a "Dineh (Navajo) Indian man who believes Dineh orthodox religion [and] has knowledge of North American Indian Emergence and Universal Creation. [He] learned sing [ceremonial repertoire] from his dad, Begashi Beahe Biakeddy, and grandparents. [He is] a Korean War veteran, disabled, [and was] born and raised at Big Mountain."]

Up on top of Big Mountain there is a rock-pile shrine. When people went to Fort Sumner away from the Four Sacred Mountains, they went across Buffalo Pass where the automobile road goes. Protection prayers are made at this shrine. The Lukachukai Mountains are the male mountain and Black Mesa is the female mountain. We will not leave this Big Mountain area because of our religion.

[Later at the same meeting, Mr. Biakeddy addressed the group as follows:] Why we are going to stay here: 1. Religion. 2. The land. 3. We must give up something to our Hopi brothers. Our ancestors went to Fort Sumner [in 1864, where Navajos were imprisoned by the U.S. government] with Goma'a [Ganado Mucho, a Navajo headman]. We live according to customs that are in harmony with the earth, according to Blessingway. The way I learned, there is no death. On top of Big Mountain there is a house facing east. The door will open. It is Be-'ochidi, they say [a male-female deity associated with creation of game and horses, and with the moon; fair skinned and red-haired because he was the son of the Sun, he therefore has sometimes been identified with Christian deities and also with a fair-skinned Aztec ("Mexican") deity, Quetzalcoatl (Reichard 1963 [1950]:386-90)]. He commanded the wild animals on this continent. He travelled through Navajoland: [names of places along east-west alignment mentioned in chapter 7 that may relate to the equinoxes]. Window Rock, Hopis, Washington, the Supreme Court—let everyone know, we want to live in peace. Medicine men from Bodaway [far northwest reservation] and other parts of Navajoland come here to do ceremonies. Fingerprints and footprints [whorls where life essence—wind, breath—can enter and leave the body; like other things in spiral form—whirlwinds, whirlpools—they are associated with the transformation between alive and dead] are the starting points from which each person grows, the prints of our Creator. Be-'ochidi's house on the mountain is very much decorated. You're not supposed to take weapons, arrowheads to this sacred place. Where prayers are offered, do not leave traces. The Dine people have lived on the Big Mountain area longer than any other people in the world. If we are removed, a terrible thing will happen. No telling what it will be—disease, wind, drought. We trust in the federal government to correct its mistake. We also trust our Navajo Nation government, and the Hopis, our dearly beloved brothers—their religion is the same as ours. [For example, symbols and ceremonial acts associated with Be'ochidi are like those associated with two closely linked Hopi deities, Muyingwa and Taiowa, as described by Clemmer (1991:64-65).] When we do ask to stay here in peace on our ancestral land, we must give something to our Hopi brothers from our hearts and our ceremonies so that they will give us our land back.

We will discuss only the first part (paragraph), which is specifically about Big Mountain. It clearly shows that Big Mountain is related to Navajo beliefs and to a story—probably a story about the past. Just what story, however, the speaker does not explain. The statement also implies some connection of Big Mountain with an event, "when the people went to Fort Sumner." The juxtaposition of references to Big Mountain and references to other places implies some connection among those places. To understand the nature of these connections, one must ask the speaker to explain them (a process probably as tedious to the interviewer as to the speaker), or turn to geography and other records of Navajo beliefs and stories.

The reference to Fort Sumner concerns a documented event, the conquest of the Navajo people by the U.S. Army in 1863–64, and the exile to Fort Sumner of Navajos who surrendered. The reference to the shrine and protection prayers involves simultaneously Fort Sumner-period warfare and religious practices rooted in "mythology" related to warfare and to the Navajo creation stories (Wood and Vannette 1979; Reichard 1963 [1950]:594; Luckert 1977:72-87).

We have already mentioned how, during raids and warfare in pre-Fort Sumner times, and even into the early twentieth century, people living around a mountain massif would flee to its high places. People all over Navajoland have told us they still visit the tops of these mountains to pray for protection, especially when they are about to travel far from home (as during military service). Trail shrines are also common along pre-conquest routes across the region, where one offers a rock and twig with a prayer for well-being before moving on (Van Valkenburgh 1940). People have also told us that these shrines restrict certain movements of groups carrying the ceremonial stick in the Enemyway, a major Navajo ceremony rooted in warfare (see Reginald Nabahe statement in chapter 5 and Haile [1938:72-73]). Protection prayers are related to the hero twin, Monster Slayer (Luckert 1977:72-81). Evoking him also evokes his whole story, which includes his birth and upbringing in the creation stories (see Sylvia Manygoats statement in chapter 3 and Reginald Nabahe statement in chapter 5); and his role in the story of the origin of the Enemy Way (Haile 1938:91-218).

We have mentioned the four sacred mountains and how they figure in the stories of the emergence, Blessingway ceremonial repertoire, and a multitude of natural sources of power that make them symbols of the organization of the natural world, the Navajo people and their territory. If mountains in general are among the most powerful types of places, these mountains are the most powerful of mountains. References to the Lukachukai Mountains and Black Mesa also evoke the stories about the emergence and about Blessingway, which includes songs or prayers that refer to these mountains (Wyman 1970:147-69; Van Valkenburgh 1941:41-42, 1974:184). The Lukachukai Mountains represent a male figure, associated with valuables (cloth, jewels) and Black Mesa (together with Navajo Mountain and the volcanic buttes around Star Mountain) represents a female figure, associated with pollen, the substance that Navajos offer to the Holy People in almost every prayer, and which many Navajos carry in a small pouch that has been blessed with Blessingway prayers.

The overall structure of the statement is also important because it interrelates all these elements and their connotations. We have heard narratives organized like this one very often in Navajoland. The statement is not explicitly a sequence of events that most people would call a "story," with locations mentioned in connection with each event. Instead, the speaker mentions places in order of their geographical scale and the scale of the group land base with which each place is associated.[1]

The four sacred mountains surround an area in the middle of which lie the Lukachukai Mountains and Black Mesa, and in the middle of Black Mesa is Big Mountain. The sequence of landmarks is also a nested series associated with progressively smaller social groups, from the entire Navajo Nation associated with the four sacred mountains to the loosely organized network of extended families that occupy neighboring (sometimes interlocking) patches of land surrounding Big Mountain (see also discussion of study by Vannette and Wood [1979] about Big Mountain, part II).

Mentioning the landbases in this sequence has the power to evoke (without explicitly mentioning) the series of social groups and the sequence of events in the emergence and Blessingway stories that correspond to the creation of each group in the series. The land was created before the Navajo people (symbolized by the four sacred mountains), who existed as human beings before becoming differentiated into (or absorbing people from various ethnic groups into) the full range of clans. The members of each clan in a particular locality then formed the core of an extended family; hundreds of these families occupy the Lukachukai Mountains and Black Mesa, and dozens occupy Big Mountain. These extended families, and the localized part of a clan at the core of each, existed before the particular family members who settled the present land base of the speaker's immediate family.

The sequence of places also encompasses more recent time because forebears of at least some Big Mountain residents moved seasonally between the Lukachukai Mountains and Black Mesa (Left-Handed 1967:22; Mitchell 1978:38). As the descendants of the early people have filled up and subdivided the land, however, families have become increasingly localized around the part of Black Mesa known as Big Mountain. The structure of this story also implies that the bonds between the Navajos and their land are the "right" state of affairs. The order in which the speaker mentions places—first symbols of the Navajo homeland (landmark) and people's recognition of their bonds (shrine), next reference to their removal by the U.S. government (Fort Sumner), then a repetition of symbols of the Navajo homeland—parallels the documented sequence of the temporary removal. The speaker brackets the reference to the removal with allusions to protection prayers and symbols that evoke Navajo origins and the web of interconnections among the Navajos, their deities, and the land. He thereby plants the idea that the persistence of the Navajos on their land is the morally imperative way foreordained since creation. Mr. Biakeddy delivered this statement at a meeting about the so-called Navajo-Hopi land dispute. He was marshaling the whole interrelated system of symbols and allusions toward this most important point.

This story, then, interrelates the speaker, his home, the Navajo social structure, the land, the origin of the present world, various Navajo deities, and the idea that these relations are morally imperative. By comparing the length of the original statement to the length of this sketchy explication, one can see how compact a speaker can make a statement, simply by naming places, events, people, and other things dense with unspoken cultural meanings that speaker and listeners share.

JOHN YAZZIE: WHERE WHITESHELL WOMAN STOPPED FOR LUNCH

[Mr. Yazzie spoke to us and a small group in June 1991. Translation by Harris Francis, reproduced with Mr. Yazzie's consent.]

My family has been moved several times over an area with a ten-mile radius. We used to live in District 6 [U.S. Soil Conservation Service district reserved for exclusive Hopi use], and when the boundary was established [1943], we were given five days to get out. Three days after the deadline, my mother was put in jail in Keams Canyon [federal government compound in the 1882 Reservation] for three days. We had to pay a fine of $300 to the range patrol. This series of moves has deeply damaged our family. Everywhere we have lived, there have been places where people have gathered medicinal things and offered prayers with corn pollen and precious stones. We have known this place for a long time and our forebears have lived here for a long time. We have moved through these places to here. About thirty-four years ago [the year before the Hopi Tribe filed the *Healing v. Jones* lawsuit], the [District 6] fence was put up. We would build sweathouses, sheep corrals, ramadas, cornfields, dwellings, and other things to make our living, then we would have to move again. We used to live at a place called Strong Cedar Tree. We just lived in a ramada there. For ten years we suffered there. All this happened when I was a boy. When we moved here [Sand Springs], I met my wife.

When I was thirteen years old I started learning traditional ceremonies, including protection prayers, uses of different medicines. That's how we used to live. Today my work is zaa'nil [a procedure involving preparation of balls of medicine in a container of a specific material that itself has power and then giving them to the patient to swallow, all accompanied by songs and prayers]. I know all the places where prayers have been offered with corn pollen and sacred stones.

[Mr. Yazzie then turned to our map and told us about several places, including the following:]

[Gives name of place.] This very sacred place is a stopping place of Whiteshell Woman. She was travelling from the Emergence Place on her final trip westward to the Ocean. She stopped here for her lunch of blue corn bread, and the crumbs turned into turquoise. [Another speaker, interrupting: She stuck her planting stick into the ground and made springs. Today this is the only place for miles around where the water comes up by itself.]

We heard an almost identical version of the story about Whiteshell Woman's stopping place during the thirteen-chapter project, except that the name of Changing Woman was used instead of Whiteshell Woman, and the stopping place was a different place. How is one to understand the significance of the place that this story is about? First one would want to know who is Whiteshell Woman. It is also clear that this story is part of a larger story, the story of her trip to the ocean, and the place is part of a larger landscape, the route of Whiteshell Woman from the Emergence Place to the ocean. One would therefore want to know about the larger story and the landscape.

One can answer these questions, again, both by asking the person who told this little story and by consulting the extensive body of Navajo stories already recorded. The creation stories, many of which are included in various statements reproduced throughout this book and which are summarized in chapter 1, contain many of the answers. This is because Whiteshell Woman is considered by many to be the same as Changing Woman, whose story culminates the creation story. Even if one doesn't consider Whiteshell Woman the same as Changing Woman, her story closely parallels that of Changing Woman.

The clearest significance of this story is like that of Jesse Biakeddy's story about Big Mountain. It interrelates a landmark that symbolizes the speaker's home; the Navajo origin story; a symbol of Navajoland in general, the east-west route across it; travel by Navajos (here, a Holy

Person) outside Navajoland and their ultimate return to Navajoland, thus establishing the inevitability of Navajos living on their land. This story, like the first one, is like an "abstract of title" in a belief system passed down by word of mouth that doesn't distinguish sacred from profane. We believe that this story would evoke these associations in most Navajos familiar with the general outlines of the creation stories.

Other possible associations with the elements of this story are perhaps more esoteric. Reichard (1963 [1950]) provides the handiest compilation of material associated with each element, much of it seemingly esoteric. (See also Spencer [1957] for synopses of the separate origin stories of various major ceremonies and an analysis of common, or "archetypal" themes in them in relation to contemporary Navajo life.) Reichard got her information directly, or indirectly through the work of other scholars, from religious specialists and from attending performances of ceremonies, many of which are rare today. We don't know how many Navajos today would actually make the associations sketched below, most of which come from Reichard or the written sources she herself used.

Story elements likely to have rich connotations are, in order mentioned in the story, Whiteshell Woman, her journey to the west, the Emergence Place, the ocean, the lunch, blue corn (bread), turquoise, the planting stick, the springs.

As already noted, some people say that Whiteshell Woman is the same as Changing Woman. Others say she is different, but related (sister, daughter). Whiteshell itself is sometimes associated with the moon. The journey to the west is associated with Changing Woman, according to Reichard's sources. It is hard not to associate this movement westward and return in the form of the originators of certain Navajo clans, the "Western Water" clans, with the cycle of depletion and renewal in nature to which Changing Woman's name itself seems to refer, and which is a fundamental concern of Navajo belief (like probably almost every other belief system). The east-to-west path, of course, is that of the sun during the day and the full moon at night. As we will show below, it is also that of the perennial rivers in Navajoland.

The reference to the Emergence Place here is noteworthy. In the versions of Navajo origin stories that we have heard and read, that is not exactly where Changing Woman was living at the time. The term is also used as a common noun, rather than a proper name, for places where ceremonies, clans, and the like originated. The speaker may have meant simply the place where First Man and First Woman settled after emerging into the present world. But if the speaker did indeed mean the Place of Emergence into the present world (and maybe even if he didn't, because of the ambiguity), associations include the following.

Few sources give an actual location of the Emergence Place, but there seems to be general agreement that the place is in or north of the sacred mountain of the north, which most Navajos today (but not necessarily in Reichard's time) recognize as the La Plata Mountains in Colorado. One place that matches the most localized description (Watson 1964:18; Van Valkenburgh 1941:136) is a lake at the highest source of one of the northern tributaries of the upper San Juan, which flows westward between the La Platas and the area where First Man and First Woman found and raised the infant Changing Woman. From there, the San Juan joins the Colorado River, which continues southwest to the ocean. The San Juan-Colorado and the northern tributaries form virtually the only perennial river system in Navajoland. There are stories in which Whiteshell Woman (as distinct from Changing Woman), left Navajoland (like Changing Woman), but she went north to the La Platas, where, (again like Changing Woman), she created progenitors of Navajo clans, but not the Western Water clans, and from corn, not from her epidermis (Reichard 1963 [1950]:495). Like Whiteshell Woman in the story here, what travels westward from the Emergence Place to the ocean is water down the San Juan and the Colorado, although the water travels by a different route than Changing Woman's overland route. The ocean itself, according to some people we have talked with, is seen as the source of all springs in Navajoland. The actual location that Mr. Yazzie may have had in mind may be where the Colorado flows into the Gulf of California. We have seen a photograph of a rock offshore, the image or home of Whiteshell Woman, which we understood is at that spot, and whiteshell probably came from there (Reichard 1963 [1950]:208). If so, the beginning and end points of this route roughly correspond to the directions of the sun at sunrise and sunset of the summer and winter solstices, respectively, in relation to Navajoland. Mentioning the Emergence Place and the ocean together, then, evokes simultaneously the journey of Changing Woman–Whiteshell Woman to her eternal home, the flow of water out to the sea, and possibly the paths of sun and full moon from rising to setting, without necessarily identifying any of these things with each other except as examples of waning powers.

The lunch of blue corn is a detail the apparent insignificance of which makes one wonder why it has been preserved in this statement. Food, along with the water mentioned at the end of this passage, is a basic material need of life that Changing Woman created, for which one offers Blessingway prayers with precious stones (whiteshell, turquoise, abalone, and jet, or perhaps just the first two). People say that Sun stops for lunch in the sky at high noon. It might also refer to the noon rise of the waxing moon at the first quarter or the noon setting of the waning moon at the third quarter. The color blue and the turquoise stone are associated with the sun, among many other associations, some of which are contradictory. The places that the various versions of this story concern have bluish rocks or soils like the blue corn bread or crumbs. The sun is also associated with an offering of a whiteshell disk in the story about the origin of horses (see chapter 5). The horse-origin story is also associated with landmarks, like this one, that have blue or banded clays that look like the banded, translucent mirage stone, which in turn looks like the "life stuff" (mingled air, moisture, light) and is also associated with long-distance travel because its resemblance to mirage links it to the power to obscure things—a power the traveller in alien territory may need. Corn is another element with a very dense set of associations. Whiteshell Woman transformed it into human flesh. In the First World, First Man and First Woman were originally corn, at least in some versions of the emergence stories (Matthews 1897:69). Corn animated by sun and lightning became human flesh. Corn, and especially its pollen, which embodies not only reproductive power but light, among other things, figure in almost all Navajo ceremonies.

The color blue, and blue corn and turquoise stones, are usually associated with the south. Blue (the word for this color also covers deep green) is associated with "the fructifying power of earth, especially domesticated plants" (Reichard 1963 [1950]:192). The color blue and turquoise stones are also associated with high noon and the (male) sun. Sometimes they symbolize the earth as a female, but usually in contexts paired with black for the sky as a male. Blue in contexts paired with the color white, and turquoise paired with whiteshell, as here, seem to symbolize male and female respectively, or, taken together, sex and the process of reproduction (Reichard 1963 [1950]:187-213). In some stories, Changing Woman is associated with two other, alter-ego-like deities, Whiteshell Woman and Turquoise Woman (said in some stories to be her daughters [Reichard 1963 (1950):496]). Turquoise is associated with Changing Woman's son Born-for-Water, and the color blue is used in a ceremonial (Shooting Chant) sandpainting that depicts the rejuvenation of Changing Woman, with blue-colored deities called Water People on the west side of the painting. Blue and turquoise therefore seem to be associated with water and western water Holy People, as well as with an alter ego of Changing Woman.

The term for planting stick can also be translated as "cane." It may therefore be associated with both the planting of seeds and old age. In Reichard's account, Changing Woman gave people canes (of turquoise, incidentally) to stick in the desert ground to get water, and when they stuck the canes in, certain clans originated. "It seems to be a symbol of ritualistic power" (Reichard 1963 [1950]:531; see also Farella 1984: 178-82). Intensive research into associations with the "cane," we believe, would show a rich symbolism, and might shed light on the symbolism of possibly related paraphernalia, such as "talking prayer-sticks." One type of prayerstick, Navajo custom says, should be carried for safe travel (Reichard 1963 [1950]:308-13), perhaps to use in prayers to immortals in unfamiliar territory. (These are made of "mirage stone," whose power is useful in travel.)[2]

Springs are symbols of life and are gifts of the Holy People, as one expects in dry country where springs are rare. As mentioned above, together with food, here symbolized by the blue corn bread, water is a basic need that is one object of Blessingway prayers. Some ceremonies require water collected from various springs and other natural sources. Moisture is an essence of the Holy People, along with light and air (Farella 1984:30; J. McNeley 1981:24-26; Reichard 1963:264). Springs (or the rain to renew them) are the subject of the rain requesting ceremony, part of the Blessingway that Changing Woman gave to the Navajos.

The associations with each element in the story form a jumble of sometimes related, sometimes contradictory, material. Some associations do interconnect particular groups of elements in a consistent way, whereas others make contradictory interconnections among the elements. The larger organization of the story provides a way of deciding which of a set of contradictory associations best fit into the whole, but they are not necessarily the ones most likely to come to a particular Navajo listener's mind.

The elements seem to fall into two groups. The first group, including Whiteshell Woman, the journey to the west, the Emergence Place, and the ocean are interrelated by the movement from (north)east to (south)-west, the flow of water from the land to the sea, and possibly the movement of sun and full moon across the sky to the ends of their courses. The second group, including the lunch, blue corn, turquoise, the planting stick or cane, and the springs, are all associated with agriculture, reproduction, and the future event of the return of people from the west. These are the two halves of the cycle of depletion and regeneration, specifically, here, as manifest in the regional hydrological cycle.

This synthesis of the statement's connotations and structure may seem anticlimactic to anyone for whom the term "hydrologic cycle" evokes high school science classes. But in the arid Southwest, the effects of this cycle pervade the lives of the many Navajos who raise livestock, farm, and live on the land without benefit of grand transregional water diversion projects or even water from a faucet. People show respect to the huge moisture-bearing air masses that sweep in from the southwest, with rain, thunder, and lightning, and to even the smallest spring. These people see water in its various forms as not only controlled by, but outer forms of, immortals who can hear and respond to human prayers and other ceremonial acts performed season after season, year upon year, century after century, to keep the cycle going. Because people have experienced long droughts when the hydrological cycle seemed to have stopped, they believe their acts, performed pure-heartedly, are necessary to keep it going.

The associations with the sun seem not as well integrated with each other or with the associations tied to the cycle of moisture. Fewer elements are associated with the sun than with water, and those that are don't fit together in a very complete way. The Emergence Place and ocean, taken together as references to the solstices, could refer, respectively, to the sunrise at the summer solstice and sunset at the winter solstice, its strongest and weakest points. The lunch, blue, and turquoise could refer to the sun at midday. If so, however, the story doesn't tie these very clearly to the idea of regeneration, since it does not offer symbols in a series that replicates the annual weakening and strengthening of the sun.

Also, traces of associations linking Mirage stone-(Twins)-Sun-War seem dimly evident. Mirage stone and horses seem to fit into the cluster, not only because the story of the origin of horses links them to the sun and the Twins, but also because they are linked to long-distance travel, which logically, at least, includes raiding. According to Reichard (1963 [1950]:412), when the Sun tried to get Changing Woman to move west, she refused until Monster Slayer rattled his flint war armor at her. Flint, however, is also associated with lightning strikes. The rattling may refer to thunder or hail, and this perhaps esoteric detail may evoke the paraphernalia and acts of rainmaking procedures.

An unresolved contradiction may lurk here between beliefs about war and the peaceful emphasis of Blessingway, especially as Navajos used Blessingway in pre-Fort Sumner trading expeditions outside their own territory (Hill 1948). Ceremonial procedures and other behavior (even storytelling) connected with these two sets of beliefs are ordinarily kept separate (Wyman 1970:4, 50). In pre-Fort Sumner times, raiding was a way of getting wealth that was at odds with the prayer and peaceful trade with other tribes that Blessingway accompanies. Navajo relations with neighboring tribes were ambivalent, but Navajos probably used the places described in this statement for Blessingway prayers during trading expeditions that followed the route along which the places lie. The statement therefore perhaps suppresses the war elements in favor of Blessingway.

13.

A Story about "Where Whiteshell Woman Stopped for Lunch"

Elements of the second story in the preceding chapter, "Where Whiteshell Woman Stopped for Lunch," refer to both general and esoteric Navajo beliefs that, to many Navajos, probably symbolize Navajo ethnicity itself. But these elements, and many of their associations and interrelations, are also found in the stories of neighboring groups. This chapter first sketches what symbolism and beliefs Navajos share with other groups. Then we offer our own story, or "hypothetical reconstruction," about how symbols of Navajo ethnicity could be so widespread among other groups. We remind the reader that these story elements, in common with other groups, relate to Navajo places and landscapes because they are parts of the stories that go with those places and landscapes. Cross-cultural comparisons of these story elements may therefore provide some insights not only into the Navajo past, but also into the significance of geographical locations associated with the Navajo past.

Story Elements among Navajo Neighbors

A thorough canvassing of recorded oral tradition from the neighboring Apache groups, Hopi, Zuni, Acoma, Laguna, and Rio Grande Pueblo Indian communities, to mention only those geographically closest to Navajoland, is both beyond the scope of this work and a feat that would take decades. Even a preliminary look at readily available information about the oral traditions of these groups, however, reveals so many parallels that the groups seem to share a common stock of oral tradition and ceremonial elements, although each group combines them in different ways. The following snippets merely hint at the density of the web.

An important Hopi deity is "Hard Substance Woman," a sometimes old, sometimes young immortal who lives where the Colorado River flows into the ocean and controls the precious shell, turquoise, and coral offering stones (Courlander 1971:84–86, 204–205). In Zuni belief, Whiteshell Woman lives in a house in the western ocean with Sun Father and is his mother or mother's mother (his wife is the Moon Mother) (Tedlock 1979:499). At Cochiti and other Keresan pueblos, creation was accomplished by a great mother deity and two daughters, a trinity reminiscent of the Changing Woman–Whiteshell Woman–Turquoise Woman group of the Navajo stories mentioned above (Benedict 1981 [1931]:1; Hoebel 1979:412). One of the daughters, incidentally, is the mother of the Navajos while the other is the mother of the Cochiti people.

Various Apache groups have a pre-eminent immortal figure called White Painted Woman (Opler 1983a:416; 1983b:433) or Changing Woman (Basso 1983:477). The Apache and Navajo languages are closely related subdivisions of the Athabaskan language group, and the name White Painted Woman is almost a cognate for the name Changing Woman (LaFarge 1963:xxiv–xxv). La Farge relates Changing Woman to the Northern Athabaskan personification of Earth and Whiteshell Woman to the Northern Athabaskan personification of the moon. One of the most important events in the stories of White Painted Woman and Changing Woman is her menarche, for which she was dressed in whiteshell (Opler 1983a:416; Reichard 1963[1950]). An association with the moon (with whiteshell as its symbol) does not seem far-fetched here. These associations may be traces of an earlier female immortal associated with, maybe personifying, the moon (who in present Navajo tradition is male, or at least is a disk carried by a male immortal).[1]

The overlapping webs of associations with Changing Woman, Whiteshell Woman, and the Hopi, Zuni, Keresan, Apache, and Northern Athabaskan immortals suggest that Changing Woman synthesizes attributes of important immortal women in the beliefs of the Athabaskan and Pueblo Indians, peoples whose ancestors were also among the ancestors of the Navajos.

A Hopi story tells of a young man who leaves Navajo Mountain (which, incidentally, forms the Navajo female pollen figure together with Black Mesa mentioned in the Big Mountain story of the preceding chapter) and goes down the Colorado River in a hollow log. This story has its counterpart in a Navajo story about the origins of the Nightway, Navajo Windway, Waterway, and Plumeway ceremonial repertoires (Courlander 1971:82–84; Matthews 1897:160–94; Wyman 1962; Spencer 1957:107–16, 164–76).[2] In the Hopi story, the young man's purpose is to get precious stones for his village for prayer offerings, in exchange for which he carries prayer sticks, a frequent Hopi offering made, like the similar Navajo offerings, to the relevant custodial immortals before taking things from the earth (Heib 1979:580).

This route begins on the Colorado River downstream from the possible location of the Navajo Emergence Place, far north of Changing Woman's (or the Navajo Whiteshell Woman's) cross-country route. The story seems to be the prototype for possibly actual (prehistoric) pilgrimages to the Colorado's mouth to gather precious shells (or to other places in that direction to trade with others who had brought the shells inland). Actual pilgrimages would have used a land route, since southwestern Indians lacked boats. The places associated with the journey of Changing Woman and Whiteshell Woman to the west, or with the return of the western water clan people, may mark this pilgrimage route. Some, if not all, of these places are on trading trails that run west and southwest from the Little Colorado River basin (Colton 1964:93, Cordell 1984:282). These places are likely to be orienting landmarks and offering points. It is worth noting that, in pre-Fort Sumner times, Navajos may have gotten most of their whiteshell and turquoise from trade with Keresans, Jemez, Hopis, and Zunis (Hill 1948:376). If all these peoples used this route, it must have been a sort of neutral, "international" corridor where peace ideally prevailed for pilgrims, even those from groups with whom the Navajos had hostilities at the time. Perhaps the Blessingway-associated Talking Prayer Sticks that people carried on such pilgrimages were their passport.

The Navajo symbolic recreation of the region's hydrological cycle has its parallel in the Hopi belief that the kachinas, masked immortals (like the Navajo haashch'ééh—the sound of the word itself seems a possible variant of "kachina") leave the Hopi villages in July and move southwest to the San Francisco Peaks, where, induced by the proper

Hopi ceremonies, they form rain clouds that move northeast into Hopi-land to water the crops (Heib 1979:577, 580; Courlander 1971:97). Zunis and Keresans also say the kachinas take the form of moisture and (at least some) have their origin place or home in the west (Lange 1979b:384, Tedlock 1979:499).

Holmes (1989) whose main work has been at Zuni, shows many common elements among Navajo beliefs and those of the Pueblos of Zuni, Acoma, and Laguna involving twin war gods, mountains as territorial boundary markers, and trails across the region. Much closer to Puebloan villages are rock-pile shrines, which look like the Navajo trail shrines but symbolize Pueblo boundary mountains. Courlander (1971) gives a number of Hopi stories with these elements also found in Navajo stories. Among many Puebloan groups, certain clans or religious societies maintain shrines to the twin war gods on certain mountains that symbolize the traditional territory, to renew which clan members make annual pilgrimages across ancient routes.

Probably the best known "facts" about Pueblo Indian belief are the associations of colors and precious stones with each of the four directions (and sometimes zenith and nadir, directions also recognized in the Navajo symbolic system.) There are many, many other natural and supernatural phenomena attached to this basic symbolic framework. The colors and stones most commonly associated with each direction vary from one Puebloan group to another. Especially noteworthy are the Zuni association of white with the east and blue with the west, and the Hopi association of white with the northeast and turquoise with the southwest (the four directions in Hopi tradition are to the sunrise and sunset at the two solstices) (Tedlock 1979:501; Heib 1979:577, 579). Apaches also have four directions with associated colors (Opler 1983a:416; Basso 1983:479; cf. Campbell 1969:148).

Puebloan ceremonial paraphernalia include "sticks" for many purposes, including as a symbol of authority of the clan head at Hopi (Connelly 1979:546). This link between clans and "sticks" may have the same roots as the Navajo link between sticks, the creation of clans, and ceremonial authority. If Navajo talking prayer sticks have some relevance here, it is worth noting that at Zuni, sticks painted with faces (like the Navajo talking prayer sticks) are surrogate human sacrifices offered along with prayers for riches and well-being (Tedlock 1979:501). This sounds like the purpose of Blessingway ceremonies, in which (like many other Navajo ceremonies), talking prayer sticks are important paraphernalia that some say symbolize a boy and girl killed, dismembered, and made into a bundle used to create new life (Farella 1984:97–99, 178; Klah 1942:41–42; compare Campbell 1969:421).

Courlander (1971:64–68; compare Campbell 1969:190) provides a Hopi story about a prayer-stick-carrying boy and girl sacrificed to the giant flood-causing snake, a relic of whom (from the back of the neck, a body part that is also a focus of the life force in the Navajo accounts cited) seems to be used in rainmaking.[3] Puebloan parallels to Navajo talking prayer sticks and their associated stories, then, seem concerned with rainmaking, fertility, and creation, rather than with long-distance travel. Where such procedures require pilgrimages, however, long-distance travel is tied in. These associations make us wonder whether the ancestors of both modern Navajos and modern Puebloans used talking prayer sticks or some other wandlike token as a passport across "alien" lands. Tokens of clanship could have served this purpose, since according to Navajo stories, at least, many Navajo clans originated in various Pueblo and other groups (Matthews 1897:135–59; Preston 1954; Mitchell 1978:184–85; Sapir 1942:80–96; Haile 1981:169–74; see also Forbes 1966:337–45). Hopis, like Navajos, have western Water Clans, the originators of which, according to both some Navajos and some Hopis, crossed the ocean in boats (Mitchell 1978:180–81; Courlander 1971:56, 70–71, 204–205).

As in Navajo belief, in Puebloan belief, water, moisture, and clouds are essences of the immortals (Heib 1979:577; Tedlock 1979:499). The Puebloan immortals called kachinas are like Navajo haashch'ééh in that masked dancers impersonate them. The Puebloan belief that the kachinas are somehow immortalized ancestors calls to mind the Navajo belief that haashch'ééh inhabit Anasazi ruins (see Mitchell quotation about the Anasazis, chapter 5). It also reminds one of the references to the pre-eminent haashch'ééh, Talking God, especially, as maternal grandfather—not only as in "Grandfather of the Gods" (the name of the public masked dances), but also as the Twins address him and, as some Navajos tell young children, he will call them "grandchild" if they develop good habits like getting up early.

Another Version of Navajo Origins

The parallels between Navajo and other Southwestern U.S. Indian symbolism, stories, and beliefs given in the preceding section suggest the following story about the development of Navajo culture and ethnicity. We offer this also to present, in another way, our idea that scholarly formulations are just as much stories as the stories that this particular story is about. We believe that our story is consistent with the evidence of the Navajo past available to us. Accepted scholarly procedure would then require a systematic look at this and other evidence (including comparable processes of change in other societies). Although we plan such an effort, it is beyond the scope of this work, and we hope to make our point without it.

The stories about the origins of the Navajo people and their customs rarely mention things that Navajos got from contact with Spanish, Mexican, and U.S. colonists. Even references to livestock are rare, despite their importance to Navajo family subsistence, documented by about 1700 (Kelley and Whiteley 1989:13–20). The story about the origin of horses in chapter 5 is unusual in this respect, and isn't included in many accounts of the creation that we have heard or read. This absence suggests that modern versions of Navajo stories about the past have a lot in common with their pre-conquest forms. These stories go back to the days when the extended family produced food and most other things for itself—by agriculture, hunting, and gathering. This is the period beginning hundreds of years before Fort Sumner, when the Navajos were a politically independent tribe led by a network of local headmen, or even earlier.

The idea that stories may be close to their pre-conquest form seems to contradict our idea that even origin stories reflect the people's current conditions of life. But according to Connerton (1989:56–60, 66), stories passed down by word of mouth may keep archaic material if they are bound to ceremonial procedures that must be performed exactly right if they are to work. Navajo origin stories have such links to ceremonial procedures. A ceremonial performance consists of one or a series of procedures, each of which must be performed according to fairly rigid specifications and must go in a prescribed order. The medicine person must reproduce the songs, prayer litanies, and sandpaintings that are part of each procedure exactly as he or she learned them (see Faris [1990:6–16] about the complexities of this phenomenon). The word-perfect songs and prayer litanies, as well as the sandpaintings, refer verbally or visually to one or another of these stories. The songs, prayers, and names of sandpaintings often include the names of specific places associated with the immortals whose help is being sought (see, for example, Gill 1981:13–15; Matthews 1902:74, 80–81, 94, 130, 269–79; Wyman 1962:193–202).

Another, more basic, reason that the stories may be close to their pre-conquest forms is that certain basic conditions of Navajo life changed little even after Fort Sumner, when the national market economy engulfed the Navajos. These stories and the practices that preserve them have survived changes in the dominant political economy to which the Navajos are subject. They have survived, we believe, because large, extended families have continued to support themselves from their customary land bases, even though, after Fort Sumner, families increasingly produced for markets and increasingly met their own needs with store-bought goods. These families have sponsored the ceremonies that anchor the stories. Only since World War II have many families seen their relationship to their lands, and their own internal cohesion, disrupted, thereby threatening the material and social basis for the ceremonies. The old people who still tell these stories grew up in the time before the disruptions.

The stories that go with each ceremonial repertoire probably have various sources, some older than others, just like the various elements of the repertoire itself, as the stories themselves make clear. Many stories common to both Navajos and various modern Pueblo Indian communities probably are earlier than the Navajos or any of the modern Pueblos as distinct, self-conscious ethnic groups (see Matthews 1897:41). Such stories may go back to the earlier inhabitants of Navajoland, the Anasazis. These people are widely recognized as ancestors of the modern Pueblo Indians. They are also, at least indirectly, among the ancestors of the modern Navajos. Both Navajos and modern Pueblo Indian communities are ethnic groups that have developed from fragments of various earlier communities. The ethnic distinctiveness of modern Pueblo and Navajo groups does not go back into time immemorial.

Anasazi is a Navajo name often translated as "Enemy Ancestors." According to Walters (1991b; see also Walters 1991a), however, it is more accurately translated as (ancestral) "foreigners" or non-Navajos. It is a term that archaeologists apply to prehistoric inhabitants of a large area in the southwestern United States that encompasses, and extends beyond, the Navajo pre-conquest use area. A cautionary note: the term Anasazi, as archaeologists use it, applies to particular material remains (architecture, basketry, pottery, and so forth) in a particular area of the southwestern United States in a particular time period (about A.D. 1 to A.D. 1540—dates of Anasazi remains are often guesses based on assumptions about the ages of certain styles in pottery and architecture). Many archaeologists also assume corresponding social, political, and cultural uniformity, but such an assumption isn't warranted. The pre-Columbian (or pre-Coronado) inhabitants of Navajoland could just as easily have made up small polities speaking different languages, having different places of origin and different histories of shifting socio-political fragmentation and recombination, and holding beliefs and customs that reflected these episodes of diverging and converging histories (see also Cordell 1984:356).

Having criticized archaeologists for oversimplifying interpretations of the archaeological record, we will nevertheless oversimplify further to tell the reader what we think their various interpretations tend to have in common.[4] What archaeologists call "Anasazi culture" evolved in this region in the centuries around A.D. 1, they suggest, as hunter-gatherers there began to grow corn for a large part of their subsistence. From then until about A.D. 1300, they say, the archaeological evidence suggests that population grew, and in most places people moved around less and depended more and more on farming. In the late 1200s, however, a notion still common among archaeologists is that these people left most of what became the pre-conquest Navajo use area. Archaeologists of today tend to see the causes as population pressure together with an extremely severe, long-lasting drought on top of the latest in a series of episodes of down-cutting in drainages (lowering of the water table). Earlier archaeologists' notions that invading Athabaskans or war among the Anasazis themselves caused the apparent Anasazi abandonment have fallen from favor (Cordell 1984:304–12). Cordell, however (1984:312–25) questions the very notion of large-scale abandonment, suggesting instead that a shift of people into the uplands and political decentralization have created the illusions of depopulation. Archaeological studies suggest to us (and others; see, for example, Brew 1979 and Cordell 1984:328) that most "Anasazis" moved to where other "Anasazis" (or at least other farming people) were already living—to the south and east, where the descendants of the mixed groups now inhabit Zuni, Acoma, Laguna, and the Pueblos along the Rio Grande. Others converged on the middle of the former Anasaziland, the southern fingers of Black Mesa, where they joined a small population already living there and became (along with later migrants from other pueblos and elsewhere) the modern Hopis (Cordell 1984:330–35; Plog 1979:129–30; Garcia-Mason 1979:454; Brew 1979:514–15).

This prehistoric shift in Anasazi settlement may have been like many later Pueblo Indian migrations recorded in colonial documents and the stories of the migrants' descendants. Most of these later displacements were responses to Spanish conquest and colonization, but some were evidently responses to drought (see numerous examples in Ortiz, ed., 1979). If the earlier displacements were like these later ones, "Anasazi" villages would have broken up and groups of extended families would have gone their separate ways (Cordell 1984:334, 352, 356; Plog 1979:129–30). The families in these groups might have been related but more likely were not, so that they could marry among themselves and maintain their customs. They would have sought refuge with friends, ceremonial or trading partners, and in-laws, in various other villages, settling on the outskirts and becoming integrated only gradually, always ready to move back to their old home if conditions there improved (see, for example, Connelly 1979:540).

The families that made up a particular village or group of villages at any one time, then, probably had disparate origins and formed only an uneasy, fragile polity. If so, the territory of a village, or group of villages delineated by the sacred places of all its constituent families, would overlap with the territories of other villages made up of other families from the same places as the families of the first village(s). Probably lineages, clans, or other groups within a village had their own sacred places that the elders or ceremonial specialists of the group were supposed to "take care of" through periodic visits and procedures, including previous homes and other places mentioned in the story of the group's "migration" to its present home.

The widespread idea about Navajo origins is based on the clear relationship between the Navajo language and languages of Northern Athabaskan Indians of Canada and Alaska. The idea is that Athabaskans migrated from the north into the Southwest, where they split up into the Navajos and various Apache groups (Brugge 1983; Cordell 1984:356–60; see also Forbes 1960:xx–xxi for a critique of this view). Recent archaeological discoveries of early Navajo-type pottery in the general vicinity of Dinetah suggest the presence of Navajos in the region shortly after the "Anasazis" left (Brown and Hancock 1991; Hogan 1989; Brugge 1992). Also, typical Navajo-style dwellings dated by the tree-ring method to the 1400s were recorded (in connection with the Navajo pre-conquest land claim before the Indian Claims Commission) in the extreme southeastern part of the Navajo pre-conquest use area (Stokes and Smiley 1966).

Archaeologists interpret these remains as evidence of Athabaskans. The pottery, quite unlike Anasazi or Puebloan pottery, resembles pottery on sites in the general area dating to the 1100s–1200s (Cordell 1984:357) and is close enough in time to this early pottery to raise the possibility of even earlier Athabaskan or Athabaskan-Anasazi communities in the region (Walters 1991a; see also Matthews 1897:41). One also wonders whether archaeologists have missed some scant evidence of isolated groups of "Anasazis" who never left the area (Cordell 1984:358; Winter 1986:24, cited in Brugge 1992:33 has evidently raised this question). During the next few centuries, the Navajos' Athabaskan ancestors traded with, lived around, married, and possibly shared ceremonies with their "Anasazi"-Puebloan neighbors, probably trading when they came to a pueblo for a ceremony. Early Spanish observers saw Athabaskans camped on the outskirts of various pueblos during the winter (the ceremonial season) for trade (Forbes 1960:282). The process intensified at the end of the 1600s, when the Pueblo Indians overthrew the Spanish colonists, only to be reconquered by them, and many sought refuge among their Navajo neighbors (Brugge 1992; Forbes 1960; Hill 1948; McNitt 1972:10–22; Sando 1979:422; Courlander 1971:184). Less widely recognized than this movement of Puebloans into Navajo communities has been the reverse movement of Navajos into pueblos.

> Bandelier stated in the 1880s: "Jemez is more than half Navajo, and one of their leading men, whom unsophisticated worshipers are wont to admire as typical and genuine Pueblo, the famous Nazle, was Navajo by birth, education, and inclination. We ought to consider, for instance, the Indians of Zuni have married with, and plentifully absorbed Navajo, Tegua (Tewa) and Jemez blood." (Van Valkenburgh 1941:80)

From these roots emerged a people of mixed Athabaskan and Puebloan ancestry and what we now think of as Navajo culture, a synthesis of mainly Athabaskan and Puebloan forms. We emphasize that we aren't talking about Navajos "borrowing" Puebloan cultural forms after the Pueblo Revolt, but about common roots of both Navajos and Puebloans in earlier, prehistoric peoples.

Through these contacts, the Athabaskan and Puebloan stories came together. They probably already had elements in common (some of which they probably shared with stories all over the hemisphere and even the world—we don't assume, as Luckert [1975:11, 1979:4, for example] seems to, that most story elements related to hunting are Athabaskan, and elements from Puebloan sources tend to relate to agriculture). The processes that led to this combining of stories may have included medicine people and other ceremonialists from one group learning ceremonial procedures from those of the other. Puebloan practitioners may have performed their own curing and other procedures for Athabaskan families and communities, and Athabaskan practitioners may have done the same for Puebloans. Members of one group might have contributed performers to ceremonial performances (especially public ones) organized by the other. Such sharing might have occurred when Athabaskan groups settled near a pueblo for trade, the winter ceremonial season, or a particular ceremonial performance, or when members of one group sought refuge with the other, or when intermarried families lived sometimes in Athabaskan communities and sometimes in pueblos. Mixed Athabaskan-Puebloan communities, such as Jemez and Zuni noted by Bandelier, might have organized large public performances with contributions from both traditions to bind their members together which influenced the stories about the origins of these types of ceremonial performance.

However Athabaskan and Puebloan ceremonialists shared what they knew, they then trained apprentices and so would have started handing down the commingled beliefs, practices, and stories about the origins of those beliefs and practices. The references to clans in these stories are perhaps clues to which Athabaskan and Puebloan communities contributed to them. Stories of the many Navajo ceremonial repertoires tell of the wanderings of Navajo clans, including residence at or near certain Anasazi archaeological sites, and how these clans gradually joined up during their travels until they all found themselves in Dinetah. For example, as Gishin Biye' told the stories of the Upward Moving and Emergence Way to Haile in 1908,

> That day some strangers visited them [western water clan people who were camped near Chaco Canyon] who spoke the same language. Asked where they had come from and where they were going, they replied that they were Pueblos from the east in search of food. And these were Coyote Pass (Jemez) People, and Black-house (Black-sheep) People and Blue-house (Salt) People [Black House and Blue House are two Chacoan Anasazi archaeological sites]. The Jemez came to the Tabaa dine (Water-shore People) and shook hands, while the To dik'ozhi (Salt Water clan) addressed the Ashiihi (Salt People) and Black-sheep People as relatives and friends. And all the Pueblo People and Navajos made friends and lived together, as is witnessed by their dwellings throughout the country. (Haile 1981:174)

Still other stories emphasize the clan, place of origin, and wanderings of the person (often with siblings or descendants) responsible for putting a particular ceremonial repertoire together (see, for example, Matthews 1902:159, Faris 1990:177).

But even as communities and ethnic groups have broken up and recombined to form new ones, the stories themselves, we suggest, have stayed with the land. They have come down by word of mouth, originating in earlier communities that used the land, passing down through the fragments of those communities after they split up, passing into the later groups that formed from the fragments of the earlier ones. Many of these stories are like verbal maps of how to get to places with important, rare resources and other sacred significance. They mention series of places that form trails across the whole Colorado Plateau. Knowledge of these stories can only be gained with the consent of the teller—one doesn't give such maps to enemies. Such knowledge is evidence, we believe, of harmonious relations between the teller and the told. It is evidence of orderly transfer of entitlement to use and care for the land—the "keys to the kingdom," or at least a duplicate set of keys. This isn't the same, of course, as saying that relations among every emerging Navajo community and every Puebloan group that remained Puebloan were all sweetness and light. Today, therefore, and owing to the recent history of conquest and colonization, Navajos are still reticent to tell such stories to non-Navajos, especially non-Indians.

In addition, old Athabaskan and Puebloan stories about other places would also get attached to new landmarks as the people moved into new localities and wanted to keep alive the stories that they have brought from elsewhere. This "claiming by naming" (Eliade 1965:15) is another way that people bond themselves to their land. It is reflected in the tendency of certain place names to be duplicated in various Navajo communities. Important vehicles for this process are the ceremonial song sets, prayer litanies, and sandpaintings in Navajo ceremonial repertoires. Many of these name places and describe their appearance (rock bridge at the junction of two rivers, for example), thereby allowing more than one place that meets the description to carry the name and become identified with the ceremonial repertoire. These names, however, don't become freely attached to just any place that meets a particular description. The location must also make geographical sense in the sequence of other places named in the song set or prayer litany, and many of the other place names in the set are attached to one and only one place—the names of the four sacred mountains, for example (Matthews 1902:269–79; Newcomb and Reichard 1975 [1937]:69–74; Wyman 1957:65–97, 1962:193–202; 1970:147–60). Finally, of course, new stories would grow up, often incorporating elements from older ones, to explain (or obscure) the new social relations that grew up as these Puebloan-Athabaskan communities formed.

The formation of Navajo culture is also evident in the origin story of Blessingway, which is also a good part of the Navajo creation stories summarized in chapter 1. Walters (1991a) proposes that most versions of Blessingway developed at the beginning of Puebloan and Athabaskan contact before A.D. 1400 (even as early as the 1100s), as did most other Navajo ceremonies. He says that they must date to the time before contact with the Spanish (late 1500s) because nothing of European origin, even the livestock that became so important to Navajo life later, is mentioned in any but what he considers the later ceremonies of the Blessingway group. Brugge (1963) proposes that this story developed after the Pueblo Revolt period of the late 1600s, and even later, after a generation or two of Navajo farmers had held off Ute raids and had turned to the more mobile pastoralism. Brugge thinks that Blessingway represents a "nativistic" reaction against the Puebloan immigration and a reassertion of Athabaskan culture. Farella (1984:183–84) sees these "Athabaskan" elements as possibly Puebloan ones simply relabeled as Athabaskan.

We have dreamed up another possibility: that Blessingway stories and associated beliefs synthesize older Athabaskan and Puebloan (and other) stories and react against Puebloan culture—not necessarily all of Puebloan culture, but at least cultural symbols of the Puebloans who had become "Christian" and, however unwillingly, were serving the Spanish as auxiliaries in raids against their refugee relatives and the (Puebloan?-)Athabaskans who gave them refuge. The synthesis of the stories might have started as early as Walters thinks, if that is when the Athabaskans and "Anasazi"-Puebloans met. The aspects of Blessingway that seem like reactions against Puebloan culture might be later, from the Spanish period. A possible mechanism for these changes in beliefs, especially the anti-Puebloan reaction, is the "nativistic" movement that Brugge suggests. The leaders of such a movement could have expressed the new synthesis of some cultural forms and rejection of others in the way that Gill (see chapter 6) says American Indian leaders now express a new intertribal synthesis of different tribal beliefs. As a result, modern Navajo and Puebloan story elements could have come from the same earlier stories, but as the peoples diverged, they retold those stories in different ways. The modern variants on the originals have come to symbolize separate groups.

One doesn't have to move very far from a "literal" interpretation of some versions of Navajo creation and ceremonial origin stories to see a similar sequence of change in culture and ethnicity. In the stories of Tall Chanter that Matthews (1897) recorded, for instance, the people (still immortals—death hasn't been invented yet) who emerge onto the present earth's surface include both Anasazis and other people who are going to be Navajos. At the Emergence Place, First Man and First Woman invent some customs that distinguish these people from the Anasazis (house form, the sweathouse). But few of these people will survive the depredations of the monsters to join the not yet created progenitors of Navajo clans. It's tempting to see these not-yet-Navajos as Athabaskans. The monsters, or more literally translated, alien gods, start destroying and eating these people, Anasazi and not-yet-Navajo. Other Navajo stories to explain what happened to the Anasazis say that natural disasters like whirlwinds and floods killed them off (see Mitchell quote on the Anasazis in chapter 5), in some accounts because the Anasazis made rectangular houses and painted sacred designs on pottery (Wyman 1970:58–59)—obvious symbols of ethnicity that survive in the archaeological record.

In the middle of this time of trouble comes the birth of Changing Woman, whose first mission was to give birth to the Twins so they could kill off the alien gods. And the alien gods they kill include Big God, the Sun's son (like the Anasazi ruler the Great Gambler in the Navajo stories; see chapter 7 and Matthews 1897:80, 82–97, 195–208; also Haile 1981:175–76); a giant eagle (a more benevolent version of which appears in a Navajo Beadway ceremony origin story about the Anasazi custom of gathering eagles for ceremonial use [Matthews 1897:196–98]); travelling rock (which, we learn from Reginald Nabahe [chapter 5], was once a crystal—reminiscent of the crystals and whiteshell discs and turquoise discs that, in other Navajo stories, are Anasazi images of or offerings to the sun [Goddard 1933:142; Matthews 1897:80, 86, 195–208; Wyman 1975:163–64]); twelve human-eating antelopes; a rock that kicks people off a cliff; slashing reeds; beings that kill with their eyes; an engulfing vagina; crushing rocks; and a giant centipede or snake.

Once cleared of the Anasazis and most of the not-yet-Navajos and the alien gods that did them in, the land is repopulated by the Western Water clans, whom Changing Woman has created after moving to the west and who move back east to Changing Woman's original home, Dinetah, where they find a few (remnant "Anasazi"-Athabaskan?) survivors of the alien gods. Another band of (remnant "Anasazi"-Athabaskan?) survivors migrates eastward into the same area from Black Mesa (Matthews 1897:145–46; place referred to was located during the thirteen-chapter project [Downer and others 1988:103]). Still other small bands from various pueblos and from the Apaches and other tribes come into the area. All these small bands become clans of the emerging Navajo people.

Finally, Changing Woman takes two Navajo children and teaches them Blessingway ceremonies. It is tempting to identify these children with the leaders of a nativistic movement that might have offered a single belief system—Blessingway, with its emphasis on peace—to unite the small bands. And the movement could have enjoined people from marrying within their own band, thereby redefining the bands as exogamous clans that intermarriage would bind into one people. The norms that forbid marriage into clans of fathers and grandfathers and into other clans that stories "link" to these clans would have sped up this binding together even more. The origin story of the Mothway ceremony (Haile 1978) is a cautionary tale of a local group whose travels are like those of the early clans. Their members intermarry and then suffer illness, prompting the first application of the ceremonial procedures that became the Mothway and the prohibition of marriage between "brothers" and "sisters." It's tempting to see a "nativistic" effort to discredit symbols of Puebloan ethnicity in favor of an Athabaskan-Puebloan synthesis in the destruction of the Anasazis for producing two obvious symbols of ethnicity (rectangular houses and painted pots), and in the killing of the alien (Puebloan?) gods by an immortal that combines attributes of both Athabaskan and Puebloan immortals and who is the child of another such immortal.

And using this conception of "nativistic" beliefs, it is tempting to interpret other Navajo origin stories. The story of Downy Home Man beating the Great Gambler (see chapter 7 and Goddard 1933:140–46) might be an earlier version of the story of Monster Slayer killing Big God. Downy Home Man is like Swan, a hero of many Northern Athabaskan stories whose exploits are like those of Monster Slayer—who is abandoned by his father on an island (perhaps evoking anxiety of teenage boys in connection with the Northern Athabaskan custom of the vision quest) and survives by lining a hole with feathers of migratory birds (Ridington 1981:354–55; 1988:126–38). Both the monster slaying story and the Great Gambler story suggest desecration of Anasazi deities or their representations. So do stories like the origin stories of the Frenzy Way, Water Way, Enemy Way, Beauty Way, and Mountaintop Way (Kluckhohn 1967 [1944]; Haile 1938, 1979; Wyman 1957, 1975) in which a young Navajo man (or a war party) abducts or lures from an underground room (a Puebloan ceremonial kiva?) two virgins, then seduces or kills them. The two virgins might be two perfect ears of corn covered with kernels over the tips, representing Puebloan immortals White Corn Girl and Yellow Corn Girl or White and Blue Corn Maidens. In a story related to the talking prayer sticks, the virgins are called White Corn Girl and Yellow Corn Girl (Haile 1947:95), and in one of the Mountaintop Way stories, the hair of one girl is bejeweled with turquoise and the hair of the other is bejeweled with whiteshell (Wyman 1975:165–66). In some versions of this story, Navajos take twin gods associated with warfare (Wyman 1975:132).

In origin stories of many ceremonies, like Frenzyway, the hero is a Navajo boy who scavenges around the dump of a pueblo but in the end gains wealth and power at the expense of the Puebloans. These stories might be transformations of a typical Puebloan story plot that is much the same except that the hero is a Puebloan boy first despised and later venerated by his own community. The substitution of the Navajo boy for the Puebloan boy evokes the early Spanish observations of Athabaskans camping outside various pueblos in winter. One can imagine the villagers in their snug rectangular dwellings laughing (over feasts spread out in painted bowls) at the hunters in their wretched tents (all dipping food from one miserable plain pointed-bottom pot), only to have the erstwhile wretched hunters use a "nativistic" story to turn the tables on them.

Finally, the story of the origin of horses might serve to mystify the raiding necessary to get horses. One must get them from Mirage Stone Man, who symbolizes both the life essence and its generative power, and the power to become obscure, the power to sneak unobserved into alien territory. It might be necessary to use Mirage Stone Man to befog the real activity, raiding to increase one's wealth, or getting horses for warfare, because Blessingway belief, so necessary to bring about the unity among offshoots of many tribes (the future Navajo clans) that would confer survival, idealizes peace and increase through engaging the generative power of life. War isn't supposed to be mentioned in connection with Blessingway. Therefore the origin stories of Blessing-way, which are the same as the creation stories, omit the story of the Twins going to their father to get weaponry to use against the alien gods (or even more bluntly, in the Gishin Biye' stories about Upward Moving and Emergence Way, to use against the Anasazis [Haile 1981:217–19]). Blessingway tradition substitutes a story in which the Twins go to their father to get horses (Wyman 1970:420–22). The story about Mirage Stone Man and the horses says it wasn't the kachina-like haashch'ééh, it wasn't the sun, and it wasn't Changing Woman by herself that gave people horses. It was a mystified activity requiring mirage stone (raid-ing?), together with Changing Woman's (Blessingway's?) power to create, that gave people horses. This story, then, perhaps tries to resolve contradictory elements: get the breeding stock by means best left obscured, but then let them reproduce peacefully. The story, appropri-ately enough, places Mirage Stone Man, an ambiguous embodiment of the power to increase through both peaceful and warlike means, squarely to cover up a contradiction between the ideals of Blessingway and what people really do.

14.

The Land, the People, and Culture Change

Is the preceding analysis carrying the effort to establish the fullness of a place's significance too far? Comparative analysis may reveal hidden insights into how Navajo culture developed, but are those insights of interest to Navajos, or just to scholars who like to play mind games with folklore? We believe that these insights are of interest to many Navajos, even if they do result by applying a scholarly framework that has come into Navajoland ultimately on the back of colonialism. Navajo culture is a living framework that has always incorporated things from outside itself.

If stories like ours are of interest to many Navajos, then each bit of evidence that can be used to construct or reconstruct, interpret or reinterpret the story of the Navajo past, is important. This evidence includes the stories of various tribes and their constituent kin groups and religious specialists; colonial documents; the landmarks, archaeological sites, and other places on the ground to which these stories apply. Scholars who are Navajos are increasingly using all these things to study Navajo culture and the Navajo past, including a kit full of analytical tools.

One of the tools is a critical perspective on each story. Taking a critical look at the construction of a story, as Silverman (1983:278) points out, doesn't necessarily mean exposing falseness in it, but rather revealing how the story reinforces cultural meanings. A critical analysis would lay out connotative meanings in the story, and in doing so is supposed to expose unresolved contradictions. The nature of these contradictions, and the way the story conceals them, would show whether and how the story serves the interests of a dominant class or other segment of society by denying or artificially resolving contradictions that really can't be resolved within the framework of social relations most favorable to the group whose interest the story serves (Hanks 1989:104–105; Silverman 1983). In this way, a critical analysis can show how people conceptualize what stories that originate with a dominant class or group are intended to hide: the social relations involved in how people make their living (relations of production), and the relations that actually allow one group to exploit another.

Our discussion of the two stories in chapters 12 and 13 is an example of a critical approach that doesn't find falseness in the stories, but does try to show how the tellers conceptualize certain social relations that enmesh them as they try to make their living. We've laid out connotative meanings, showing how the tellers invoke sources of power in Navajo belief, culture and life to assert an irreducible unity of the land and the Navajo people, and therefore their right as Navajos to occupy the land. This is how the tellers see some of the relations of production in which they are enmeshed—relations between Navajos and non-Navajos, the U.S. government, or the Hopis, that amount to the struggle over who controls the land. Our discussions reveal little evidence in the stories of contradictions unacknowledged by the tellers. One of the tellers says that Hopi "religion is the same as ours," an idea consistent with our discussion of beliefs that symbolize Navajo ethnicity, beliefs that neighboring groups, including the Hopis, see as symbols of their own ethnic identities. Then we constructed a story of how these elements could have come to be shared.

This, our own story, has grown within the same general political context (which includes the Navajo-Hopi "land dispute") as the two stories that we are discussing. Our story, however, is rooted within an anti-exploitation framework somewhat different from the Navajo cultural framework of those two stories. Our story, too, is not immune to a critical analysis, which we leave to the reader. We're trying to make the point, following Althusser (1969, 1971) and Mugubane and Faris

(1985) that you can analyze a story and the cultural framework that it reinforces, but only from the standpoint of another cultural framework. Some analytical frameworks are better than others for bringing out certain patterns in a "text," but each framework does so at the expense of obscuring other patterns.

There is, indeed, a contradiction at the core of both the stories and this very book—the contradiction of hostilities between ethnic groups that have both common roots and a common experience of conquest and colonization. These hostilities between Navajos and Puebloans, and especially, today, Hopis, are like both a family feud and a bitter fight between strangers. The ethnic boundary crosscuts and obscures the common roots of both peoples. But many Navajos (and apparently, also Hopis) acknowledge this contradiction. They see that the ideology of ethnicity in this situation in the long run serves mainly the corporations (and related interests) whose profits from exploiting reservation lands would be reduced by intertribal unity.

Maybe it's not so much Navajos (or Hopis) as these corporations, their associates in government, and many professionals who study Navajo culture, who choose to see ethnic identities as fixed from time immemorial. As ethnicity scholar Werner Sollors says,

> Ethnic groups are typically imagined as if they were natural, real, eternal, stable and static units. . . . The studies that result from such premises typically lead to an isolationist, group-by-group approach that emphasizes "authenticity" and cultural heritage within the individual, somewhat idealized group—at the expense of more widely shared historical conditions and cultural features, of dynamic interaction and syncretism. . . .
>
> [E]thnicity is not so much an ancient and deep seated force surviving from the historical past, but rather the modern and modernizing feature of a contrasting strategy that may be shared far beyond the boundaries within which it is claimed. . . .
>
> Looking at ethnicity as modern does not imply that ethnic conflicts thereby appear less "real" simply because they may be based on an "invention," a cultural construction. . . . However, focusing on the differences out of the historical context of their emergence and at the expense of transethnic similarities—even when this effort stems from an act of self-defense or from an understandable grudge against those who, out of bias or ignorance, would deny the validity of any ethnic enterprise or misinterpret it persistently—may be exactly what sets off the ethnic mechanism . . . of dividing the x's and the y's. (Sollors 1989: xiv–xv)

And even Isaacs (1989:11–16), who seems to see the tendency to make ethnic distinctions as deeply rooted in human nature, mentions many examples of nation states, especially former colonies and remnants of empires, that resulted when a ruling class drew their boundaries to combine groups, or parts of groups, with different histories and cultures—apparently intentionally to divide the ruled, and pit the fragments against one another, thus insuring their own elite hegemony.

Studies like that of Sollors cited above emphasize ethnic enclaves in urban society and therefore ignore the role of land struggles in ethnic self-awareness. But as David Muga points out,

> . . . [I]t has recently become fashionable to view Indigenous Americans merely as ethnic minorities in a pluralist framework. This view, however, is profoundly erroneous, since aboriginal rights to land provide an incontestable sovereignty which no other ethnic minority can claim. This sovereignty must be interpreted to include the power of indigenous communities to determine their own membership and concept of "citizenship" as well as sovereignty over politico-administrative affairs. (Muga 1991:63–64)

Throughout this book we have tried to show that Navajos see in their homeland an essential source of sustenance both for themselves, materially, and for their culture, without which they can't survive as a society. If Sollors is right, Navajos displaced from the land might form ethnic enclaves in cities or elsewhere, either by themselves or merged with other Indians, the process that Gill sees evidence of. But they wouldn't be the same as the Navajo people in Navajoland today. And after centuries of struggle against colonialist powers to keep, or regain, control of the land, Navajos understandably respond to queries about the cultural significance of particular places with statements that either openly or by implication assert their right to the whole landscape. The story of the origin of the Navajo people, both as passed down among generations of Navajos and in the version we have constructed, shows that the Navajo people and their culture came into being through the struggles of their forebears to keep control of the land, and that the culture has survived because people have stayed on the land and adapted things that inevitably come from outside into an ongoing way of life to form a distinctive, integrated cultural whole.

This brings us to our last word about why keeping Navajo cultural landscapes and the stories that go with them alive is important: because one can look at those stories from several different points of view, each of which will show a story about the past origins and evolution of Navajo life, culture, and people. And the changes of the past have lessons for coping with change today. But if the places are lost, the stories will go with them.

NEVY JENSEN

*[The last word here should belong to our teacher, Blessingway singer Nevy Jensen,
who spoke at Fort Sumner in February 1992. Translation by Harris Francis and Klara
Kelley, reproduced with Mr. Jensen's consent.]*

What I'm going to tell about is the history of how generations of people have come from way back. In this way, these
stories, traditions way back have always come down. I don't
know from how far back they have come down, just way back,
they always come down. And this is the case today, you see
things coming down the same way. And then there are the
goals, the purposes. You had to think of yourself and everything
around you. You had to make an effort to achieve your goals,
this was your power. You had to work hard to get along in life.
This is what I mean by going back, everything has a purpose.
One day what we do today will have a purpose in the future.

Our planning in our life, we are taught these things, with
this we make a life. Our thinking is our desire, this is how we
continue life. The stories began way back, I don't know where
or when.

A man called Doo Dint'ii' [Scout?] this was his story. My
maternal grandfather told about [how] this is the way it was.
There was a woman called Baa', [Warrior Girl], this is her story.
The story has been handed down for generations. Also one
called Nabaa' [Warrior], this was his story. This is just the tip of
the story I will tell you about. This is so we will know who we
are.

There are about three hundred Indian tribes on the earth today. We aboriginal Navajos, Eskimos, northern Athabaskans I'm
talking about, maybe three different kinds on the land. As our
language is evolving, I don't know how far it is passed down
from one generation to another, maybe ten generations of us.
You know about the ones nearby, they are just called the
Apaches. There are several different ones, some in Colorado,
some here in New Mexico, in Arizona, the ones I'm talking
about I count about ten of. I don't know how much of a gap
there is between us, generation-wise. Now these other tribes of
Indians, who were our enemies [Puebloans], we integrated with
them as we went along. Migrants of Taos, Tewa clan have been
among us for I don't know how many generations. They are
now—I don't know what they're called, really the Tewa people

are the Tahneeszahnii clan. They became related, Tewa people
and Tahneeszahnii, we aboriginal Navajos, our Tahneeszahnii
relatives. That's how those clans came to be. They have been
among us for generations, and also different Rio Grande Puebloans, and the aboriginal Puebloans and the Puebloans in general, and these Zunis also, these are known here. And thus the
Zunis became the present Zuni clan. They spend generations
with each other, they call them relatives, they intermarry. They
become interrelated.

Still farther back I will say something about what happened
over there at the Emergence Place. The story over there is the
same. These now what we call the Holy People, and what we
call various creatures. There are the Wind People, and also
Water Creature People, and also Winged Creature People. These
we mention in ceremonies, how back then they came into existence one by one. They [Holy People] made a plan, they made a
plan for us way back at the bottom of time. So the story about
them, they made a sweathouse, the way to make a sweathouse
came into being, and that way became the custom. And again,
they built a dwelling, they made a hogan. They made a planning hogan. And according to that, that plan, it is being carried
out. According to that, by means of it there is teaching. They
Holy People made the plan. That which we will plan for the future was set in motion back then. What we plan by was already
made. And by means of it things progress today.

So back then, this is how these things that were created
came about. What we call the Holy People, maybe the Red Ant
People, maybe the Winged Creature People, these we call the
Holy People and they reach anywhere in the four directions.
Thus we tell about them. Out of them have come prayers. Out
of them have come ceremonies. Thus by means of this there is
teaching, by means of it we teach other. That's how things keep
going.

Back then troubles were developing. They are going on
now, today they are going on. And because of that Changing
Woman came into being in holiness on top of a sacred place.
Thus they came about, this history. Thus things are unfolding
and from there things were made, things that are kept going by
means of Blessingway ceremony. Likewise, according to it—that
Blessingway ceremony—they were made, the things that were
kept going according to it. And back then, birth, growth, that

increase, that teaching came into being. It is the teaching. In that way there is teaching.

And back then, the Dine [Navajos] too were recreated, we five-fingered people were thus recreated. The ones that were created over there back then. So with turquoise we were created Dine. With Whiteshell we were created Dine. With abalone we were created Dine. With jet we were created Dine. These only, with them we were created. In order for peace to spread they were created thus. In order that peace came about and is spreading we were placed thus. And that line is the main stalk of the Navajo people, we tell about it.

Today, according to it, that plan is named. And now from out of that it is taught. The Holy People are taught about. Whiteshell Woman taught it. And from there, this is how we've passed it down.

And as time passed, there were those various foreigners that one knows about. The ones that were previously mentioned, probably about ten different ones. And we were all at peace. And they [continued to?] live, and among them there came to number three hundred [groups of] Indians, as I said. And these were the only ones to be found, these generations, back then, maybe in 14.., 14.., that's the story.

Then the Europeans came among us.

APPENDIXES

LIST OF NAVAJO STORIES
AND STATEMENTS

MAMIE SALT

SYLVIA MANYGOATS

REGINALD NABAHE

TEDDY DRAPER, SR.

WHITE ROCK

THE ORIGIN OF HORSES

CRANE PETROGLYPHS AND MASSACRE SITE

ROSE FRANCIS

THE ORIGIN OF THE FRENZY WAY CEREMONY

THE COAL MINING ON BLACK MESA

TIMBER CUTTING IN THE NAVAJO FOREST

OLD NAVAJOLAND

EL MALPAIS

ASBESTOS WASTE DUMP COMING TO MY BACKYARD

AN OPEN LETTER

JESSE BIAKEDDY: BIG MOUNTAIN

JOHN YAZZIE: WHERE WHITESHELL WOMAN STOPPED FOR LUNCH

NEVY JENSEN

TABLE 1. Indicators of Involvement in Non-Navajo World, Thirteen Chapters

	Area (sq. mi.) per mile of paved road	No. of businesses	Large employer	Paved road distance to nearest: Bordertown	Agency
Navajo Nation	11.6	*	various	5–160 mi.	0–90 mi.
Two Gray Hills	6.5	2	—	75	45
Sheep Springs	8.5	1	—	45	60
Tsaile-Wheatfields	8.5	1	Navajo Community College	75	45
Beclabito	9.0	1	—	20	50
Tuba City	9.3	45	Navajo Nation, federal govt.	75	0
Leupp	9.5	3	—	25	90
Indian Wells	11.8	1	—	40	15
Sanostee	15.0	2	—	65	35
Kayenta	15.8	c.20	Peabody Coal	160	85
White Rock	17.2	1	—	50	30
Blue Gap	18.1	1	—	100	40
Nenahnezad	18.3	3	BHP Utah coal	15	15
Navajo Mountain	no pavement	1	—	80	85

*Ratio of chapters with 10 or more businesses to total number of chapters is 1 : 18 (CANDO 1988:49–58)

TABLE 2. Field Methods Data, Thirteen Chapters

	People interviewed	Area (sq. mi.)	Places identified	Weeks per interview team	Places per: Interviewee	Week	Area per place (sq. mi.)	People interviewed per wk.
Total	60*	4316	164	17.5	3	9	26	3
Blue Gap	4	181	17	2	4	8	11	2
Indian Wells	4	355	8	1	2	8	44	4
Kayenta	6	789	11	1	2	11	72	6
Leupp	6	475	12	2.5	2	5	40	2
Navajo Mt.	16	608	23	2.5	1	9	26	6
Tsaile-Wheatfields	2	254	7	1	4	7	36	2
Tuba City	2	371	17	1	8	17	22	2
Beclabito	3	135	10	1	3	10	14	3
Nenahnezad	2	183	6	1	3	6	31	2
Sanostee	6	490	19	1.5	3	12	26	4
Sheep Springs	2	170	12	1	6	12	14	2
Two Gray Hills	4	133	13	1	3	13	10	4
White Rock	3	172	9	1	3	9	19	3

*People who identified specific places only; excludes people who discussed only their concerns about policies.

TABLE 3. Types of Places Classified According to How They Look, Thirteen Chapters (by percentage of total number of places identified)

	Total No.	Total Pct.	Natural area	Places with cultural features Navajo	Anasazi	Historic* non-Navajo
Total	164	100	66%	9%	4%	21%
Small locations/single sites	92	100	46	13	5	34
Large areas/districts	72	100	93	3	2	2
Blue Gap	17	100	82	18		
Indian Wells	8	100	38		25	38
Kayenta	11	100	64		10	27
Leupp	12	100	25		8	67
Navajo Mountain	23	100	74	17	4	4
Tsaile-Wheatfields	7	100	100			
Tuba City	17	100	35			65
Beclabito	10	100	70	30		
Nenahnezad	6	100	83			17
Sanostee	19	100	74	16	5	5
Sheep Springs	12	100	83	8		8
Two Gray Hills	13	100	69			31
White Rock	9	100	78			22

*"Historic" as contrasted with "prehistoric" (Anasazi)—most are public buildings.

TABLE 4. Field Methods Data, Various Studies

	People interviewed	Area (sq. mi.)	Places identified	Places per interviewee	Places per week	Area per place (sq. mi.)	People interviewed per wk.	Area per interviewee
Chapter survey	60(a)	4,316	164	3	9	26	3	72
Pre-conquest claim		60,000	88			682		
Hopi Part. Lands I		1,450	80			18		
Arizona Forests	56?		42	1	10?		14?	
Navajo Forest I		209	15			14		
Anasazi San Juan Basin			44					
4 Corners powerline	82(b)	1,730	20(c)	<1	2?	87	8?	21
Ute Mt. exchange	10?(d)	14	16(c)	2	1?	1	1?	1
De-Na-Zin Wash		20	20(c)				1	1
NW New Mex. coal leases	120	500	156(e)	1	4	3	3	4
1934 Navajo Res.		6,008	689			9		
Navajo Forest II	6	57	27	5		2		10
Canyon de Chelly	16	65	154	10	31	<1	3	4
Hopi Partitioned Lands III	54	1,450	222	4		7		27
	37(f)		200(f)	5	50		9	

(a) Excludes people who did not identify specific places.
(b) Includes 35 residents of outlying areas who apparently provided little information on specific places; counts spouses present at same interview.
(c) Includes family graves, abandoned homesites, and other archaeological sites that land users identified as significant.
(d) Estimated number of people who seem to have provided most of the information on specific places.
(e) Includes 46 family graves, abandoned homesites, other archaeological sites.
(f) Excludes 17 people interviewed at Teesto in earlier years and 22 places identified by those people.

TABLE 5. Types of Places Classified According to How They Look, Various Studies

Project	Total No.	Total Pct.	Natural area All	Natural area Large	Natural area Small	Navajo	Anasazi	Other	Misc.
Chapter survey	164	100	66%	41%	25%	8%	4%	21%	
Aboriginal land claim	88	100	90	72	18	1	8	1	
HPL I	80	100	97	58	40	1	1		
Arizona National Forests	42	100	100	95	5				
Navajo Forest I	15	100	87	87		13			
4 Corners powerline	20	100	40	35	5	60			
Ute Mt. land exchange	16	100	44	6	38	56			
De-Na-Zin Wash	20	100	5		5	95			
NW New Mex. coal leases	110*	100	73	52	21	24	3		
1934 Nav. Res.	689	100**	94	54	40	6			
Navajo Forest II	27	100	95	85	10	3			2
Canyon de Chelly	154	100	47	14	33	40	7		6
HPL III	222	100	82	29	53	13	1	<1	4

*Excludes 46 archaeological sites and graves related to individual family histories.
**Estimated percentages.

TABLE 6. Place Name Studies

	Canyon de Chelly (ours)	HPL III	Chaco Canyon	Anasazi San Juan	Alamo	Tsegi Canyon	Canyon de Chelly (Jett)
Total number of places	154	222	*	44	126	54	153
Type of place classified according to appearance (percent of total)							
Natural area	47%	82%			81%**	76%	47%
Navajo cultural feature	40	13			8	20	42
Anasazi cultural feature	7	1					5
Other cultural feature		<1			6	2	1
Multiple, misc., uncertain	6	4			3	2	5
Places with names							
Total number	131	174	270	21	93	54	144
% of all proper names	90%	80%	90%	30%	78%	72%	98%
% of all generic names	6%	14%	5%	25%	11%	17%	2%
Uncertain	4%	6%	5%	45%	11%	11%	
Type of place suggested by name (percent of all places with names)							
Natural area	49%	79%	59%		74%	74%	45%
Navajo cultural feature	27	9	11		1	20	40
Anasazi cultural feature	6	1	11	55			5
Other cultural feature			1		8	2	1
Unclear	18	10	18	45	17	4	10

*Many names are variants for a single place.
**Includes places with names only; source provides too little information on places without names to classify them by their actual characteristics.

NOTES

1. Background

1. The Navajo Nation Historic Preservation and Archaeology Departments matched grants from the Arizona and New Mexico State Historic Preservation Offices to fund this work.

2. The following summary of Navajo documented history is based mainly on the sources used by Kelley and Whiteley (1989). Useful overviews are by Bailey and Bailey (1986), Brugge (1983), Correll (1979), Iverson (1981), Weiss (1984), and Young (1978). The background material on Navajo culture is based on our own experiences and on the works of Benally (1982), Farella (1984), Faris (1990), Franciscan Friars (1910), Frisbie (1987), Gill (1981), Goddard (1933), Haile (1938, 1943, 1947, 1978, 1979, 1981), Klah (1942), Kluckhohn and Wyman (1969 [1940]), Luckert (1975, 1977, 1978), Luckert and Cooke (1979), Matthews (1897, 1902), J. McNeley (1981), Mitchell (1978), Newcomb and Reichard (1975 [1937]), Reichard (1963 [1950]), Spencer (1957), Wyman (1957, 1962, 1970, 1975), and Yazzie (1984). Our summary is so general and most of these sources are so particular that we list them here rather than clogging the text with references to substantiate every statement.

3. Our summary of the creation stories outlines mainly what the following sources have in common: Benally (1982), Goddard (1933), Klah (1942), Matthews (1897), Mitchell (1978), Wyman (1970), and Yazzie (1984). See also Zolbrod (1984).

2. The Project to Consult Navajo Communities

1. Later, in planning this book, we sought and received written consent from each person to reproduce his or her statement and to use his or her name in print.

3. Interpretation of Results

1. Sources of stories related to ceremonies are as follows: Benally (1982); Faris (1990); Fishler and Goldtooth (1953); Clinton (1990); Goddard

(1933); Haile (1938, 1943, 1947, 1950, 1978, 1979, 1981); Hill and Hill (1943a, 1943b); Klah (1942); Kluckhohn (1967 [1944]); Luckert (1975, 1977, 1978); Luckert and Cooke (1979); Matthews (1887, 1897, 1902); Newcomb (1940); Newcomb and Reichard 1975 [1937]); Oakes, King, and Campbell (1943); O'Bryan and Sandoval (1956); Preston 1954; Reichard (1944); Sapir (1942); Stephen and Gishin Biye' (1930); Wheelwright (1945, 1946a, 1946b, 1951, 1956, 1958); Wyman (1957, 1962, 1965, 1970, 1975); and Yazzie (1984).

2. We excluded from our review the hundreds of reports of archaeological surveys that have occurred in these communities because the level of effort required to synthesize them was out of proportion to our purpose, which was to get a general idea of what interviewees were leaving out. We also excluded more general regional syntheses of prehistoric archaeology. Finally, we excluded historical narratives not focused on places in the thirteen chapter areas. The remaining general sources are works by Van Valkenburgh (1941, 1974); Watson (1964); Brugge (1964, 1972); McNitt (1962, 1972); Kelley (1977); Luckert (1975, 1977); Navajo Nation (n.d.a, n.d.b, 1962); Stokes and Smiley (1963, 1964, 1966, 1969); Crampton (1959); Hafen and Hafen (1954); Richardson (1985); Colton (1946, 1964); Gregory (1916); Walker and Shepherd (1964); Threinen (1981); Fransted (1979); Condie and Knudson, eds. (1982); York (1984); York and Winter (1988); Etcitty (n.d.); Bingham and Bingham (1979:39). A useful future effort would be to return to the thirteen chapter areas with lists of places mentioned in these sources (and in the regional syntheses of prehistoric archaeology as well) and find what local people have to say about them.

4. Other Studies

1. The background information on the historical context of the various studies is our own interpretation of what we have read and experienced. We can't pretend to present authoritative summaries of the complex details and different interpretations of events and records. Overviews of the Navajo-Hopi disputes are by Indian Law Resource Center (1979), Kammer (1980), Redhouse (1985), and Whitson (1985). Overviews of development in the Checkerboard area are by Brugge (1980), Gerlach and Dulles (1982), Kelley (1982), Radford (1986), and York (1990).

2. At the time of this writing, mediation had stalled over several issues, including refusal of Navajos still living on HPL to accept 75-year leases from the Hopi government to live on what they consider their own lands.

5. Stories and Types of Places in the Other Studies

1. According to Hill (1938:161), traditional Navajo eagle-catching occurred between November and January.

2. Many Anasazi sites for which Fransted failed to find Navajo stories do figure in stories that go with Navajo ceremonies, recorded in literature from fifty or more years ago (see chapter 3, note 1), but references in the stories are often to a residence near a landmark, rather than the name of the ruin itself. Other Anasazi sites that Fransted doesn't list also figure in Navajo stories that go with ceremonies.

7. The Hidden Reservoir

1. More insights about the storied landscapes might come from comparing the short versions of stories that people tell while expressing their public policy concerns with the longer versions that people tell for their own sake. What people leave out in the short versions may be the "embellishments" that, according to Faris (in Washburn—esthetic systems) mark parts of an esthetic creation that embody particularly important beliefs.

2. This ceremony (Navajo name ajilee) has been called in the literature "Prostitutionway," "Lustway," and "Excess Way." Many Navajos object to the first two terms in particular, because they don't cover the range of maladies that the ceremony was used to cure. Many anthropologists object to the last term because it seems too general. We have used the term "Frenzyway" because it seems to cover a broader range of the ailments for which the ceremony is used and because the customary explanation of most of these ailments seems to have been a type of witchcraft that Kluckhohn (1967 [1944]) calls "frenzy witch-craft."

11. Analytical Framework

1. This may be a modest example of analytical methods integrated in somewhat the way Hanks seems to suggest, using symbols (or elements most heavy with connotations) as units of analysis to study the internal form of the text and locate the text in its cultural context. These methods also flow from Faris's (1983:92) idea that, in an esthetic system, the elements that show the most redundancy or elaboration may cover the most significant ideas (or conflicts) in the society itself.

12. Hidden and Manifest Landscapes in Two Stories

1. Compare "typical oral formulaic narrative structure that juxtaposes structural elements" (Foley 1988:59, 78).

2. The association of sticks with getting water from dry land is found in traditions elsewhere in the world (for instance, the Old Testament; compare also the practice of dowsing). It may be a logical response to a very ancient belief that the terrestrial earth floats on the ocean. In one of the Navajo Emergence stories, a flood preceded the creation of the present earth surface; then a bird dove into the ocean and brought up some mud, which was enlarged to make the terrestrial earth.

13. A Story about "Where Whiteshell Woman Stopped for Lunch"

1. But then, Navajo symbolism often requires things in pairs that represent complementary principles needed together to sustain life. These are usually identified with male and female, according to their relative attributes, the more aggressive or forceful or larger one being male and the quieter or gentler or smaller being female.

2. Another part of this story, the Downy Home Man episode, resembles a Northern Athabaskan story (Ridington 1981:354-55), which seems to be rooted in the custom of vision quests for boys at puberty, with migratory birds to symbolize death and rebirth.

3. This idea, along with the phrase "Eat my brain" in the Frenzyway origin story as given by Kluckhohn (1967 [1944]) and excerpted in chapter 7, may reflect an ancient, worldwide belief connecting brain tissue to fertility (La Barre 1984).

4. See overviews of prehistory in Ortiz, ed. (1979). Cordell (1984) offers critical summaries of past syntheses. Dean and others (1985) is a useful supplement to Cordell's book.

REFERENCES

Althusser, Louis. 1969. Marxism and Humanism. In *For Marx*, pp. 219–48. London: Verso.

———. 1971. Lenin and Philosophy. In *Lenin and Philosophy and Other Essays*, pp. 23–70. New York: Monthly Review Press.

American Association for Indian Affairs. 1990. Briefing Document: American Indian Religious Freedom. Ms. distributed at National Sacred Sites Caucus, Denver, Colorado, November 15–16.

Andrews, Tracy J. 1991. Ecological and Historical Perspectives on Navajo Land Use and Settlement Patterns in Canyons de Chelly and del Muerto. *Journal of Anthropological Research* 47(1):39–67.

Attakai v. United States. 1990. CIV 88–964 PCT EHC, February 29.

Badonie v. Higginson. 1981. 638 F. 2nd 172 (10th Cir. 1980), cert. denied, 452 U.S. 954 (1981).

Bailey, Garrick, and Roberta Glenn Bailey. 1986. *A History of the Navajos.* Santa Fe: School of American Research Press.

Barboncito. 1868. Statement in minutes of the Navajo Treaty Council, Fort Sumner, New Mexico, May 29. In Navajo Nation, Proposed Findings of Fact on Behalf of the Navajo Tribe of Indians, Docket 229 before the Indian Claims Commission (undated), p. 171. On file, Navajo Nation Research Library, Window Rock, Arizona, and Gallup (New Mexico) Public Library.

Bartlett, Michael H. 1980. *Archaeological Resources in the Twin Buttes/Summit Pine Forests, Navajo Nation.* Navajo Nation Papers in Anthropology 2. Window Rock, Arizona: Navajo Nation Cultural Resource Management Program.

Basso, Keith. 1983. Western Apache. In *Handbook of North American Indians*, vol. 10: *Southwest*, ed. Alfonso Ortiz, pp. 462–88. Washington, D.C.: Smithsonian Institution.

———. 1990 (1983). Stalking with Stories. In *Western Apache Language and Culture.* Tucson: University of Arizona Press.

Begay, Adella, and McQueen Suen-Redhouse. 1992. Letter to the Editor, *Navajo-Hopi Observer*, Flagstaff, Arizona, August 5.

Begay, Daryl R. 1991. Navajo Preservation: The Success of the Navajo Nation Historic Preservation Department. *CRM* 14(4):1–4. Washington, D.C.: National Park Service.

Begay, Richard M., Loretta Jackson, and Kurt Dongoske (with contribution by Alexa Roberts). 1992. Navajo, Hualapai, and Hopi Cultural Resources for the Glen Canyon Environmental Studies. Ms. submitted to National Park Service Anthropology Division, Washington, D.C.

Bell, Charlotte R. 1985. *Federal Historic Preservation Case Law.* Washington, D.C.: Advisory Council on Historic Preservation.

Benally, Clyde. 1982. *Dineji Nakee Naahane'—A Utah Navajo History.* Monticello, Utah: San Juan School District.

Benedict, Ruth. 1981 (1931). *Tales of the Cochiti Indians.* Albuquerque: University of New Mexico Press.

Bindell, Stan. 1991. Effort Continues to Save Tuba City BIA Historical Buildings. *Navajo-Hopi Observer,* Flagstaff, November 20, p. 1.

Bingham, Sam, and Janet Bingham. 1979. *Navajo Farming.* Chinle, Arizona: Rock Point School.

Brew, J. O. 1979. Hopi Prehistory and History to 1850. In *Handbook of North American Indians,* vol. 9: *Southwest,* ed. Alfonso Ortiz, pp. 514–23. Washington, D.C.: Smithsonian Institution.

Brown, Gary M., and Patricia M. Hancock. 1991. The Dinetah Phase in the La Plata Valley. Paper prepared for inclusion in *Cultural Diversity and Interaction: Prehistory of the Upper San Juan Drainage, Northwestern New Mexico,* ed. Lori Stephens Reed and Paul F. Reed. Cultural Resources Series, USDI Bureau of Land Management, New Mexico State Office, Santa Fe. Forthcoming. Ms. in authors' possession.

Brugge, David M. 1963. *Navajo Pottery and Ethnohistory.* Window Rock, Arizona: Navajo Tribal Museum.

———. 1964. Vizcarra's Navajo Campaign of 1823. *Arizona and the West* 6(3):223–44.

———. 1972. *Navajo and Western Pueblo History.* Tucson: Tucson Corral of the Westerners.

———. 1980. *A History of the Chaco Navajos.* Reports of the Chaco Center 4. Albuquerque: National Park Service.

———. 1983. Navajo Prehistory and History to 1850. In *Handbook of North American Indians,* vol. 10: *Southwest,* ed. Alfonso Ortiz, pp. 489–501. Washington, D.C.: Smithsonian Institution.

———. 1992. Thoughts on the Significance of Navajo Traditions in View of the Newly Discovered Early Athabaskan Archaeology North of the San Juan River. In *Why Museums Collect: Papers in Honor of Joe Ben Wheat,* ed. Meliha S. Duran and David T. Kirkpatrick, pp. 31–38. Albuquerque: Archaeological Society of New Mexico 19.

Bruner, Edward M. 1986. Ethnography as Narrative. In *The Anthropology of Experience,* ed. Victor W. Turner and Edward M. Bruner, pp. 139–55. Urbana: University of Illinois Press.

Cahn, Ninibah. 1982. Appendix. In *By Executive Order: A Report to the American People on the Navajo-Hopi Land Dispute,* vol. 2, by Edgar S. Cahn. Washington, D.C.: Citizens Advocate Center.

Campbell, Joseph. 1969 (1959). *The Masks of God: Primitive Mythology.* New York: Penguin.

CANDO. 1988. *Navajo Nation FAX 88: A Statistical Abstract.* Window Rock, Arizona: Navajo Nation Commission to Advance Navajo Development Opportunities, Navajo Nation Division of Economic Development.

Carroll, Charles H. 1982. An Ethnographic Investigation of Sites and Locations of Cultural Significance to the Navajo People to Be Affected by PNM's Four Corners to Ambrosia to Pajarito 500 kV Transmission Project. Albuquerque: Public Service Company of New Mexico.

———. 1983. Ute Mountain Land Exchange Ethnographic Study. Albuquerque: Public Service Company of New Mexico.

Christenson, Andrew L. 1990. Navajo Place Names—Tsegi Canyon Arizona. Ms. in authors' possession.

Cleeland, Teri A., and David E. Doyel. 1982. Ethnic, Religious, and Scientific Significance of NFPI Compartment 9 Sites. In *Archaeological Survey of the*

Forest Highlands of the Defiance Plateau and Chuska Mountains, Navajo Nation, by Laurance D. Linford. Navajo Nation Papers in Anthropology 6. Window Rock, Arizona: Navajo Nation Cultural Resource Management Program.

Clemmer, Richard O. 1991. The Relation of Hopi and Ute Social Organization, History, Cosmology, and Religion to Land, with Special Regard to the Upper Rio Grande and San Juan River Valleys and Nearby Areas. Appendix B in An Investigation of AIRFA Concerns Relative to the Fruitland Coal Gas Development Area, Draft, by David M. Brugge. Ms. Albuquerque: Office of Contract Archaeology, University of New Mexico.

Clinton, Alvin. 1990. Interview. In I Am a Child of This Sacred Land, by the Teesto Navajos Affected by the Relocation Efforts. Ms. Window Rock, Arizona: Navajo-Hopi Land Commission

Colby, Benjamin N., David F. Aberle, and Richard Clemmer. 1991. The Hopi-Navajo Situation under the New Commission. *Anthropology Newsletter,* February.

Colton, Harold S. 1946. *The Sinagua: A Summary of the Archaeology of the Region of Flagstaff, Arizona.* Flagstaff: Museum of Northern Arizona Bulletin 22.

————. 1964. Principal Hopi Trails. *Plateau* 36(3):91–94.

Condie, Carol, and Ruthann Knudson, eds. 1982. *The Cultural Resources of the Proposed New Mexico Generating Station Study Area, San Juan Basin, New Mexico.* Albuquerque: Quivira Research Center Publication 39.

Connelly, John C. 1979. Hopi Social Organization. *Handbook of North American Indians,* vol. 9: *Southwest,* ed. Alfonso Ortiz, pp. 539–53. Washington, D.C.: Smithsonian Institution.

Connerton, Paul. 1989. *How Societies Remember.* New York: Cambridge University Press.

Cordell, Linda S. 1984. *Prehistory of the Southwest.* Orlando: Academic Press.

Correll, J. Lee. 1979. *Through White Men's Eyes* (6 vols.). Window Rock, Arizona: Navajo Nation Museum.

Courlander, Harold. 1971. *The Fourth World of the Hopis.* New York: Crown.

Crampton, C. Gregory. 1959. *Outline History of the Glen Canyon Region 1776–1922.* University of Utah, Department of Anthropology, Anthropological Paper 42 (Glen Canyon Series 9).

Dean, Jeffrey S., Robert C. Euler, George J. Gumerman, Fred Plog, Richard H. Hevly, and Thor N. V. Karlstrom. 1985. Human Behavior, Demography, and Paleoenvironment on the Colorado Plateaus. *American Antiquity* 50:497–520.

Deloria, Vine. 1991. Sacred Lands and Religious Freedom. In *Native American Rights Fund Legal Review* 16(2):1–6.

Detienne, Marcel. 1986 (1981). *The Creation of Mythology.* Trans. Margaret Cork. Chicago: University of Chicago Press.

Dine BiWilderness Society. 1991. Open letter to Navajo Nation President Peterson Zah. Ms. in authors' possession.

Doe, John. 1988. *Speak into the Mirror: A Story of Linguistic Anthropology.* Lanham, Maryland: University Press of America.

Downer, Alan S. 1989. Anthropology, Historic Preservation and the Navajo: A Case Study in Cultural Resource Management on Indian Lands. Ph.D. diss. in anthropology, University of Missouri, Columbia.

Downer, Alan S., with contributions by Richard Begay, Harris Francis, Klara Kelley, and Alexandra Roberts. 1988. Navajo Nation Historic Preservation Plan Pilot Study: Identification of Cultural and Historic Properties in Seven Arizona Chapters of the Navajo Nation. Ms. on file, Navajo

Nation Historic Preservation Department, Window Rock, Arizona and Arizona State Historic Preservation Office, Phoenix.

Downer, Alan S., with contributions by Stella Clyde, Harris Francis, Klara Kelley, Alexandra Roberts, and Loretta Werito. 1989. Navajo Nation Historic Preservation Plan Pilot Study: Identification of Cultural and Historic Properties in Six New Mexico Chapters of the Navajo Nation. Ms. on file, Navajo Nation Historic Preservation Department, Window Rock, Arizona, and New Mexico State Historic Preservation Office, Santa Fe.

Downer, Alan S., Alexa Roberts, Harris Francis, and Klara Kelley. 1993 (in press). Identification of Historical Resources: Traditional History and Alternative Conceptions of the Past. In *Reconfiguring the Cultural Mission: Issues and Case Studies in Cultural Conservation,* ed. Mary Hufford. Champaign: University of Illinois Press.

Draper, Teddy, Sr. 1973. Teddy Draper Sr. In *Navajo Stories of the Long Walk Period,* ed. Ruth Roessel, pp. 43–57. Tsaile, Arizona: Navajo Community College Press.

Einbender, LeGrand. 1990. Navajo Social Forestry Research Data, Phase II, June. Ms. in authors' possession.

Einbender, LeGrand, and Donald Wood. 1991. Navajo Social Forestry. *Journal of Forestry* 89(1):12–18.

Eliade, Mircea. 1965. *The Myth of the Eternal Return.* Bollingen Series. Princeton: Princeton University Press.

Etcitty, Juan. N.d. *An Oral History of the Lake Valley and Whiterock Communities.* Crownpoint, New Mexico: Lake Valley Navajo School.

Ewen, Stuart. 1988. *All Consuming Images.* N.p.: Basic Books.

Farella, John R. 1984. *The Main Stalk: A Synthesis of Navajo Philosophy.* Tucson: University of Arizona Press.

Faris, James C. 1983. From Form to Content in the Structural Study of Aesthetic Systems. In *Structure and Cognition in Art,* ed. D. Washburn, pp. 90–112. Cambridge: Cambridge University Press.

———. 1990. *The Nightway: A History and a History of Documentation of a Navajo Ceremonial.* Albuquerque: University of New Mexico Press.

Faris, James C., and Harry Walters. 1990. Navajo History: Some Implications of Contrasts of Navajo Ceremonial Discourse. *History and Anthropology* 5:1–18.

Fishler, Stanley A., and Frank Goldtooth. 1953. *In the Beginning: A Navaho Creation Myth.* University of Utah Anthropological Paper 13. Salt Lake City: University of Utah Press.

Foley, John Miles. 1988. *The Theory of Oral Composition: History and Methodology.* Bloomington: Indiana University Press.

Forbes, Jack D. 1960. *Apache, Navaho and Spaniard.* Norman: University of Oklahoma Press.

———. 1966. The Early Western Apache, 1300–1700. *Journal of the West* 5:336–54.

Forest Lake Dine Rights Movement. 1990. Dine Bikeyah. September. Newssheet.

Francis, Harris. 1988. Teesto Sacred Places Study. Confidential ms. Navajo Nation Historic Preservation Department, Window Rock, Arizona.

Francis, Harris, and Klara Kelley. 1990. Traditional Places in Canyons de Chelly and del Muerto. Confidential ms., National Park Service, Canyon de Chelly National Monument, Chinle, Arizona; Southwest Regional Office, Santa Fe, and Navajo Nation Historic Preservation Department, Window Rock, Arizona.

———. 1992. Sacred Places in Canyons de Chelly and del Muerto, Phase II, draft. Confidential ms. on file, Navajo Nation Historic Preservation Department, Window Rock, Arizona.

Franciscan Friars. 1910. An Ethnologic Dictionary of the Navajo Language. St. Michaels, Arizona: Franciscan Friars.

Fransted, Dennis. 1979. An Introduction to the Navajo Oral History of Anasazi Sites in the San Juan Basin Area. Navajo Ageing Services, Fort Defiance, Arizona. Ms. in authors' possession.

Fransted, Dennis, and Oswald Werner. N.d. The Ethnogeography of the Chaco Canyon Area Navajo. Ms. in authors' possession.

Frisbie, Charlotte J. 1987. *Navajo Medicine Bundles or Jish: Acquisition, Transmission, and Disposition in the Past and Present.* Albuquerque: University of New Mexico Press.

Frisbie, Charlotte J., and Eddie Tso. 1993. The Navajo Ceremonial Practitioners Registry. *Journal of the Southwest* 35(1):53–92.

Gal, S. 1989. Language and Political Economy. In *Annual Review of Anthropology* 18:345–67.

Garcia-Mason, Velma. 1979. Acoma Pueblo. In *Handbook of North American Indians,* vol. 9: *Southwest,* ed. Alfonso Ortiz, pp. 450–66. Washington, D.C.: Smithsonian Institution.

Gerlach, Ernest J., and John F. Dulles II. 1982. *Energy Development in Northwestern New Mexico: A Civil Rights Perspective.* New Mexico Advisory Committee to the U.S. Commission on Civil Rights.

Gill, Sam D. 1981. *Sacred Words: A Study of Navajo Religion and Prayer.* Westport, Connecticut: Greenwood Press.

———. 1987. *Mother Earth.* Chicago: University of Chicago Press.

Goddard, Pliny Earle. 1933. *Navajo Texts.* New York: American Museum of Natural History.

Greenberg, Henry, and Georgia Greenberg. 1984. *Carl Gorman's World.* Albuquerque: University of New Mexico Press.

Gregory, Herbert. 1916. *The Navajo Country: A Geographic and Hydrographic Reconnaissance of Parts of Arizona, New Mexico, and Utah.* U.S. Geological Survey Water Supply paper 380. Washington, D.C.: Government Printing Office.

Hafen, Leroy R., and Ann W. Hafen. 1954. *Old Spanish Trail, Santa Fe to Los Angeles.* Glendale, California: Arthur H. Clark.

Haile, Father Berard. 1938. *Origin Legend of the Navaho Enemy Way: Text and Translation.* Yale University Publications in Anthropology 17.

———. 1943. *Origin Legend of the Navaho Flintway.* University of Chicago Publications in Anthropology, Linguistic Series.

———. 1947. *Head and Face Masks in Navaho Ceremonialism.* St. Michaels, Arizona: St. Michaels Press (AMS reprint 1978).

———. 1950. *Legend of the Ghostway Ritual and Suckingway.* St. Michaels, Arizona: St. Michaels Press.

———.1968. *Property Concepts of the Navajo Indians.* Catholic University of America, Anthropological Series 17.

———. 1978. *Love Magic and Butterfly People: The Slim Curly Version of the Ajilee and Mothway Myths.* Flagstaff: Museum of Northern Arizona.

———. 1979. *Waterway: A Navajo Ceremonial Myth told by Black Mustache Circle.* Flagstaff: Museum of Northern Arizona Press.

———. 1981. *The Upward Moving and Emergence Way: The Gishin Biye' Version.* Lincoln: University of Nebraska Press.

Hanks, W. F. 1989. Texts and Textuality. In *Annual Review of Anthropology* 18:95–156.

Hardeen, George. 1990. Apaches, Zunis Join Navajos, Hopis in Opposing

Developing of Sacred, Historical Landmark. *Navajo Times* (Window Rock, Arizona), December 17.

———. 1991. Woodruff Butte Dispute. *Arizona Daily Sun* (Flagstaff, Arizona), January 8.

Healing v. Jones. 1963. 210 F. Supp. 125, 129 (D Ariz. 1962), cert. denied 373 U.S. 758 (1963).

Heib, Louis A. 1979. Hopi World View. In *Handbook of North American Indians*, vol. 9: *Southwest*, ed. Alfonso Ortiz, pp. 577–80. Washington, D.C.: Smithsonian Institution.

Hill, W. W. 1938. *The Agricultural and Hunting Methods of the Navajo Indians*. Yale University Publications in Anthropology 18.

———. 1948. Navaho Trading and Trading Ritual: A Study in Cultural Dynamics. *Southwestern Journal of Anthropology* 4:371–95.

Hill, W. W., and Dorothy W. Hill. 1943a. The Legend of the Eagle-Catching Way. *New Mexico Anthropologist* 6–7(2):31–36.

———. 1943b. Two Navajo Myths. *New Mexico Anthropologist* 6–7(3):111–14.

Hoebel, E. Adamson. 1979. Zia Pueblo. In *Handbook of North American Indians*, vol. 9: *Southwest*, ed. Alfonso Ortiz, pp. 407–17. Washington, D.C.: Smithsonian Institution.

Hogan, Patrick. 1989. Dinetah: A Reevaluation of Pre-Revolt Navajo Occupation in Northwest New Mexico. *Journal of Anthropological Research* 45(1):53–66.

Holmes, Barbara. 1989. *American Indian Land Use of El Malpais*. Albuquerque: Office of Contract Archeology, University of New Mexico.

Holt, H. Barry. 1981. Navajo Sacred Areas. *Contract Abstracts and CRM Archaeology* 2(2):45–53.

Indian Law Resource Center. 1979. Report to the Hopi Kikmongwis and Other Traditional Hopi Leaders on Docket 196 and the Continuing Threat to Hopi Land and Sovereignty. Washington, D.C. Ms. in authors' possession.

Indian Wells Chapter. 1990. Resolution of August 19. Indian Wells, Arizona, and Legislative Services Office, Window Rock, Arizona.

Isaacs, Harold R. 1989 (1975). *Idols of the Tribe: Group Identity and Political Change*. Cambridge, Mass.: Harvard University Press.

Iverson, Peter. 1981. *The Navajo Nation*. Albuquerque: University of New Mexico Press.

Jett, Stephen C., Chauncey M. Neboyia, and William Morgan, Sr. 1992. Navajo Placenames and Trails of the Canyon de Chelly System, Arizona. Draft. Ms. in authors' possession.

Judd, Neil M. 1954. The Material Culture of Pueblo Bonito. *Smithsonian Miscellaneous Collections* 124.

Kammer, Jerry. 1980. *The Second Long Walk*. Albuquerque: University of New Mexico Press.

Kelley, Klara. 1977. Commercial Networks in the Navajo-Hopi-Zuni Region. Ph.D. diss. in anthropology, University of New Mexico.

———. 1982. *The Chaco Canyon Ranch: Ethnohistory and Ethnoarchaeology*. Navajo Nation Papers in Anthropology 8. Navajo Nation Cultural Resource Management Program, Window Rock, Arizona.

———. 1985a. *The Archeology of McKinley Mine*, vol. 2: *Navajo Ethnohistory of the North Lease: Site Formation Processes*. Cultural Resources Management Division, Sociology and Anthropology Department, New Mexico State University, Las Cruces, New Mexico, Report 621.

———. 1985b. Ethnoarchaeology of Navajo Trading Posts. *The Kiva* 51(1):19–37.

————. 1986a. Draft Technical Report: Socioeconomic Conditions around the Dineh Power Project Area: Navajo Traditional Ways of Life. Ms. on file, Navajo Nation Archaeology Department, Window Rock, Arizona.

————. 1986b. *Navajo Land Use: An Ethnoarchaeological Study*. Orlando: Academic Press.

————. 1987. An Archaeological Survey for the IHS Chambers-Sanders Trust Lands ("New Lands") Phase I Water System. NNCRMP–87–090. Ms. on file, Navajo Nation Archaeology Department, Window Rock, Arizona.

————. 1988. *San Augustine Coal Area, Archaeological Investigations in West-Central New Mexico,* vol. 2, *Historic Cultural Resources.* Cultural Resources Series No. 4, U.S. Department of the Interior, Bureau of Land Management, New Mexico State Office, Santa Fe.

Kelley, Klara, Alan S. Downer, and Alexa Roberts. 1993. American Indians and Archaeologists Two Years after NAGPRA. Ms. in authors' possession.

Kelley, Klara, Harris Francis, and Peggy F. Scott. 1991. Navajo Sacred Places on Hopi Partitioned Lands. Confidential ms. on file, Navajo-Hopi Land Commission and Navajo Nation Historic Preservation Department, Window Rock, Arizona.

Kelley, Klara, Peggy F. Scott, and Harris Francis. 1991. Navajo and Hopi Relations. Ms. on file, Navajo-Hopi Land Commission, Window Rock, Arizona.

Kelley, Klara, and Peter M. Whiteley. 1989. *Navajoland: Family and Settlement and Land Use.* Tsaile, Arizona: Navajo Community College Press.

Kemrer, Meade F., and Kenneth J. Lord. 1984. *Cultural Resources Overview for the Navajo Forest.* Albuquerque: Chambers Consultants and Planners.

Klah, Hosteen. 1942. *Navajo Creation Myth.* Recorded by Mary C. Wheelwright. Santa Fe: Museum of Navajo Ceremonial Art.

Kluckhohn, Clyde. 1967 (1944). *Navaho Witchcraft.* Boston: Beacon Press.

Kluckhohn, Clyde, and Leland C. Wyman. 1969 (1940). *An Introduction to Navaho Chant Practice.* Memoirs of the American Anthropological Association No. 53. Menasha, Wisconsin.

La Barre, Weston. 1984. *Muelos: A Stone-Age Superstition about Sexuality.* New York: Columbia University Press.

La Farge, Oliver. 1963. Preface. *Navaho Religion,* by Gladys Reichard. Bollingen Series. Princeton: Princeton University Press.

Lange, Charles H. 1979a. Cochiti Pueblo. In *Handbook of North American Indians,* vol. 9: *Southwest,* ed. Alfonso Ortiz, pp. 366–78. Washington, D.C.: Smithsonian Institution.

————. 1979b. Santo Domingo Pueblo. In *Handbook of North American Indians,* vol. 9: *Southwest,* ed. Alfonso Ortiz, pp. 379–89. Washington, D.C.: Smithsonian Institution.

Left-Handed. 1967 (1938). *Son of Old Man Hat.* Recorded by Walter Dyk. Lincoln: University of Nebraska Press.

Linthicum, Leslie. 1992. The Huerfano Holy War. *Albuquerque Journal,* June 14, p. F–1.

Luckert, Karl W. 1975. *The Navajo Hunter Tradition.* Tucson: University of Arizona Press.

————. 1977. *Navajo Mountain and Rainbow Bridge Religion.* Flagstaff: Museum of Northern Arizona Press.

————. 1978. *A Navajo Bringing-Home Ceremony: The Claus Chee Sonny Version of Deerway Ajilee.* Flagstaff: Museum of Northern Arizona.

Luckert, Karl W., and Johnny C. Cooke. 1979. *Coyoteway: A Navajo Holyway Healing Ceremonial.* Tucson: University of Arizona Press.

Lyng v. Northwest Indian Cemetery Protective Association. 1988. No. 86–1013, U.S.

Sup. Ct., April 19, 1988. Full text in *Indian Law Reporter*, May 1988, 15:1017–27.

Magubane, Bernard, and James C. Faris. 1985. On the Political Relevance of Anthropology. *Dialectical Anthropology* 9:91–104.

Masayesva v. Zah. 1992. Federal District Court, Phoenix, Final Judgment (as amended December 18, 1992) (Appealed 1993, U.S. Court of Appeals, Ninth Circuit, No. 93–15109).

Matthews, Washington. 1887. The Mountain Chant: A Navajo Ceremony. In *Fifth Annual Report of the Bureau of American Ethnology for the Years 1883–1884*, pp. 37–467. Washington, D.C.: Smithsonian Institution.

———. 1897. *Navaho Legends.* New York: American Folklore Society.

———. 1902. *The Night Chant: A Navaho Ceremony.* Memoirs of the American Museum of Natural History 6. New York: Knickerbocker Press (AMS Reprint 1978).

McNeley, Grace. 1987. Home: A Family of Land and People. *Dine Be'iina* 1(l):161–64. Shiprock, New Mexico: Navajo Community College.

McNeley, James Kale. 1981. *Holy Wind in Navajo Philosophy.* Tucson: University of Arizona Press.

McNitt, Frank. 1962. *Navajo Traders.* Norman: University of Oklahoma Press.

———. 1972. *Navajo Wars.* Albuquerque: University of New Mexico Press.

Mitchell, Edward. 1991. Appendix B—Supplemental Ethnographic Reports. In A Cultural Resources Inventory of Compartments 34, 28, 45, and 50, Navajo Nation Forest, The Whiskey Creek/Ugly Valley Timber Sale, by Greg L. Bowen, Dennis Yazzie, Harold Yazzie, and Edward Mitchell. Report number HPD–91–109. Ms. on file, Navajo Nation Historic Preservation Department, Window Rock, Arizona.

Mitchell, Edward, and Jane King. 1990. Statement presented to the American Association for Indian Affairs Annual Board of Directors meeting, Camp Verde, Arizona, November 30. Navajo Nation Historic Preservation Department, Window Rock, Arizona. Ms. in authors' possession.

Mitchell, Frank. 1978. *Navajo Blessingway Singer: The Autobiography of Frank Mitchell, 1881–1967,* ed. Charlotte J. Frisbie and David McAllister. Tucson: University of Arizona Press.

Morse, Frances. 1990a. Tribes Say Woodruff Butte "Sacred." *Gallup Independent,* November 8, p. 3.

———. 1990b. Owner of Sacred Butte Says He'll Sell Land. *Gallup Independent,* November 24, p. 2.

———. 1991. Woodruff Butte Sale Put on Hold. *Gallup Independent,* August 23, p. 2.

Muga, David A. 1992. Indigenous Americans and the U.S. Constitution. *Nature, Society, and Thought* 5(1):51–67.

Nageezi Chapter. 1991. Resolution of Nageezi Chapter, April 21. Nageezi, New Mexico and Legislative Services Office, Window Rock, Arizona.

National Park Service and Navajo Nation. 1990. Joint Management Plan, Canyon de Chelly, Arizona. National Park Service, Southwest Regional Office, Santa Fe, New Mexico.

Navajo Nation. 1962. Proposed Findings of Fact in Behalf of the Navajo Tribe of Indians in Area of Havasupai Overlap. Docket 91 Before the Indian Claims Commission.

———. 1977. Untitled, list of Navajo sacred places on Hopi Partitioned Lands, submitted to U.S. District Court for Arizona in re: *Sekaquaptewa v. McDonald,* May 13, 1977. Confidential ms. on file, Navajo Nation Historic Preservation Department.

———. N.d.a. Forms for archaeological sites in the area of the Navajo Land

Claim before the Indian Claims Commission, Docket 229. Mss. on file, Navajo Nation Research Library, Window Rock, Arizona.

———. N.d.b. Proposed Findings of Fact on Behalf of the Navajo Tribe of Indians, Docket 229 before the Indian Claims Commission. On file, Navajo Nation Research Library, Window Rock, Arizona, and Gallup (New Mexico) Public Library.

Navajo Nation Council. 1958. Archaeology Permits. Title 16, Chapter 7, *Navajo Tribal Code*.

———. 1972. Removal and Destruction of Antiquities. Title 17, Chapter 3, *Navajo Tribal Code*.

———. 1977. Creation of Navajo Nation Archaeology Department and Navajo Tribal Museum. Title 19, Chapter 11, *Navajo Tribal Code*.

———. 1978. Desecration or Unlawful Destruction of Relics and Artifacts Associated with Traditional Navajo Spiritual Beliefs. Navajo Nation Council Resolution CF–20–78, February.

———. 1986. Navajo Nation Policies and Procedures Concerning Protection of Cemeteries, Gravesites, and Human Remains. Navajo Nation Council Resolution ACMA–39–86, May.

———. 1987. Adopting Navajo Nation Historic Preservation Department Plan of Operation. Navajo Nation Council Resolution ACJA–15–87, January.

———. 1988. Cultural Resources Protection Act (Replaces All Previous Titles and Resolutions). Navajo Nation Council Resolution CMY–19–88, May.

Navajo Nation Historic Preservation Department. 1990a. Draft Navajo Nation Policy to Protect Tradtional Cultural Properties. Window Rock, Arizona.

———. 1990b. Statement of the Navajo Nation about Woodruff Butte before the Navajo County Board of Supervisors meeting, September 4, Holbrook, Arizona. Ms. in authors' possession.

Navajo Times (Window Rock, Arizona). 1990 (May 3). Letters to the Editor.

———. 1990 (May 10). Letters to the Editor.

———. 1990 (December 27). Letters to the Editor.

———. 1991 (February 7). Letters to the Editor.

———. 1991 (July 18). Letters to the Editor.

Newcomb, Franc Johnson. 1940. Origin Legend of the Navaho Eagle Chant. *Journal of American Folklore* 53:50–77.

Newcomb, Franc Johnson, and Gladys Reichard. 1975 (1937). *Sandpaintings of the Navajo Shooting Chant*. New York: Dover. (Originally published by J. J. Augustin, New York.)

Oakes, Maud, Jeff King, and Joseph Campbell. 1943. *Where the Two Came to Their Father: A Navaho War Ceremonial*. Bollingen Series I. Princeton: Princeton University Press.

O'Bryan, Aileen, and Sandoval. 1956. *The Dine: Origin Myths of the Navaho Indians*. Bureau of American Ethnology Bulletin 163. Washington, D.C.: Government Printing Office.

Olin, Caroline, with Sally Hadlock. 1980. Recording the Roots of Navajo Culture. *Exxon USA* 19(2):26–31.

Opler, Morris E. 1983a. Chiricahua Apache. In *Handbook of North American Indians*, vol. 10: *Southwest*, ed. Alfonso Ortiz, pp. 401–18. Washington, D.C.: Smithsonian Institution.

———. 1983b. Mescalero Apache. In *Handbook of North American Indians*, vol. 10: *Southwest*, ed. Alfonso Ortiz, pp. 419–39. Washington, D.C.: Smithsonian Institution.

Ortiz, Alfonso, ed. 1979. *Handbook of North American Indians*, vol. 9: *Southwest*. Washington, D.C.: Smithsonian Institution.

Parker, Patricia L., and Thomas F. King. 1990. Guidelines for Evaluating and

Documenting Traditional Cultural Properties. *National Register Bulletin 38*. Washington, D.C.: National Park Service, Interagency Resources Division.

Plog, Fred. 1979. Prehistory: Western Anasazi. In *Handbook of North American Indians*, vol. 9: *Southwest*, ed. Alfonso Ortiz, pp. 108–30. Washington, D.C.: Smithsonian Institution.

Poster, Bruce. 1992. Economic Development in the Paragon Ranch Region of Northwest New Mexico. *Navajo Nation Economic Development Forum 12* (April). Navajo Nation Division of Economic Development, Window Rock, Arizona.

Preston, Scott. 1954. The Clans. In *Navajo Historical Selections*, by Robert Young and William Morgan, pp. 23–27. Navajo Historical Series 3. U.S. Department of the Interior, Bureau of Indian Affairs, Phoenix (Arizona) Indian School Print Shop.

Radford, Jeff. 1986. *The Chaco Coal Scandal: The People's Victory over James Watt*. Corrales, New Mexico: Rhombus.

Ramah Navajo Chapter. 1989. Resolution of January 13. Ramah, New Mexico, and Legislative Services Office, Window Rock, Arizona.

Redhouse, John. 1985a. *Geopolitics of the Navajo-Hopi Land Dispute*. Albuquerque: Redhouse/Wright Productions.

———. 1985b. *Holy Land: A Navajo Pilgrimage Back to Dinetah*. Albuquerque: Redhouse/Wright Productions.

Reichard, Gladys. 1944. *The Story of the Navajo Hail Chant*. New York: J. J. Augustin.

———. 1963 (1950). Navajo Religion. Bollingen Series. Princeton: Princeton University Press.

———. 1977 (1939). *Navaho Medicine Man: Sandpaintings and Legends of Miguelito*. New York: Dover. (Originally published by J. J. Augustin, New York.)

Reid, Betty. 1990. Drilling at Aneth Protested. *Gallup Independent*, April 3, p. 1.

———. 1991a. Relocated. *Gallup Independent*, February 20, p. 1.

———. 1991b. Zah: Navajoland Not a Dump. *Gallup Independent*, August 16.

Reno, Philip. 1981. *Mother Earth, Father Sky: Navajo Resources and Economic Development*. Albuquerque: University of New Mexico Press.

Richardson, Gladwell. 1985. *Navajo Trader*. Tucson: University of Arizona Press.

Ridington, Robin. 1981. Beaver Indians. In *Handbook of North American Indians*, vol. 6: *Subarctic*, ed. June Helm, pp. 350–60. Washington, D.C.: Smithsonian Institution.

———. 1988. *Trail to Heaven*. Iowa City: University of Iowa Press.

Russell, Johnny. 1991. To The Editor: Asbestos Waste Dump Coming to My Backyard. Ms. circulated to local newspapers, and in authors' possession.

Russell, Scott Christian. 1980. Navajo oral history and ethnohistory of northeastern Black Mesa: eastern lease area. Ms. in possession of Scott Russell.

Sando, Joe. 1979. Jemez Pueblo. In *Handbook of North American Indians*, vol. 9: *Southwest*, ed. Alfonso Ortiz, pp. 418–29. Washington, D.C.: Smithsonian Institution.

Sapir, Edward. 1942. *Navaho Texts*. Iowa City: Linguistic Society of America, University of Iowa.

Schoepfle, Mark, Kenneth Bigishe, Rose T. Morgan, Angela Johnson, and Peggy Scott. 1979. The Impact of the Navajo-Hopi Land Dispute—Teesto Chapter Report. Ms. on file, Navajo Community College, Shiprock.

Schroeder, Albert H. 1965. A Brief History of the Southern Utes. *Southwestern Lore* 30(4):53–78.

Shebala, Marley. 1991. Navajos Work to Protect Huerfano Mountain from Asbestos Dump. *The Navajo-Hopi Observer* (Flagstaff, Arizona), October 9, p. 5.

――――. 1992. School Teaches Navajo Customs. *Gallup Independent,* January 21, p. 1.

Silverman, Kaja. 1983. *The Subject of Semiotics.* New York: Oxford University Press.

Sollors, Werner, ed. 1989. *The Invention of Ethnicity.* New York: Oxford University Press.

Spencer, Katherine. 1957. *Mythology and Values: An Analysis of Navaho Chantway Myths.* Philadelphia: American Folklore Society.

Stephen, Alexander M., and Gishin Biye'. 1930. The Navajo Origin Legend. *Journal of American Folklore* 43:88–104.

Stoffle, Richard W., and Michael J. Evans. 1990. Holistic Conservation and Cultural Triage: American Indian Perspectives on Cultural Resources. *Human Organization* 49(2):91–99.

Stoffle, Richard W., David B. Halmo, Michael J. Evans, and John E. Olmstead. 1990. Calculating the Cultural Significance of American Indian Plants: Paiute and Shoshone Ethnobotany at Yucca Mountain, Nevada. *American Anthropologist* 92:416–32.

Stokes, M. A., and T. L. Smiley. 1963. Tree-Ring Dates from the Navajo Land Claim: I. The Northern Sector. *Tree-Ring Bulletin* 25:8–18.

――――. 1964. Tree-Ring Dates from the Navajo Land Claim: II. The Western Sector. *Tree-Ring Bulletin* 26:13–27.

――――. 1966. Tree-Ring Dates from the Navajo Land Claim III. The Southern Sector. *Tree-Ring Bulletin* 27(3–4):2–11.

――――. 1969. Tree-Ring Dates from the Navajo Land Claim: IV. The Eastern Sector. *Tree-Ring Bulletin* 29:2–14.

Taliman, Valerie. 1992. Navajo Nation Challenges Proposed Asbestos Dump. *High Country News* (Paonia, Colorado), May 4, p. 5.

Tedlock, Dennis. 1979. Zuni Religion and World View. In *Handbook of North American Indians,* vol. 9: *Southwest,* ed. Alfonso Ortiz, pp. 499–508. Washington, D.C.: Smithsonian Institution.

Threinen, Ellen. 1981. *The Navajos and the BIA.* U.S. Department of the Interior, Bureau of Indian Affairs, Navajo Area Office, Window Rock, Arizona.

Tiller, Veronica E. 1983. Jicarilla Apache. In *Handbook of North American Indians,* vol. 10: *Southwest,* ed. Alfonso Ortiz, pp. 440–61. Washington, D.C.: Smithsonian Institution.

Tsaile-Wheatfields Chapter. 1990. Resolution of March 18. Tsaile, Arizona, and Legislative Services Office, Window Rock, Arizona.

U.S. Congress. 1934. External Boundaries of the Navajo Reservation in Arizona. June 14. Ch. 521, 48 Stat., 960–62.

――――. 1969. National Environmental Policy Act.

――――. 1974. Navajo-Hopi Land Settlement Act. Public Law 93–531. May 29. 25 USC P 640.

――――. 1975. Indian Self-Determination and Education Assistance Act. Public Law 93–638. January 4.

――――. 1978. American Indian Religious Freedom Act. Public Law 95–341. August 11. 92 Stat. 469.

――――. 1979. Archaeological Resources Protection Act. Public Law 96–95. October 31.

――――. 1990. Native American Graves Protection and Repatriation Act. Public Law 101–601.

U.S. Department of the Interior, Bureau of Land Management, Albuquerque District Office. 1990. El Malpais National Conservation Area General Management Plan, draft (April).

――――. 1991. El Malpais National Conservation Area General Management Plan, final (January).

U.S. Department of the Interior, Bureau of Land Management, Las Cruces District Office. 1990. Fence Lake Project Final Environmental Impact Statement (September).

U.S. Department of the Interior, National Park Service. 1990a. El Malpais National Monument General Management Plan/Environmental Assessment/Wilderness Suitability Study, draft (January).

———. 1990b. El Malpais National Monument General Management Plan/ Environmental Assessment/Wilderness Suitability Study, final (October).

U.S. Department of the Interior, Federal Agencies Task Force. 1979. American Indian Religious Freedom Act Report. P.L. 95–341.

Vannette, Walter M., and Alison Feary. 1981. Navajo Sacred Places and Resource Use in and near the Coconino, Kaibab, and Apache Sitgreaves National Forests. Confidential ms. on file, U.S. Department of Agriculture, Coconino National Forest, Flagstaff, Arizona.

Vannette, Walter M., and Reed Tso. 1988. Navajo Religious Use of the 1934 Reservation Area. Expert Witness report, Brown and Bain, P.A., Phoenix, and the Navajo Nation Department of Justice, Window Rock, Arizona.

Van Valkenburgh, Richard F. 1940. Sacred Places and Shrines of the Navajos: Navajo Rock and Twig Piles Called Tsenadjih. *Plateau* 13(1):6–9.

———. 1941. Dine Bikeyah. Ms. U.S. Indian Service, Navajo Agency, Window Rock, Arizona.

———. 1956. Report of Archaeological Survey of the Navajo Hopi Contact Area. Prepared for Indian Claims Commission, Navajo Hopi Land Claim. Ms. on file, Laboratory of Tree-Ring Research, University of Arizona, Tucson.

———. 1974. Navajo Sacred Places. In *Navajo Indians III*, ed. David A. Horr. New York: Garland.

Walker, Captain J. G., and Major O. L. Shepherd. 1964. *The Navajo Reconnaissance*, ed. Lynn R. Bailey. Los Angeles: Westernlore Press.

Wallach, Amei. 1991a. Indian Leaders Battle Auction of Sacred Items. *New York Newsday*, May 21.

———. 1991b. Top Bidder to Return Sacred Indian Masks. *New York Newsday*, May 22.

———. 1991c. Return Mask but to Whom? *New York Newsday*, May 23.

Walt, Henry, Denny Apachito, Jr., George Apachito, Jackson Pino, Patsy Apachito, Betsy Brandt, Mike Marshall, and Chris Musello. 1987. Alamo Navajo Place Names: Mapping Database. Ms. Alamo Navajo School District, Alamo, New Mexico.

Walters, Harry. 1991a. A New Perspective on Navajo Prehistory. B.A. thesis, Goddard College, Plainfield, Vermont.

———. 1991b. Untitled presentation at Canyon de Chelly Navajo Guides Association Training Program, sponsored by the Canyon de Chelly National Monument (National Park Service), Chinle, Arizona, February 25.

Ward, Leah Beth. 1992. New PHM Board Eager to Reshape Company. *Albuquerque Journal*, August 30, p. F–3.

Watson, Editha. 1964. *Navajo Sacred Places*. Window Rock, Arizona: Navajo Tribal Museum.

Weiss, Lawrence David. 1984. *The Development of Capitalism in the Navajo Nation*. MEP, University of Minnesota, St. Paul.

Wheelwright, Mary Cabot. 1945. *Eagle Catching Myth and Bead Myth*. Santa Fe: Museum of Navajo Ceremonial Art Bulletin 3.

———. 1946a. *Hail Chant and Water Chant*. Navajo Religion Series 2. Santa Fe: Museum of Navajo Ceremonial Art.

———. 1946b. *Wind Chant and Feather Chant*. Santa Fe: Museum of Navajo Ceremonial Art Bulletin 4.

———. 1951. *Myth of Mountain Chant and Myth of Beauty Chant*. Santa Fe: Museum of Navajo Ceremonial Art Bulletin 5.

———. 1956. *The Myth and Prayers of the Great Star Chant and the Myth of the Coyote Chant*. Navajo Religion Series 4. Santa Fe: Museum of Navajo Ceremonial Art.

———. 1958. *Red Ant Myth and Shooting Chant*. Navajo Religion Series 7. Santa Fe: Museum of Navajo Ceremonial Art.

Whitson, Hollis A. 1985. A Policy Review of the Federal Government Relocation of Navajo Indians under P.L. 93–531. *Arizona Law Review* 17(2):371–414.

Wicoff, Mary. 1991a. Navajos Fight Star Mountain Fence. *Gallup Independent*, March 27, p. 1.

———. 1991b. Disputed Star Mountain Fencing Project Goes On. *Gallup Independent*, March 28, p. 1.

Wilson v. Block. 1983. 708 F. 2nd 735 (D.C. Cir.), Cert. denied, 104 S. Ct. 371 (1983).

Winter, Joseph C. 1986. New Evidence on the Arrival of the Athabaskans in the Southwest and Western High Plains. Paper presented at the Navajo Studies Conference, Albuquerque, New Mexico.

Wood, John J., and Walter M. Vannette. 1979. A Preliminary Assessment of the Significance of Navajo Sacred Places in the Vicinity of Big Mountain, Arizona. Ms. U.S. Department of the Interior, Bureau of Indian Affairs, Navajo Area Office, Window Rock, Arizona.

Wood, John J., Walter M. Vannette, and Michael J. Andrews. 1982. *"Sheep Is Life," An Assessment of Livestock Reduction in the Former Navajo-Hopi Joint Use Area*. Flagstaff: Northern Arizona University Anthropological Paper 1.

Wyman, Leland C. 1957. *Beautyway: A Navaho Ceremonial*. Bollingen Series. Princeton: Princeton University Press.

———. 1962. *The Windways of the Navaho*. Colorado Springs: Taylor Museum.

———. 1965. *The Red Antway of the Navaho*. Navajo Religion Series 5. Santa Fe: Museum of Navajo Ceremonial Art.

———. 1970. *Blessingway*. Tucson: University of Arizona Press.

———. 1975. *The Mountainway of the Navajo*. Tucson: University of Arizona Press.

Yazzie, Alfred. 1984. *Navajo Oral Tradition* (3 vols.). Chinle, Arizona: Rough Rock Demonstration School.

York, Frederick F. 1979. An Ethnohistory of Human Occupation and Land-Use Activities on the PNM Project Area of the Bisti. In *An Inventory and Analysis of Archaeological Resources on 3.8 Sections of Land near the Bisti Badlands, Northwestern New Mexico*, ed. Margaret A. Powers, Appendix D. Bloomfield, New Mexico: San Juan County Museum Division of Conservation Archaeology Contributions to Anthropology Series 119.

———. 1982. The Results of the Ethnographic Survey. In *The Cultural Resources of the Proposed New Mexico Generating Station Study Area, San Juan Basin, New Mexico*, ed. Carol J. Condie and Ruthann Knudson. Albuquerque: Quivira Research Center Publication 39.

———. 1984. *Historic Cultural Resources in the Arch Joint Venture Project Area along the De-Na-Zin Wash*. Office of Contract Archeology, University of New Mexico, Albuquerque.

———. 1990. Capitalist Development and Land in Northeastern Navajo Country, 1880s to 1980s. Ph.D. diss. in anthropology, State University of New York, Binghamton.

York, Frederick F., and Joseph C. Winter. 1988. *Report of an Ethnographic Study and Archeological Review of Proposed Coal Lease Tracts in Northwestern New Mexico*. Office of Contract Archeology, University of New Mexico, Albuquerque.

Young, Robert W. 1978. *A Political History of the Navajo Tribe*. Tsaile, Arizona: Navajo Community College Press.

Zolbrod, Paul G. 1984. *Dine Bahane': The Navajo Creation Story*. Albuquerque: University of New Mexico Press.

Zuni Tribal Council. 1990. Resolution M70–90–1132, August 21.

INDEX

Acoma (Pueblo) Indians, 171, 174, 206, 212
Alamo Navajo Reservation, NM, 52, 59, 234
Alamo Navajo School Board, 59
Albuquerque, NM, 121, 162, 167
Allotments, Indian, 56–57, 154, 156. *See also* Checkerboard Area, NM
American Indian Religious Freedom Act (AIRFA), 4, 15–16, 57, 138, 143, 153, 156, 162, 174–76
American Indian Self-Determination Act, 58
Anasazis, 29–30, 35, 39, 40, 48, 57, 71–72, 77, 81, 82–83, 98, 110, 126, 155, 180, 188–89, 209, 211–19, 233–34. *See also* Archaeological sites; specific place names
Aneth, UT, 134, 147, 162–63, 181
Apache Indians, 188, 206–209, 213, 218, 225; Jicarilla, 78–79; Navajo, 166; Western, 170, 171; White Mountain, 143
Apache-Sitgreaves National Forest, AZ. *See* Arizona National Forests
Archaeological Resources Protection Act (ARPA), 138
Archaeological sites, 48, 107, 116, 119, 124, 146, 151, 158, 160, 168–69, 178, 180–81, 190, 221. *See also* Anasazis; Landscapes and social groups; Sacred places; specific types of sites
Archetypes, 190, 200
Arizona National Forests, 52, 58, 87, 92, 143, 233–34. *See also* United States government: Forest Service
Arizona Navajo Reservation of 1934, 52, 84, 154–55, 233–34. *See also* Navajo-Hopi disputes; Navajo-Hopi Land Settlement Act
Arts and crafts sales, 126, 127, 164. *See also* Economic development; Tourism
Asbestos, 179–81

Asdzaan Bazhnoodaa'i, 100
Athabaskan Indians, 126, 165, 188, 206, 212–19, 225
Attakai v. United States. *See* Sacred places: access to

Badonie v. Higginson. *See* Rainbow Bridge, AZ
Bandelier, Adolph, 214
Barboncito, 151
Bead Way, 82, 218
Beauty Way, 219
Beclabito, NM, 14, 25–27, 232–33
Be'ochidi, 194–95
Benavides, Fray Alonso de, 166
Biakeddy, Jesse, 194, 199
Big Mountain, AZ, 56, 61, 92, 153, 194–97, 199. *See also* Black Mesa; Hopi Partitioned Lands; Navajo-Hopi disputes; Relocation; Executive Order Reservation of 1882
Big Mountain Dine Nation, 154
Big Sheep Mountain, CO, 71, 114, 174, 201. *See also* Mountains of cardinal directions
Bisti, NM, 57, 143, 155, 174. *See also* Paragon Ranch, NM
Black Lake (Dark Lake), NM, 67, 111
Black Mesa, AZ, 29, 100, 134, 150–52, 174, 194, 196–97, 212, 218. *See also* Big Mountain, AZ; Coal mining; Navajo-Hopi disputes; Executive Order Reservation of 1882
Blanca Peak, CO, 174. *See also* Mountains of cardinal directions
Blanco Canyon, NM, 179–81
Blessingway, 21, 22–25, 35, 76, 80, 81, 83, 106, 110, 113, 115, 118, 119, 168, 194, 197, 201–204, 216–20
Bloomfield, NM, 179
Blue Gap-Tachee, AZ, 14, 25–27, 232–33
Bodaway, AZ, 195

Born For Water. *See* Twins
Boulder (Hoover) Dam, 19. *See also* Dams
Brown, Eddie, Assistant Secretary of Interior, 162
Buffalo Pass, AZ, 194
Bullhead City, NV, 150

Calling God, 40, 74
Canyon de Chelly, AZ, 52, 59, 61, 65, 68, 71–72, 83, 84, 86, 87, 89, 90, 92, 96, 106, 108, 110, 126, 134, 161, 163–64, 233–34. *See also* Tourism; United States government: National Park Service
Canyon del Muerto, AZ. *See* Canyon de Chelly
Caretaker ethic, 93–94, 99–100, 151, 158–62, 170, 184. *See also* Environment: protection of; Landscapes: and piecemeal approach; Mother Earth
Carson, Col. Christopher (Kit), 18, 167. *See also* Fort Sumner
Carter, President Jimmy, 154
Celestial bodies, 46, 80, 106, 117
Central Arizona Project, 150–51
Central places, 28, 38, 48, 130, 150, 181–83. *See also* Navajo Nation government: chapters
Ceremonialism: and healing, 22, 136–48, 180; paraphernalia of, 21–22, 25, 33–35, 36–37, 69, 72, 74–76, 80, 81, 83, 111, 131, 139–41, 144, 168, 172–73, 184, 201–204, 206–209; and plants, 21–22, 25, 33–35, 45, 81, 83, 88, 95, 107, 108, 110–11, 131, 140, 157, 161–63, 172–73, 174, 178–79, 180, 184, 198; procedures of, performances in, 10, 21–22, 25, 30–35, 62, 72, 75–76, 81, 92, 95, 116–17, 123, 129, 132, 151, 157, 161, 170, 172–73, 178, 184, 195–96, 198–99, 201–204, 206–211, 226–27; raw materials for, *see* paraphernalia of; repertoires of, 21–22, 85, 90, 108, 113, 119, 120, 126, 140, 178. *See also* Stories; names of specific paraphernalia, procedures, and repertoires
Chaco Canyon, NM, 34, 57, 59, 71, 77, 85, 105, 108, 110–13, 155, 215, 234
Chambers-Sanders Trust Lands, AZ, 134, 154–57. *See also* Navajo-Hopi disputes
Changing Woman, 22–25, 30, 38, 43, 65, 67–68, 71, 74–76, 80, 82, 106, 118, 119, 121, 122, 155, 158, 166, 179, 199–204, 206–207, 218–20, 226–27
Chanters. *See* Medicine people
Chapters. *See* Navajo Nation government: chapters

Checkerboard Area, NM, 52, 56–57, 154, 169, 171, 173, 185
Chimney Rock, CO, 166
Chinle, AZ, 182
Christians, 140, 141, 174, 182, 195, 217. *See also* Mormons
Chuska Mountains, AZ and NM, 161, 185. *See also* Navajo Forest
Citibank, 160
Claw Way, 33
Coal Creek massacre site, NM, 77–79
Coal mining, 19, 29, 55, 56–57, 89, 98, 100, 103, 107, 129, 134, 143, 150–55, 171–72, 173, 174. *See also* Economic development
Coconino National Forest, AZ. *See* Arizona National Forests; San Francisco Peaks
Colonialism, 11, 17–19, 41, 54, 98–100, 118, 167–68, 187–89, 191, 210–11, 212, 216, 221–24. *See also* Economic development; Fort Sumner
Colorado River, 18, 36, 52, 119, 134, 201, 207
Comanche Indians, 167
Cone Towards Water Man, 110
Continental Divide, 121
Corn, 29, 117, 119, 131, 212; blue corn bread, 200–203. *See also* Farming
Corn Maidens, 219
Coronado, Don Francisco de, 19, 211
Coyote, 23, 29, 36
Coyote Pass Canyon, NM, 108, 109
Coyote Way, 82
Crane petroglyphs, 76–77, 111, 155. *See also* De-Na-Zin, NM
Crownpoint, NM, 182
Crystal, NM, 65
Cultural resources, 4–5, 15, 16, 58, 62, 91, 128, 129, 146–48, 151, 163, 179, 180–81. *See also* specific types
Culture: loss of, 4, 9, 30, 33–35, 42, 46–47, 49–50, 90, 91, 97–98, 100, 105, 153, 156, 168, 188–89, 211; preservation of, 1, 5, 16, 60, 135–48, 210–11; secrecy and preservation of, 1, 3, 5, 6, 34, 50, 64, 102, 105, 145, 147, 149, 176
Customary use areas. *See* Landscapes: and social groups; Permits

Dams, 18, 33, 103, 121. *See also* names of individual dams
De-Na-Zin, NM, 52, 87, 233–34. *See also* Bisti, NM; Crane petroglyphs; Paragon Ranch, NM
Depression, 19, 148
Dine, 10. *See also* Navajo
Dine Bikeyah Committee, 154

Dine BiWilderness Society, 184. *See also* Dine CARE
Dine CARE, 159, 162, 181, 183–84
Dine Spiritual and Cultural Society, 142, 169, 181, 183. *See also* Navajo Medicine Men's Association
Dinetah, NM, 71, 119, 121, 123, 124, 134, 154, 165–69, 179, 185, 213, 215, 218
DNA legal aid, 142, 143
Documents, historical, 17, 151, 221. *See also* Research methods; Stories: forms of
Downy Home Man, 111, 219
Draper, Teddy, Sr., 65, 71
Durango, CO, 114

Earth-surface people, 24
Economic development, 3, 6, 11, 16, 50, 60, 81, 90, 101–104, 135–36, 149–64, 168–84, 188, 232. *See also* Colonialism; specific types of development
Education, 46, 100, 130, 138–39, 148, 168–69, 182–83. *See also* Culture: loss of
Electrical power generation, 18, 19, 56–57, 103, 144, 150–51, 153, 155, 174, 176. *See also* Economic development
El Malpais, NM, 171–73
Emergence (story), 23, 28–29, 36, 106, 114, 116, 118, 166, 197, 199–201, 207, 217, 226–27
Enemy Way, 69, 82, 142, 180, 196, 219
Environment: and ceremonialism, 20, 25, 141, 144–45; protection of, 9, 100, 141, 151, 158–62, 176, 183. *See also* Caretaker ethic; Mother Earth
Erosion control, 19, 96, 152–53, 158, 161, 164. *See also* Livestock reduction program
Eskimos, 225
Ethnicity, 11, 18, 24, 135, 188, 205, 209–220, 223–27
European Americans. *See* Whites
Evil Way, 82
Executive Order Reservation of 1882, 54–56, 143–44, 198. *See also* Hopi Indians; Hopi Partitioned Lands; Navajo-Hopi disputes; Navajo Partitioned Lands

Farming, 17–19, 20, 25, 34, 43, 96, 102, 164, 166–67, 198, 200–204. *See also* Corn
Father Sky, 184
Fence Lake Project, 174
First Man and First Woman, 23–25, 118, 125, 200, 202, 217
Flagstaff, AZ, 34, 71
Forest Trust, 161
Fort Defiance, AZ, 62, 182

Fort Sumner, NM, 18, 30–31, 77, 83, 113, 132, 167, 194, 195–96, 210
Fort Wingate, NM, 182
Four Corners–Pajarito transmission line, 52, 60–61, 87, 92, 233–34. *See also* Public Service Company of New Mexico (PNM)
Francis, Rose, 79
Frenzyway, 106, 108–112, 178, 219

Ganado, AZ, 34
Ganado Mucho, 194
Gilmore, Mary, 151
Gishin Biye', 215, 220
Glen Canyon Dam, 103, 143, 176. *See also* Dams
Gobernador Knob, NM. *See* Spruce Mountain, NM
Governments, state, 114, 118, 132, 169, 170, 178–79, 181. *See also* Navajo Nation government; United States government
Grand Canyon, AZ, 103, 183
Grants, NM, 171
Graves. *See* Native American Graves Protection and Repatriation Act; Navajo Nation government: laws of; Sacred places: types
Grazing. *See* Erosion control; Livestock
Great Gambler, 71, 77, 82, 105, 106, 108, 111–12

Haashch'eeh, 82, 98, 207, 209
Hadlock, Harry and Sallie, 168
Havasupai Indians, 183
Healing v. Jones, 198. *See also* Navajo-Hopi disputes
Hesperus Peak, CO. *See* Big Sheep Mountain
Historic preservation, 4, 92. *See also* Cultural resources; Culture: preservation of
History. *See* Stories
Hogans, 20–21, 23, 73, 115, 117, 124, 130, 167, 180, 198, 226
Holy People, 1, 2, 20, 21, 22, 25, 28–29, 36, 41, 45, 76, 77, 93, 95, 100, 113, 184, 226. *See also* Inner forms; Power; names of specific holy people
Homesites, 117, 125, 129. *See also* Hogans; Landscapes: and social groups
Hopi Indians, 33–34, 71, 143, 156, 170, 178–79, 188, 194–95, 198, 206–209, 212. *See also* Ethnicity; Navajo-Hopi disputes; Pueblo Indians
Hopi Partitioned Lands, 52, 63, 79, 92, 134, 150, 152–54, 156, 193, 233–34. *See also* Black Mesa; Executive Order Reservation of 1882; Navajo-Hopi disputes

Hopi villages, 108. *See also* individual villages
Horses, origin of (story), 73–76, 98, 204, 210, 220. *See also* Livestock
Houses. *See* Hogans
Huerfano Mountain (Huerfano Mesa), 30, 65, 71, 73, 143, 155, 156, 166, 167, 169, 179–80
Hunting ceremonial procedures, 82, 110

Immortals. *See* Holy People
Indian Wells, AZ, 14, 25–27, 48, 232–33
Inner forms, 10, 21, 110, 170. *See also* Holy People; Power
Insulation Contracting Unlimited (ICU), 179–81
Intellectual property, 88. *See also* Culture: secrecy and preservation of; Storytelling

Jemez Indians, 83, 108, 214, 215. *See also* Pueblo Indians
Jensen, Nevy, 113, 132, 225
Jish, 139, 140–44. *See also* Ceremonialism
Jobs, 19, 102, 103, 129, 148, 157, 161, 163, 164, 173, 183–84. *See also* Economic development

Kaibab National Forest, AZ. *See* Arizona National Forests
Kayenta, AZ, 14, 25–27, 28, 232–33
Keams Canyon, AZ, 109, 198

Laguna Pueblo Indians, 83, 171, 206, 212. *See also* Pueblo Indians
Lake Powell, UT, 35, 143, 176, 180. *See also* Dams; Rainbow Bridge, AZ
Lake That Takes Pity On Others, AZ, 80
Land disputes, 32, 163, 164. *See also* Navajo-Hopi disputes
Land ownership, 165–83, 185. 194. *See also* Allotments; Checkerboard Area, NM; Navajo-Hopi disputes; Navajo Reservation; United States government
Landscapes, 41, 42–46, 91–104; organizing principles of, 19–21, 23, 43, 72, 81, 89, 114, 115, 187–88, 196–97; and planning, 5–6, 94, 101–104, 129, 145–48, 149–84; and piecemeal approach, 42, 54, 90, 91–104, 187–88; and social groups, 43–44, 87, 90, 92–93, 96–100, 101–104, 107, 117, 129, 145–48, 149–50, 156–59, 171–73, 177, 180, 194–204, 221–24; and teaching, 140, 148; zones of, 94–96, 103, 108, 151, 157, 164, 171–73, 175, 196. *See also* Caretaker ethic; Economic development; Sacred places; Sacred preserves

Language: bilingualism in government agencies, 175; and clans, 215; figurative, 100, 187–92, 193–204. *See also* Navajo: language; Research methods
La Plata Mountains, CO. *See* Big Sheep Mountain, CO
Largo Canyon, NM, 71
Laws, 54, 137–38, 149–84. *See also* Navajo Nation government: laws of; specific titles
Lawsuits, 169–81. *See also* Navajo-Hopi disputes; specific titles
Leases. *See* Right-of-way, lease, and royalty payments
Leupp, AZ, 14, 25–27, 182, 232–33
Lifeway, 33, 77, 81
Lightning, 73, 125, 204
Little Colorado River, 52, 54, 123, 134, 207
Livestock, 17–19, 22, 25, 32, 43, 73–76, 78, 81, 93, 96, 102, 125, 155, 156, 158, 161, 163, 164, 167, 180, 203, 210, 216. *See also* Erosion control; Landscapes: and social groups; Livestock reduction program
Livestock reduction program: of 1930s, 19, 130, 156; on Hopi Partitioned Lands, 152; in Navajo Forest, 158, 161
Los Angeles, 18
Los Pinos River, 121, 166
Lower Greasewood, AZ, 141
Lukachukai, AZ, 34, 194, 196
Lunch, 200–203
Lyng v. Northwest Cemetery Protective Association, 176

Manygoats, Sylvia, 30, 64, 91, 196
Martinez, Romalo, 180
Mask, 168, 209. *See also* Ceremonialism: paraphernalia of
McKinley Mine, 174
Medicine people, 3, 21, 25, 58, 61–62, 81–82, 89, 95, 132, 136–48, 157, 168, 171, 174, 194. *See also* Navajo Medicine Men's Association
Mexicans. *See* Spaniards
Mexican War, 19
Mirage Man, 74–75
Mirage stone, 73–76, 118, 204, 220. *See also* Ceremonialism
Mitchell, Frank, 82
Moencopi, AZ, 34
Mogollon Rim, 54
Monsters, 32, 38, 40, 67–70, 106, 120, 121, 124, 217–19
Monster Slayer, 74–76, 98, 120, 196, 204, 218. *See also* Twins
Monument Valley, 127, 163

Moon, 76, 195, 200–203, 206–207. *See also* Celestial bodies

Morgan, Yanua, 163

Morgan, Bessie Adakai, 163, 181

Mormons, 68, 178, 183

Mother Earth, 29, 43, 99–100, 162, 184, 188. *See also* Caretaker ethic

Mountain soil, 23, 35, 114

Mountains of cardinal directions (sacred), 14, 20–21, 23–24, 50, 74, 96, 114, 115, 123, 134, 143, 170, 194, 196–97. *See also* Landscapes: organizing principles of; Mountain soil

Mountaintop Way, 82, 219

Mount Taylor, NM, 30, 174. *See also* Mountains of cardinal directions

Myths, 22, 189–91. *See also* Stories

Nabahe, Reginald, 65, 111, 196, 218

Nageezi, NM, 169, 179

Names, 198. *See also* Holy People; Places: names of

Narbona Pass, NM, 69

National Environmental Policy Act (NEPA), 4, 16, 57, 138

National Historic Preservation Act (NHPA), 16, 57, 138, 153, 156, 158, 170, 174, 181

National Register of Historic Places (NRHP). *See* National Historic Preservation Act

Native American Church, 140, 142

Native American Graves Protection and Repatriation Act (NAGPRA), 176–77

Nativistic movement, 188, 216–20

Navajo, NM, 160

Navajo: clans, 17–18, 24, 79–80, 82, 166, 197, 209, 213–16, 218, 225–26; communities, 7, 18, 19–20, 101–104, 130, 145–48, 150, 171–73, 179–81, 182–83, 197; language, 8, 27, 65, 105, 139, 194, 213. *See also* Ceremonialism; Culture; Ethnicity; Landscapes; Navajo Nation government; Sacred places; Stories

Navajo Ceremonial Practitioners' Registry, 137, 140

Navajo Community College, 139, 144, 168–69

Navajo–Cornell University Field Health Research Project, 136

Navajo Forest, 52, 58, 62, 134, 157–62, 233–34. *See also* Navajo Forest Products Industries

Navajo Forest Products Industries, 62, 159–62. *See also* Navajo Forest

Navajo Guides Association, 164

Navajo-Hopi disputes, 34, 54–56, 143–44, 151–57, 198, 222–23. *See also* Arizona Navajo Reservation of 1934; Executive Order Reservation of 1882; Navajo-Hopi Land Settlement Act

Navajo-Hopi Land Settlement Act, 55, 56, 154–55. *See also* Navajo-Hopi disputes; Arizona Navajo Reservation of 1934

Navajo Indian Irrigation Project, 167. *See also* Dams; Navajo Reservoir, NM

Navajo Land Claim (before the Indian Claims Commission), 52, 54, 134, 136, 143, 168, 169, 185, 213, 233–34

Navajo Medicine Men's Association, 62, 137, 140–44, 158, 167, 175. *See also* Dine Spiritual and Cultural Society

Navajo Mountain, AZ and UT, 14, 25–27, 30, 33–34, 48, 196, 207, 232–33

Navajo Nation Cultural Resources Protection Act, 137–38

Navajo Nation government, 4, 63, 128, 129, 141, 150, 164; Archaeology Department, 137; chapters, 14, 26–27, 48–49, 61, 97, 130, 141, 146–48, 154, 155, 157, 159, 163, 164, 169, 170–84; Council (legislative), 137–38, 159, 160–61; Division of Resources, 159; Forestry Department, 157–58, 162; Historic Preservation Department, 4–5, 15, 137, 179; laws of, 137–38; Navajo Health Authority, 62, 137, 140–42; Navajo Tribal Museum, 136, 169; Office of Navajo Economic Opportunity, 137; Office of Navajo Healing Sciences, 137; origin of, 19; senior citizens' programs, 174

Navajo Nation Policy to Protect Cemeteries, Gravesites, and Human Remains. *See* Navajo Nation government: laws of

Navajo Partitioned Lands, 152, 154–55. *See also* Executive Order Reservation of 1882

Navajo Rehabilitation Trust Fund, 154–55

Navajo Reservation, 14, 18, 52, 113, 150, 182, 185. *See also* Arizona Navajo Reservation of 1934; Chambers-Sanders Trust Lands, AZ; Checkerboard Area, NM; Executive Order Reservation of 1882; Treaty of 1868

Navajo Reservoir, NM, 121, 167–68. *See also* Dams

Ned Hatathle Museum. *See* Navajo Community College

Nenahnezad, NM, 14, 25–27, 232–33

Nightway, 21, 82, 106, 126, 142, 207

Ocean, 199, 200–203

Oil and gas, 19, 124, 147, 155, 162–63, 168, 170. *See also* Economic development

Old Soldier, 108
Oraibi, AZ, 34, 72
Overgrazing. *See* Erosion control; Livestock

Page, AZ, 72, 150
Paiute Indians, 183
Paragon Ranch, NM, 62, 134, 154–55. *See also* Bisti, NM; Crane petroglyphs; De-Na-Zin, NM; Navajo Rehabilitation Trust Fund; Public Service Company of New Mexico; Ute Mountain Land Exchange
Peabody Coal Company, 150–52, 174
Permits: grazing, 163, 170; land-use, 164. *See also* Right-of-way, lease, and royalty payments
Petroglyphs, pictographs, 71, 119, 166, 167, 168. *See also* Crane petroglyphs
Peyote. *See* Native American Church
Phoenix, AZ, 151, 157, 174
Piedra River, CO, 166
Places: names of, 41, 49–50, 59, 84–86, 91, 105–107, 210, 215–16, 234; related to Frenzyway, 108–112. *See also* specific place names
Planting stick, 200–203. *See also* Ceremonialism
Plants. *See* Ceremonialism
Plumeway, 207
Pollen, 75–76, 184, 196, 202. *See also* Ceremonialism
Power, 1, 10, 21–22, 45, 50, 62, 93, 98, 100, 125, 140, 151, 164, 196, 201, 203, 225. *See also* Holy People; Inner Forms; Sacred places: significance of
Power plants. *See* Electrical power generation
Prayersticks, 203, 207–209. *See also* Ceremonialism
Preference Right Lease Applications (PRLAs), 171. *See also* Right-of-way, lease, and royalty payments
Public buildings. *See* Central places
Public Service Company of New Mexico (PNM), 57, 60, 92, 155. *See also* Four Corners–Pajarito transmission line; Paragon Ranch, NM; Ute Mountain land exchange
Pueblo Indians, 17, 18, 69, 111–12, 124, 167, 206–209, 211–19, 223, 225–26. *See also* Stories: Puebloan; names of individual groups
Pueblo Revolt, 167, 216

Quetzalcoatl, 195

Railroad, 18, 156, 171
Rainbow Bridge, AZ, 33, 143, 176

Rain requesting procedures, 36–37, 106, 111, 209. *See also* Ceremonialism; Weather
Ram, 73
Ramah Navajo History Committee, 173, 183
Ramah Navajo Reservation, NM, 139, 171–74
Reagan, President Ronald, 137–38, 154, 157
Reconquest (Spanish), 167
Recreation. *See* Tourism
Relocation, 55, 144, 152–53, 194–99. *See also* Navajo-Hopi disputes; United States government: Navajo and Hopi Indian Relocation Commission
Research methods, 6–8, 11, 27–28, 39, 42, 47, 54, 60–63, 84–90, 146, 169, 187–92, 209–210, 221–23, 232, 233
Return to the earth, 140, 144, 152, 168. *See also* Culture: loss of
Right-of-way, lease, and royalty payments, 88, 129, 157, 160, 171; and grazing permit, 163. *See also* Economic development; Permits
Rio Grande National Forest, CO, 177
Rio Grande (river), 52, 54, 121, 124, 167
Road construction, 94, 95, 114, 122, 124, 128, 155, 178–79. *See also* Economic development
Rock Point, AZ, 139
Rough Rock Demonstration School, 138, 140–41
Routes: of ceremonial travel, 85, 96, 106, 108–110, 120–23, 125, 128, 143, 194–97, 199–204, 207–209, 215; and learning about sacred places, 89, 97
Royalties. *See* Right-of-way, lease, and royalty payments

Sackler, Elizabeth, 168
Sacred places: access to, 55, 150, 152–53, 174; boundaries of, 92–97, 118; defined, 2, 40; intertribal interest in, 170–84; protection measures, 101–104, 128, 146–48, 169, 175, 178–81; ranking of, 91–95; significance of, 39–40, 42–46, 50, 59–60, 61, 84–86, 90, 91–95, 98, 171–73, 178, 179–81, 191–92, 194–204, 205, 221; types, 1, 6, 9, 35, 38–39, 44–46, 58, 59–62, 79, 81–84, 98, 106–112, 113–32, 168, 172, 180, 194, 199, 233–34. *See also* Ceremonialism; Cultural resources; Landscapes; Sacred preserves; Stories; specific types; specific place names
Sacred preserves, 45, 70, 96, 118, 162,

175, 179. *See also* Landscapes: zones of;
Sacred places
Salt, Mamie, 28, 42, 91, 98, 100, 151
Salt River Project (SRP), 174
Salt Woman, 125
Sand Springs, AZ, 198
San Francisco Peaks, AZ, 58, 94–95, 110,
123, 143, 170–71, 174, 176, 207. *See also*
Mountains of cardinal directions
San Juan Basin, NM, 52, 56–57, 77
San Juan Basin Wilderness Protection Act,
154
San Juan–Chama Diversion Project, 167.
See also Navajo Reservoir
San Juan Mountains, CO, 166
San Juan National Forest, CO, 177
San Juan River, 36, 52, 119, 121, 166, 167,
180, 201
Sanostee, NM, 14, 25–27, 232–33
Savings and loan crash, 157
Schools. *See* Central places; Education
Scott, Peggy Francis, 79
Seasons, 197, 200–204, 208, 214; and use
of sacred place, 80, 82, 106. *See also*
Celestial bodies; Storytelling; Weather
Separation of the Sexes (story), 23, 37–38
Sheep Springs, NM, 14, 25–27, 232–33
Shiprock, NM, 69, 182
Shooting Way, 83
Slave trade. *See* Warfare
Snake, 112, 125
Spaniards, 17–18, 71, 79, 90, 124, 188,
210, 217, 219. *See also* Whites
Spider Woman, 111
Springs, 200–203. *See also* Rain request-
ing procedures; Sacred places: types;
Weather
Spruce Mountain, NM, 24, 166
Star Mountain, AZ (Crystal), 68, 70–71
Star Mountain, AZ (Hopi Partitioned
Lands), 79–80, 153, 196
Stars. *See* Celestial bodies
Stony Butte, NM, 108. *See also* White Rock,
NM
Stories: forms of, 2, 22, 49, 106, 136, 139,
188–92, 210–11; and ceremonialism, 7,
10, 49, 106, 120, 126, 151, 206–211;
and history, 2–3, 6, 189–92; intertribal,
188, 205–209, 214–20, 221; and landscape, 187–88, 191–92, 205–209, 215–
16; about origins, 2, 22–25, 113, 119,
120, 126, 165–67, 187–91, 209–220,
224–27; Puebloan, 169, 178, 188, 205–
209; and social classes, 222. *See also*
specific names of ceremonies, people,
places, and stories
Storytelling, 22, 49, 89, 97, 137, 148, 214–

15; and seasons, 28, 35–36, 88; situa-
tions of, 64–65, 68, 116, 123, 132
Sun, 24, 32, 38, 65–67, 74, 76, 106, 161–
62, 200–204, 218–20. *See also* Celestial
bodies
Surface Mining Control and Reclamation
Act (SMCRA), 172. *See also* Coal mining
Sweathouse, 23, 66, 68, 97, 116, 180, 198,
226. *See also* Storytelling
Symbolism. *See* Language: figurative

Talking God, 40, 74, 82–83, 110
Tall Chanter, 217
Taos: Blue Lake of, 92; Pueblo Indians of,
225. *See also* Pueblo Indians
Taylor Grazing Act, 19, 156
Teesto, AZ, 154
Tewa Indians, 214, 225–26. *See also* Pueblo
Indians
Timber cutting, 58, 94, 143, 157–62, 176.
See also Economic development
Toadlena, NM, 14, 25–27; see also Two
Gray Hills
Tonalea, AZ, 34
Tourism, 28, 40, 48, 58, 59, 94, 96, 121,
126, 127, 143, 155, 161, 163–64, 168,
170–73, 174, 176, 183
Trading posts, 18, 34, 130, 180, 182. *See
also* Central places
Treaty of 1868, 18, 54, 113, 132, 151, 167
Tsaile-Wheatfields, AZ, 14, 25–27, 159,
232–33
Tsegi Canyon, AZ, 85, 234
Tso, Ed, 62
Tuba City, AZ, 14, 25–27, 34, 48, 182–83,
232–33
Tuba City Cultural Projects, Inc., 182–83
Tucson, AZ, 151
Turquoise, 36–37, 73–76, 184, 200–203,
206, 227. *See also* Ceremonialism
Twins, 24, 30, 32, 38, 40, 65–70, 71, 82,
106, 118, 119, 121, 161–62, 166, 168,
204, 208, 218–20
The Two Came To Their Father (story), 24,
32, 38, 65–67, 82, 106
Two Gray Hills, 232–33. *See also* Toadlena,
NM

United States government: Army, 18–19,
125, 196; Bureau of Indian Affairs
(BIA), 55, 58, 62, 96, 128, 130, 152–53,
159, 162, 182–83; Bureau of Land Management (BLM), 18, 57, 124, 154, 167,
168, 169–75; Bureau of Reclamation,
121; Economic Development Administration (EDA), 160; Federal Communications Commission (FCC), 167;

Forest Service, 18, 58, 94, 96, 114, 167, 169–70, 175–77; Indian Claims Commission, *see* Navajo Land Claim; Indian Health Service (IHS), 136–37; National Park Service, 59, 163–64, 167, 169–77; Navajo and Hopi Indian Relocation Commission (NHIRC), 56, 156; Office of Economic Opportunity, 137; Office of Navajo-Hopi Indian Relocation, 56, 156; Soil Conservation Service, 198. *See also* Colonialism; Laws; Warfare; names of specific dams, forests, parks, and reservations

Upward Reaching Way, 82, 215, 220
Uranium mining, 19, 56–57, 143, 171
Ute Indians, 18, 72, 77, 121, 124, 167, 216
Ute Mountain land exchange, 62, 87, 92, 233–34. *See also* De-Na-Zin, NM; Paragon Ranch, NM

Vandalism, 124, 146, 168–69, 182. *See also* Sacred places: protection measures

Walpi, AZ, 109
Walters, Harry, 168–69
Warfare, 17–18, 30, 36, 69, 71, 77–79, 83, 90, 113, 121, 124, 143, 166–67, 188, 196, 204, 207–208, 220
Water Monster, 23, 28–29, 36–37
Waterway, 106, 178, 207, 219
Watson, Tom, Sr., 62
Watt, James, 154
Weather, 32–33, 72, 77, 106, 200–204, 207–209, 212; and ceremonialism, 36–37, 61, 81; and sacred places, 46, 61, 69

Western Water Clans, 79–80, 82, 106, 123, 124, 200–203, 209, 215, 218
Wheatfields Lake, AZ, 161
Wheelwright Museum, 139
White Butterfly, 111–12. *See also* Great Gambler
White House Ruins, AZ, 126
White Rock, NM, 14, 25–27, 72–73, 130, 232–33. *See also* Stony Butte, NM
Whites, 17–18, 31, 33, 34, 71, 72, 90, 99, 180, 181, 188, 227. *See· also* Spaniards
White shell, 36–37, 73–76, 106, 184, 198–203, 206–207, 227. *See also* Ceremonialism; Changing Woman; Water Monster
Whiteshell Woman, 199–200. *See also* Changing Woman
Wilson v. Block. *See* San Francisco Peaks, AZ
Window Rock, AZ, 97, 139, 174, 180, 182, 195. *See also* Navajo Nation government
Windways, 21, 81, 83, 207
Wolf Creek Pass, CO, 166
Woodruff Butte, AZ, 110, 178–79
World War II, 19, 148, 211
Wupatki National Monument, AZ, 71

Yazzie, John, 198–99
Yellowman, Louise, 183

Zah, President Peterson, 100, 162, 184
Zuni Indians, 69, 143, 156, 170, 171, 174, 178–79, 188, 206–209, 212, 214, 226. *See also* Pueblo Indians